Earth for Sale

Earth for Sale

Reclaiming Ecology
in the
Age of Corporate Greenwash

by Brian Tokar

South End Press   Boston, MA

Library of Congress Cataloging-in-Publication Data

Tokar, Brian.
Earth for sale : reclaiming ecology in the age of corporate greenwash / by Brian Tokar.
    p.   cm.
Includes bibliographical references and index.
ISBN 0-89608-558-9. — ISBN 0-89608-557-0 (pbk)
1. Environmentalism. 2. Green movement. 3. Environmental policy— United States. I. Title.
GE195.T63   1997
363.7'05—dc21   97-3513
                                                                              CIP

South End Press, 116 Saint Botolph Street, Boston, MA 02115

03 02 01 00 99 98 97   1 2 3 4 5 6 7 8

Table of Contents

Introduction

Environmental Politics at the Crossroads

On an unusually warm November morning in the politically volatile year of 1994, environmental activists in the northeastern corner of North America awoke to some long-awaited but entirely unexpected news. The new nationalist prime minister of the province of Quebec, Jacques Parizeau, had announced the indefinite postponement of the hotly contested Great Whale hydroelectric project, which would have flooded hundreds of square miles of Arctic wilderness in the James Bay region of northern Canada. The project, Parizeau said, was *"sur la glace"*—on ice—and would be for a long time to come.

For several years, opposition to Quebec's mammoth hydroelectric project had brought together activists from many walks of life and varying political outlooks in the northeastern United States and Canada. Hydro-Quebec, the province-owned utility that for two decades had staked its future on damming all the major rivers in the vicinity of James Bay, had become an international symbol of ecologically devastating development, injustice toward traditional native populations, and high-stakes financial and political manipulations. International grassroots coalitions of environmentalists, supporters of indigenous sovereignty, and advocates of sustainable energy and fiscal responsibility had joined together to pressure electric utilities and regulatory boards throughout the northeastern United States to reject power contracts with Hydro-Quebec.

While Parizeau's announcement was clearly not the last word on Great Whale—and plans were under way for numerous smaller scale hydro projects throughout Quebec's Indian Country—it was the culmination of more than five years of a campaign that was more diverse, colorful, and decentralized than anything the region had seen for some time. Throughout New England and New York, where Hydro-Quebec was planning to sell much of the project's electricity, activists petitioned state officials and regulatory agencies. There were demonstrations, presentations, and theatrical performances in the state capitals, at utility hearings, and in cities and small towns alike. Students at major universities initiated divestment campaigns. Speakers from the Cree nation appeared regularly throughout the region, and Cree and Inuit canoeists traveled from James Bay to New York City, holding public receptions all along the way. Where local utilities were publicly owned, voters were mobilized against the Hydro-Quebec contracts. Labor activists decried job losses resulting from the transfer of billions of dollars of utility funds across the Canadian border. People developed alternative energy plans for their towns, and curricula about James Bay and the Cree for their local schools. One town in Vermont established an ongoing student exchange program with a school in the Cree and Inuit town of Great Whale.

All of these efforts resulted in a steady erosion of political support for the Hydro-Quebec contracts. Probably the most decisive blow was the cancellation in the spring of 1992 of a $13 billion contract with the New York State Power Authority. Ultimately, the gargantuan Great Whale project, once the crown jewel of Hydro-Quebec's plans, had become a serious embarrassment for a provincial government committed to Quebec's political and cultural independence. Representatives of the Cree nation made it known throughout North America, and Europe as well, that if Quebec were to secede from Canada, then the native peoples of the region were ready to secede from Quebec.[1]

* * *

For several years, companies based in San Diego and Los Angeles illegally dumped sewage sludge containing highly toxic chemicals on Native-American land in southern California's desert country. The groundwater became contaminated with arsenic, lead, and other toxic metals, and members of the Torres-Martínez Desert Cahuilla band experienced frequent storms of sludge-laden dust, terrible odors, and serious health problems. The companies responsible for the dumping claimed exemption from federal hazardous waste laws on the grounds that they were allegedly recycling and composting the sludge. Both the Environmental Protection Agency (EPA) and the Bureau of Indian Affairs (BIA) refused to enforce laws prohibiting the illegal dumping of sludge in the area.

Two one-day blockades of the sewage trucks during the summer of 1994 began to attract support from local farmworkers, who experienced the daily effects of the sludge, and from urban environmentalists as well. The situation grew more tense. It took a tragic turn when the nephew of one outspoken opponent of the sludge dumping was found shot dead, and another activist's home was raked by gunfire late at night. One October morning, Cahuilla people and their supporters barricaded the entrance to the sludge facilities, and began a longer-term nonviolent human blockade of the site. Despite numerous provocations from Riverside County sheriffs, two unsuccessful armed attacks against the barricades, and a dubious compromise offered by the BIA, the blockade held for fifteen days and nights. Nightly bilingual community rallies featured traditional songs and stories, as well as active participation from the Latino farmworker communities nearby. Supporters came from Greenpeace, the Southwest regional environmental justice network, urban environmental health groups, the United Farm Workers, and the American Indian Movement.

After fifteen days, a federal judge signed a temporary restraining order against the sludge operations. The sludge site has since remained closed. Activists with the Indigenous Environmental Network are mobilizing against continuing efforts by EPA and BIA officials to encourage the dumping of waste on native lands, and local activists are still pressing for the removal of nearly a million tons of illegally dumped sludge.[2]

*   *   *

Stories such as these reflect a very different kind of environmental outlook from what we read in the daily papers or see on the evening news. While final victories at James Bay, Torres-Martínez, and countless other sites of grassroots resistance are far from certain, these campaigns seem a world away from the news stories that originate in the halls of power in Washington, D.C. They reflect a newer, more expansive grass-roots approach to environmental issues that has emerged in the 1990s, even as environmentalists face an incessant and powerful attack on the edifice of protective laws that have largely defined the agenda of the movement for more than twenty years. In both cases, local activists had little hope that their concerns would be adequately addressed in the leg-islative arena, and so they acted accordingly.[3] They strove to highlight the frequently obscured social and economic dimensions of environ-mental issues, and in doing so, raised issues and forged long-standing al-liances that reach far beyond the limits of traditional environmental politics.

The 1990s began amid widespread optimism that the tide of environ-mental destruction was beginning to turn. The twentieth anniversary of Earth Day in the spring of 1990 was marked by what organizers termed the largest outpouring of public support for environmental protection in U.S. history. Environmental sentiments were at an all-time high, and polluting companies were clearly on the defensive. Even Republican President George Bush proclaimed himself a champion of the environ-ment and, for some time, sought to distance himself from the anti-envi-ronmental excesses of Ronald Reagan's administration. The '90s, we were repeatedly told, would be the environmental decade, a time when humanity would rediscover how to live in harmony with the earth.

By mid-decade, however, this optimism had all but faded. Substan-tive legislative victories were few and far between, and environmental atrocities continued unabated. Even before the congressional elections of 1994, when the Republican Party took control of Congress for the first time in forty years, the ability of the traditional, Washington-based voices of environmentalism to wield political influence was much in doubt. While membership in many national environmental groups was declining, anti-environmental legislation and quasi-populist "property rights" or "wise use" movements were gaining disproportionate visibil-ity in the mainstream media.

Today we are faced with stepped-up logging in the National Forests, persistent chemical assaults on the health and safety of millions of people, the collapse of coastal fisheries, and the refusal of corporations and governments alike to take meaningful steps against global climate change. Though people across the United States and around the world continue to work against formidable odds to protect their communities and natural ecosystems from the forces of destruction, their struggles are far less visible now than they were a few short years ago. Politicians and media pundits repeatedly dismiss the environmental movement as "extremist," despite numerous polls suggesting that an overwhelming share of the U.S. public still supports increased environmental protection.

How and why has this unfortunate turn of events come to pass? The reasons are political, economic, and even cultural, reflecting broader changes in the sociopolitical climate in the United States and throughout the industrialized world. As this book will seek to demonstrate, however, the problem is also closely linked to developments within the environmental movement itself.

In recent years, there has been an intensely polarized struggle for the very heart and soul of the environmental movement. This struggle emerged as the movement grew rapidly during the 1970s and '80s, becoming much more apparent in the 1990s as the influence of the largest national groups began to wane, and as grassroots activists all across the country sought new ways to halt environmental devastation and work toward a greener future.

In the view of many dedicated local activists, the high-profile national environmental groups—from the Sierra Club to the National Wildlife Federation—are incapable of adequately defending the integrity of the natural environment. In their pursuit of influence among the decision-makers and power brokers of Washington, D.C. and in the corporate world, these groups have staked their reputations on a politics of moderation and compromise. They have institutionally tied themselves to the political and policymaking establishment, accepting as inevitable a declining public role in environmental protection and seeking accommodation with the powerful interests responsible for environmental destruction. They have adopted a limited agenda focusing on the efficient management of environmental problems within the limits imposed by present political and economic realities. Thus, they are unable to acknowledge a reality that is becoming more widely accepted by grassroots environmental activists—that the protection of public health and the conservation of natural ecosystems may ultimately require more comprehensive changes in society.

The declining effectiveness of the mainstream environmental groups reflects, in part, the dominant political culture, which has become ever more subservient to the dictates of corporate America, with its reckless pursuit of unlimited financial gain. In such a setting, an environmentalism that is unwilling to challenge established political and economic institutions is, at best, confined to waging endless defensive battles to sustain the most minimal protections of public and environmental health.

A very different kind of ecological activism has emerged over the past two decades in communities all across the United States. In direct response to some of the most immediate threats to public health and the integrity of natural ecosystems, people have been organizing. Campaigns against toxic incinerators and landfills, plans to store nuclear waste in remote rural areas, destruction of unique natural areas, and excessive urban development have brought thousands of people into direct conflict with the corporate-dominated status quo. Often, these campaigns are run entirely by volunteers, on minuscule budgets, garnering little if any national media attention. While larger organizations may play a supporting role, they are frequently supplanted by less formal networks of grassroots eco-activists that are far more willing to give local campaigns the support and assistance they really need. In the best of cases, this kind of holistic ecological activism reaches beyond the imperative of responding to immediate crises. Sometimes, it inspires systemic critiques of the causes of environmental destruction and long-range visions of a cooperative and truly ecological society.

This resurgence of local grassroots activism on behalf of endangered ecosystems and communities of people has engaged individuals from all walks of life, many of whom would never before have thought of themselves as environmental activists. All across the United States, chemical workers are fighting to protect their families and communities from the effects of toxic exposure, fishing and trapping enthusiasts are working to decommission hydroelectric dams that threaten fish and wildlife habitats, and suburban dwellers are opposing unneeded highway projects. Mothers are demanding chemical-free food for their children, hikers and snowmobilers alike are questioning suburban developments that would impact important trails, and people of diverse socioeconomic backgrounds are uniting against the government's plans to store nuclear waste in isolated communities all across the country. All these efforts challenge the popular perception that public environmental concern is on the decline.

This perception is substantially tied to the increasing political submissiveness of the leading national environmental groups. During the Clinton years, the environmental vote has been largely taken for granted by an administration thoroughly beholden to corporate interests. While Bill Clinton has fallen far short on every environmental promise he has made, it has been easy for Democrats to paint themselves as an alternative to the virulently anti-environmental Republican Party. Those who seek influence within the established political structures of Washington often see little choice but to continue supporting the administration, despite its sellouts of environmental interests on issues ranging from logging in the National Forests to protecting the ozone layer, from food safety to international trade. The nature of these policy shifts and the inadequacy of the environmental movement's official response to them are an important focus of the chapters that follow.

Two additional developments have contributed to the increasing political disengagement of the environmentally concerned public: the emergence of so-called corporate environmentalism and the rise of environmental consumerism. These two closely related phenomena contribute to the co-optation of environmental concerns by convincing millions of people that ecological problems will be adequately addressed by means that lie entirely outside of political sphere. Together, they constitute what has come to be known as the corporate "greenwash." Each in its own way has contributed to the heightened visibility of anti-environmental interests.

The term "corporate environmentalism" is generally attributed to Du Pont CEO Edgar Woolard, who, in a speech following the 1989 Exxon oil spill in Alaska, called for a "corporate environmental stewardship fully in line with public desires and expectations."[4] Corporate environmentalism, however, is more often an expression of the public relations department than a policy supported by any other branch of the corporate hierarchy. It seeks to assuage public concerns about pollution and resource depletion, while casting environmentally destructive corporations as environmental innovators. As author Tom Athanasiou has described it, "corporate environmentalism offers a misleading win-win fantasy of environmental protection in which tough choices will not be necessary."[5] It furthers the notion that environmental issues are largely a technical matter, a set of problems to be solved without regard to underlying institutional, social, and political considerations. Corporate environmentalism arrived on the international stage in 1992, when organizations such as the Business Council for Sustainable Development played a dominant behind-the-scenes role at the UN "Earth Summit" in Rio de Janeiro, and successfully intervened to quell discussions of the central role of transnational corporations in the destruction of the earth's environment.[6]

The concept of "green consumerism" appeared during the leadup to the 1990 Earth Day anniversary. It is based on the myth that environmental problems are largely the result of individual consumer choices, neglecting all the ways in which these choices are shaped and constrained by decisions made in corporate boardrooms, well beyond the reach of public scrutiny. Indeed, corporate managers make the vast majority of decisions about what is produced and how, seriously limiting individual choices and shaping patterns of consumption in countless unacknowledged ways.

Green consumerism instead views all of life as one big shopping mall. If everyone is equally responsible for the destruction of the earth, the solution is merely to buy more natural and recycled products, and companies are more than willing to make such products available at a premium price. Not only does green consumerism dilute the challenge that an ecological ethic might pose to the very idea of a consumer society, but the corporate promotion of fashionable "green" products makes life more difficult for small, local producers of everything from organic food to hand-sewn clothing. Further, as "natural" products have become a niche market for those affluent enough to pay for them, the goods available to everyone else are even shoddier and more toxic than before. In a highly individualistic, economically driven society such as ours, green consumerism makes it possible for people to feel they are doing something for the earth without questioning the lifestyles or the economic system that have actually brought us to the brink of ecological collapse.

Thus, three closely related phenomena—the absorption of the mainstream environmental movement by the political status quo, the emergence of corporate environmentalism, and the proliferation of "ecological" products in the marketplace—have all helped fuel the perception of a declining popular commitment to environmental protection. Indeed, they have helped set the stage for today's anti-environmental backlash. To better understand the backlash against environmentalism, and its considerable popularity among corporate managers and political operatives, will require a look at some unique and widely misrepresented economic realities.

Conventional wisdom suggests that many people, discouraged by a stagnant economy and rising taxes, have simply rejected environmentalism, viewing it as a source of excessive constraints on economic growth. Yet the real story is far more complex. While the news media portray public policy as limited by the compelling necessity to reduce public spending, a look beneath the surface reveals unprecedented corporate profit-taking and a sweeping redistribution of wealth from middle-income sectors of the population to the very wealthy. After steady declines in corporate profits during the late 1970s and 1980s, especially in manufacturing, profits rose dramatically in the early 1990s as companies globalized production. Domestic employment remained stagnant, and the United States achieved the discomfiting distinction of having the most unequal distribution of wealth in the industrialized world.[7] A centerpiece of corporate strategy is to reduce the role of government in the economy, thereby eviscerating public constraints on the pursuit of private profit.

While mainstream environmental groups have been courting favor with the powers-that-be, the powerful interests that generally dominate economic policy have become increasingly hostile to environmental protection, even as many have embraced the public relations agenda of corporate environmentalism. The 1990s are a period of unprecedented cost-cutting and "downsizing" of corporations, often misleadingly described as a necessary defensive response to global competition. While working people across the United States and around the world face the most obvious negative effects of economic globalization, corporate managers have fueled the myth of widespread public concern over the costs of complying with environmental regulations. Companies such as Du Pont and Monsanto often try to have it both ways—publicly proclaiming their commitment to reducing pollution and saving the environment, while simultaneously helping to sustain the opposition to environmental protection.[8]

Anti-environmental interests have been able to rally the support of many middle-class people who are simply fed up with the current state of affairs. For three decades, government policies have dramatically shifted the burden of taxation from corporations to individuals, and from the wealthy to those of more modest means. Quasi-populist crusades against increased taxation and for the unlimited rights of private property owners have sustained an assault on environmental protection that would have been inconceivable just a few short years ago. Anti-environmental advocates have learned to wield the rhetoric of freedom and individual rights. Their actions, however, merely confer popular legitimacy to the demands of a global corporate power structure that rejects all constraints on the limitless expansion of its greed-driven practices.

Traditional environmentalists have responded to this anti-environmental backlash in a variety of ways. Some even support efforts to "streamline" existing regulations. "Yes," they will argue, "we can make regulations more flexible, replace mandates with incentives, and prohibitions with statistical assessments, but we must do so in an environmentally responsible way." Since it is impossible, in their view, to resist corporate demands, they will press to moderate them, tempering their most damaging effects. This is the only recourse offered by an insider, interest group-oriented approach to politics. Some environmental groups, such as the "free market"-oriented Environmental Defense Fund, have taken this strategy of accommodation several steps further, supporting corporate efforts to replace regulations with measures that rely on the workings of the marketplace to curtail pollution and conserve natural resources.

One of the central themes of this book is that neither government regulations nor the capitalist market is capable of providing adequate protection for natural ecosystems or communities affected by environmental pollution. It will take a broad-based, popular ecological movement to reach beyond today's self-limiting policy debates. Such a movement asserts the integrity of communities of people, and of all life on earth, as an overriding principle for society. While compromise is often inevitable in politics, people seeking to change society should not allow their agenda to be shaped by whatever seems most "realistic" at any given moment. When they do, as we will see in the chapters that follow, it becomes increasingly difficult to regain the initiative from those who wish to tear down both the environmental and social safety nets.

In recent years, the environmental mainstream has begun to acknowledge the need to return to the grassroots, but its commitment to procedural, short-term solutions, to a narrow pragmatism in the face of unfettered corporate expansion, makes it all but impossible for these groups to facilitate such a return. In a 1994 interview in the quarterly publication of the Boston-based Conservation Law Foundation, Interior Secretary Bruce Babbitt was asked what the environmental community should do about the growing "wise use" property rights movement. "Public support for the environment is broad but not terribly intense," he responded. "The other factor is that the opponents of the environment have learned the importance of grassroots organizing." Babbitt continued:

> The national environmental organizations, during the sixties and seventies, went to Washington with lawyers, economists, really wonderful scientific, economic and legal resources, and they took their grassroots support for granted. And all of a sudden, their opponents are doing a better job at the grassroots level.[9]

Babbitt is right, and much of the environmental mainstream knows it. But the problem cannot be addressed merely by trying to shore up grassroots support for pro-environment lawyers, economists, and lobbyists in Washington. Nor can it be adequately addressed with more direct mail fundraising, advertising campaigns, or alerts broadcast over the Internet. Grassroots eco-activists have raised a much more sweeping critique of environmental business-as-usual. They know that corporations are systematically poisoning the water, air, soil, and food. They know that corporations are clear-cutting the world's forests at an astounding rate, and expanding economic practices that violate the earth's atmosphere and climate. And a growing number of grassroots eco-activists recognize that this expansion is absolutely central to an economic system based on unprecedented concentrations of private wealth and an ethic of unlimited private gain.

The only adequate response is to build a broad-based, politically conscious ecology movement that is committed to justice, equity, and a very different kind of relationship between human communities and the natural world. Ecological activists in the coming period will need to develop a clearer understanding of the social and economic causes of environmental problems, as well as the institutions that are most responsible for the destruction of the earth and our communities. They will need to express this understanding with bold and creative direct action campaigns, alliance-building, political pressure, and the creation of ecological alternatives. This undertaking is one of the most central challenges that environmentally aware people face as we approach the 21st century.

* * *

The chapters that follow will draw upon the examples of many different kinds of environmental campaigns, movements, and organizations, and highlight the ways they have developed and changed during the 1990s. Part I addresses the limits of traditional environmentalism from a number of perspectives. The Prologue and Chapter One examine the origins of mainstream environmentalism and the emergence of a grassroots critique of the leading national environmental groups. We will see how revelations of corporate contributions to these groups played a role in the debates surrounding the twentieth anniversary of Earth Day, and how leading foundations serve to channel the environmental debate toward a self-limiting mainstream agenda.

Chapter Two chronicles the growing influence of corporate ideology within the environmental movement, including debates over tradable "rights" to pollute, energy efficiency measures, "industrial ecology," and campaigns to privatize public lands. Chapter Three examines the long-standing debate over the nature of regulation, highlighting some of the disturbing environmental compromises of the Clinton administration as well as the anti-regulatory agenda of the Republican-led Congress. Finally, Chapter Four looks at the highly polarized debate over forestry in the United States, particularly in the Pacific Northwest. The western "timber wars" may offer the clearest illustration of the limits of traditional environmentalism and the need for a grassroots alternative. Readers who prefer to begin their exploration of specific policy issues with a more descriptive case study might wish to pass by the more general policy discussions in Chapters Two and Three, and go right to Chapter Four.

Part II of this book highlights the growing diversity of grassroots alternatives to the mainstream environmental agenda. Chapter Five offers an historical perspective on the development of ecological approaches to social transformation. Chapters Six and Seven focus on the two most significant domestic grassroots environmental movements of recent years: the environmental justice movement and the resurgence of grassroots forest activism. These chapters explore many of the unique qualities and campaigns of these movements, their troubled relations with the environmental mainstream, and their emerging perspectives on the systemic roots of environmental problems.

Chapter Eight looks beyond the United States and the industrialized world for a perspective on the emerging ecological movements of the South. These movements offer a unique challenge to conventional environmental thinking, along with a comprehensive ecological critique of the agenda of "sustainable development." Chapter Nine addresses a variety of efforts to unify grassroots eco-activists in both theory and practice, focusing on movements such as Green politics and bioregionalism, the philosophical outlooks of ecofeminism, social ecology, and deep ecology, and the emergence of an ecological critique of economics. We will conclude by examining ecological movements in the wider context of social activism, and asking what kind of ecological activism might help to realize the promise of a new politics of democracy and community.

It is important at the outset to clarify some terms. On many occasions, I will refer to "mainstream environmentalism," "traditional environmentalism," and "national environmental groups." These phrases refer to the most influential national environmental groups, those which emerged from the 19th-century conservation movement (Sierra Club, National Audubon Society), from mid-20th-century sportsmen's and hikers' clubs (National Wildlife Federation, Wilderness Society, Izaak Walton League), and from the more policy-oriented efforts of the 1970s (Natural Resources Defense Council, Environmental Defense Fund, Friends of the Earth). The spokespeople and CEOs of these groups will often be referred to as the voices of "official environmentalism." Each of these groups remains unique in many ways: the Sierra Club and Audubon Society still maintain scores of active chapters around the country; the NWF has the closest ties to the Republican Party; the EDF has established itself as a link between the environmental movement and advocates of corporate environmentalism. Many political differences among these groups have emerged during the 1990s, particularly around highly charged issues, from food safety to trade policy. Yet they remain united around their "insider" political stance and moderate political priorities as well as their fundraising methods, organizational style, media image, and other qualities.

Today, there are considerably more environmental organizations based in Washington, D.C., than ever before. The vast majority of these are issue-oriented policy think tanks, which are not directly linked to environmental activist constituencies, except in an important information-gathering capacity. Others, like the U.S. Public Interest Research Group (USPIRG), are directly engaged in lobbying and policymaking but often adopt a more independent, consumer-oriented approach than that of the core mainstream groups.

Some issue-oriented groups in Washington do maintain a closer working relationship with grassroots activists around the country. Save America's Forests, which is referred to in Chapter Four, is one leading example. On the West Coast, the San Francisco-based Earth Island Institute provides organizational support for a rather decentralized network of specific activist projects, and the Rainforest Action Network has developed its own unique synthesis of national and international media work and support for local activism. Greenpeace remains an influential player on the national as well as international scene. At some periods in its history, it has acted like one of the Group of Ten (except for its frequent forays into high-visibility direct action); at other times, it has maintained closer links with grassroots activists. Other large groups, such as the Nature Conservancy (which advertises itself as "nature's real estate agent"), claim to eschew overt political involvement and focus on specific land preservation efforts, albeit on a national and even worldwide scale.

The grassroots environmental movement is also rather complex in its institutional structures. The real heart of the various movements we will discuss, particularly in Chapters Six and Seven, is made up of the countless groups of self-organized volunteers that come together around immediate local concerns and continually reinvent themselves as local conditions and issues evolve. Some have offices and small staffs and even receive an occasional foundation grant to support their work, while others operate entirely out of living rooms, churches, and community centers. Various larger networks have been formed primarily to help support such groups, from the regional environmental justice networks in the South and Southwest to Heartwood and the Native Forest Network. Finally, groups as diverse as the Alliance for the Wild Rockies, Food & Water, and the Oregon-based Native Forest Council initiate and develop focused campaigns around specific issues but remain in contact with large networks of activists that give their campaigns an effectiveness far beyond the scope of the organizations' limited resources.

It is these dedicated grassroots activists—many of whom I have had the incomparable pleasure of knowing and working with during my own nearly twenty-five years of activism—who are working every day to reclaim ecology from the insidious influences of the corporate greenwash. The very future of life on earth may lie in their hands. The chapters that follow are dedicated to all of them.

* * *

I would also like to take this opportunity to thank all the wonderful people without whose help and encouragement this book would never have come to pass. First, I'd like to thank Mike Albert and Lydia Sargent of *Z Magazine*, where portions of several of these chapters first appeared, for helping to support my writing over the past seven years and encouraging my ongoing explorations of the myriad dimensions of environmental politics. Second, thanks to my editors at South End Press: Sonia Shah, who offered numerous invaluable editorial suggestions during some of the most difficult stages of this project, and Cynthia Peters, who patiently and masterfully helped usher it toward its conclusion. Greta Gaard, Steve Chase, Zoë Erwin, and Roy Morrison all read major portions of the manuscript at various critical stages, offering their clear thinking, editorial insights, and personal encouragement.

Others who shared their ideas and insights—and offered critical information when I needed it the most—include Orin Langelle, Anne Petermann, Jeff St. Clair, Andy Mahler, Leah Garlotte, Michael Colby, Susan Meeker-Lowry, Carmelo Ruiz, Bob Buchanan, Suzanne Richman, Chaia Heller, Howard Hawkins, Tom Shor, Fred Friedman, and others far too numerous to mention. Finally, deepest thanks to all my friends and *compañeros* in the activist community here in Vermont, as well as all my colleagues and students at the Institute for Social Ecology and Goddard College in Plainfield, Vermont. These are the people who really kept me focused on the obstacles to, and the promise of, an ecological future, and who demonstrated the care and flexibility to periodically allow me to put other pressing commitments aside in order to bring this project to its final completion.

PART I

The Limits of Environmentalism

Prologue

The Challenge of Environmentalism

A rushing mountain stream calls to us as we awaken. A great blue heron rises amid the treetops, reflected in still water. The rising sun radiates a glorious hue that unfolds to embrace the whole sky. For countless eons, experiences like these have reminded people of our most fundamental connection to the rhythms and harmonies of life on earth.

In our time, though, close observation of the natural world often has a bittersweet quality. The songbirds are not as abundant as they were in our earliest memories. In some years, there are almost no monarch butterflies to be found in the fields and forests, in the parks or above the rooftops. Every year, the weather seems just a little bit more out of balance. Damaging floods follow periods of persistent drought. In wintertime, there is less snow than there used to be or, in some years, dramatically more. Where we once traveled to see vast expanses of intact original forest, there are now empty hillsides, stripped bare of nearly all their trees. We are even advised to stay indoors during midday hours to protect ourselves from the sun's harmful ultraviolet rays.

For the 45 percent of human beings who live in the world's urban centers, the outlook is considerably bleaker. The air is unhealthy to breathe, sometimes for weeks at a time. Children are hospitalized with extreme cases of asthma, emphysema, and highly resistant forms of tuberculosis. Others contract rare genetic diseases, or allergies and autoimmune conditions that defy traditional diagnosis. Worldwide, hurricanes and other violent storms arrive with increasing frequency and severity, making life in crowded and often makeshift urban settlements more insecure than ever before.

We live in a time when civilization's manifold assaults on the integrity of the earth's living ecosystems have escalated to an unprecedented degree. For the first time in four million years of human history, it can be said that no living being on earth is unaffected by the consequences of human intervention. For the first time in 10,000 years of civilization, we live in a world thoroughly dominated by a global economic system, a consumption-driven culture, and an entire way of life that accepts no natural limits to the continual expansion of its reach. For the first time in the 200-year history of capitalism, nearly all of the world's peoples and natural ecosystems are subject to the whims of a global economy that would appropriate life itself to satisfy the insatiable wants of a powerful few.

In the face of such extraordinary assaults on the integrity of the natural world and human cultures and communities, powerful social movements have emerged to raise fundamental questions about our civilization's relationship to nature. For some, the fear of impending apocalypse has inspired a profound new commitment to the sanctity of life and a deeply felt need to question all aspects of the way of life we have been taught to take for granted. For more than half a century since the dawning of the nuclear age, the threat of annihilation, whether through nuclear catastrophe or ecological collapse, has shaken people out of their complacency, and compelled them to commit their lives to the creation of more peaceful and humane ways of living. From Albert Einstein and many of the other pioneering scientists of the nuclear age, to countless anti-nuclear and environmental activists around the world today, people have been propelled into action by the urgency of both near-term and long-range threats to the survival of life on earth.

Yet many more people, especially in these cynical times, have merely grown weary. The profound adaptability of the human species has transformed what was once a sense of widespread alarm into a willful disregard for what social critic Susan Sontag has termed "a catastrophe in slow motion."[1] Ecological philosophies that question conventional as-

sumptions about the relationship of human beings and human civilization to the rest of life are shunned in many circles. Ecological values are
often overwhelmed, either by an ethic of fast living, personal advantage,
and the elevation of acquisitiveness and greed to the status of moral
"virtues," or by a shortsighted form of environmentalism that mirrors
our society's predilection for simple formulas and easy solutions. Large
portions of the U.S. environmental movement are resigned to the Si-
syphean task of struggling to ameliorate some of the worst excesses of
current corporate practices without addressing the underlying causes of
ecological and social problems. Some of the best-known and most well-
funded environmental groups have virtually abandoned their critical
role, seeking instead to demonstrate that environmental integrity can
somehow be made compatible with the relentless drive for profits.

Since 1990, when hundreds of thousands of people celebrated the
twentieth anniversary of the original Earth Day, there has been a widespread awareness that all is not right with the environmental movement
in the United States. By the middle of the decade, this awareness had become a serious crisis of confidence, with all of the most basic environmental protections in U.S. law under attack, and the mainstream
environmental movement strikingly ill-equipped to reverse the tide.
Twenty years of working within the system, of lobbying for a seat at the
table of official deliberations, have brought little of lasting value in the
face of a far-reaching corporate assault on the public regulation of environmentally damaging practices.

An environmental movement that once seemed to embody the hopes
of millions of people for a safer, healthier, more harmonious future, today finds itself under attack, vilified by politicians and the media, and
mired in countless defensive and often demoralizing legislative and legal battles. The defeat of many of the most extreme anti-environmental
measures that have been proposed in recent years could prove to be little
more than a temporary hiatus unless the ecology movement can regain
people's confidence in its ability to raise larger questions and inspire
hope in the possibility of a greener future. Before we can move forward,
it is necessary to understand just how the movement came to find itself
in such a discouraging situation.

In U.S. history, the origins of environmental thought and action are most often traced to the works and deeds of Henry David Thoreau and John Muir. While these figures are usually associated with a more inward, contemplative form of rebellion, inspired by the transcendentalist writings of Ralph Waldo Emerson and others, their example helped set the stage for today's environmental activists. From Thoreau's famous refusal to pay the local poll tax to Muir's call for a greater unity between humanity and wild nature, both of these men encouraged deep questioning of the assumptions of a society that valued conformity over self-expression, and blind obedience to industrial rhythms over the close observation of the natural world. Muir denounced "[t]he galling harness of civilization" that daily constrains people's relationship with the natural world and empowers "devotees of ravaging commercialism" to create a society founded on a "perfect contempt" for all of nature.[2]

While figures such as Thoreau and Muir were awakening readers to new ways of thinking about society and its relationship to the natural world, a very different kind of conservationist agenda was becoming entrenched in the halls of power in Washington, D.C. This approach, most often associated with President Theodore Roosevelt and his chief forester, Gifford Pinchot, sought to transform the public lands of the American West from an untamed frontier, recently captured from "savage" bands of "Indians," into a productive landscape of efficient, well-managed tree farms and feedlots for cattle, all in the name of conservation. Historian Donald Worster describes Pinchot's outlook in this way:

> There was . . . no doubt about his utilitarian bias toward nature. Prosperity, argued Pinchot, could never be made secure in a society that wasted its natural wealth in the traditional frontier style . . . It required instead a program of long-range, careful management that would put resource development on a thoroughly rational and efficient base.[3]

This utilitarian approach helped to define today's mainstream environmentalism. While Pinchot sought to introduce ideas of rationality and efficiency into the environmental debates of his time, he and other progressive land managers ultimately did little more than streamline and justify the conquest of the West, only briefly moderating the unchecked abuse and exploitation of western lands. More than a billion acres of land had been transferred to private interests by the federal government in the forty-odd years since the Homestead Act of 1862, leading to massive speculation, haphazard timber cutting and overgrazing, and devastating mining practices that sometimes left a sterile landscape for miles around. One of the first recorded citizen environmental actions in the United States was a protest by local farmers near Marysville, California against a local mining company. The miners, in their reckless pursuit of fortune, were diverting the Mary River into huge pipes and nozzles, exposing veins of gold by rapidly washing away as much soil as possible, and scattering massive amounts of gravel, rock, and debris in their wake, much to the chagrin of those who sought to make their living from the land.[4]

Then, as now, the primary agenda of federal agencies was to promote development. A century ago, this meant the fullest possible settlement of the western frontier, aided most dramatically by federal projects to harness water resources for irrigation, flood control, and soon, for electric power generation. Regulation was a tool to temper the worst effects of uncontrolled development and, in the hands of progressives like Pinchot, to democratize development in the hope that more people might benefit from its rewards. "The purpose of Forestry," Pinchot wrote, "is to make the forest produce the largest possible amount of whatever crop or service will be most useful, and keep on producing it for generation after generation of men and trees."[5] When not exploited for their timber, the nation's public forests were seen as playgrounds for members of elite hunting clubs, such as the Boone and Crockett Club, to which Roosevelt and Pinchot both belonged. A massive federal program to exterminate predators such as wolves and coyotes was justified as a measure to protect livestock and also to sustain populations of desirable game species. Although this program peaked in the 1930s, it continues to this day, especially in the Southwest. Wider ecological values, extolled by pioneering naturalists such as Aldo Leopold or Vermont's George Perkins Marsh, had little place in such a plan; nor did the aesthetic and spiritual values espoused by the likes of Thoreau and Muir.

The period of rapid economic growth that followed World War I made it difficult for even moderate conservationists to find allies in the U.S. government. Agencies such as the Forest Service and the Bureau of

Reclamation (which had been established to promote a "scientific" approach to western water development) once again staked out a role in promoting the availability of western lands for the exploitation of their resources. As author Robert Gottlieb has explained:

> Through the 1920s and into the 1930s, the language of conservationism was increasingly appropriated by the resource-based industries and other industrial interests . . . [T]he historic tension between conservationism as an anticorporate social movement and as an effort to rationalize a resource-based capitalism had disappeared. By the close of the Progressive Era in the 1920s, conservationism as expertise and rational management of resources for business uses had emerged as the movement's conventional ideology, an ideology eagerly embraced by the very industries an earlier generation of conservationists had so forcefully challenged.[6]

In the 1990s, anti-environmental publicists and property rights agitators would call for the "wise use" of resources to disguise their subservience to the resource-extraction industries that most generously supported their activities.[7]

There was much more to the environmental debates of a century ago than issues of land use and western resource management. Gottlieb, for example, has documented the emergence of a widespread movement for public health and safety in many urban areas in the early 1900s. From smoke control leagues that called attention to the dense clouds of soot emitted by coalburning furnaces, to Dr. Alice Hamilton's campaigns against workplace pollutants such as phosphorus, lead, and carbon monoxide, these campaigns came to influence the strategies of trade unionists, social reformers, and others concerned about the social consequences of the emerging industrial order.[8]

Despite these early stirrings, however, the various groups that now constitute the mainstream of the environmental movement have origins quite removed from the world of social activism. Though they may demonstrate a considerable diversity of priorities and political orientations, the environmental groups that are now household names were, from their beginnings, far more allied with the tradition of elite resource management than with the progressive farmers, health workers, and conservationists who prepared the way for today's grassroots environmentalists.

The oldest of these groups, the Sierra Club and the National Audubon Society, are also the only two that still support active chapters of members/activists all across the country. The Sierra Club traces its origins to John Muir's turn-of-the-century battles to protect California's Yosemite Valley from timber and ranching interests, and to stop the damming of the Hetch Hetchy Valley, high in the Sierra Nevada, by interests seeking to supply drinking water to the rapidly growing city of San Francisco. Muir and his colleagues, including several prominent Berkeley academics, were ultimately unable to save the Hetch Hetchy from development. The project was approved in 1913, but Muir's legacy was renewed several decades later. The Sierra Club had become a rather staid, elite social club until David Brower carried it—amid considerable resistance—to the leading edge of environmental controversy during the 1950s and 1960s.[9]

The Audubon Society was founded in 1886, some thirty-five years after the death of its namesake, the legendary wildlife painter John James Audubon. In its first, short-lived incarnation, the society was the project of big game hunter and magazine editor George Bird Grinnell, who was alarmed by the indiscriminate hunting of birds for feathers and other commercial uses. A decade later, the organization was revived by a group of society women in Boston. Their rather limited purpose: "To discourage the buying and wearing for ornamental purposes of the feathers of any wild birds except ducks and gamebirds, and to otherwise further the protection of native birds."[10] By the turn of the century, there were thirty-five state societies, which would play an important role in the establishment of National Wildlife Refuges across the United States. Still, for much of its history, the Audubon Society, like other conservation groups of its time, largely served what journalist Philip Shabecoff describes as a "rich, white, male, Protestant" clientele.[11]

Hunters and other sportsmen concerned about the contamination of streams and rivers in the upper Midwest founded the Izaak Walton League in the 1920s and the National Wildlife Federation (NWF) in 1936. The NWF began as a federation of state societies of hunting enthusiasts, largely funded by ammunition suppliers such as Du Pont and

Remington; it only began to assume a wider role in public education around wildlife issues during the 1960s.[12]

The Wilderness Society embraced a more activist agenda right from its founding in 1935 by the renowned wilderness hiker and social crusader Bob Marshall. Marshall was one of the few early environmentalists who eschewed elitism and embraced a philosophy linking social justice to the liberation of nature.[13] Along with the Sierra Club, the Wilderness Society was in the forefront of developing a legislative approach to wilderness preservation, leading to the passage of the Wilderness Act in 1964.

The end of World War II brought an unprecedented wave of consumerism and massive industrial development. Major industrialists were concerned that the rapid development and accompanying increases in resource use might raise public demands for greater regulation of business practices. At the same time, corporate America was alarmed about possible shortages of basic raw materials. Two important organizations that emerged from this period were the Conservation Foundation and Resources for the Future, both commissioned to study ways to mitigate resource shortages, population growth, and water pollution without impeding the engines of economic growth. Laurance Rockefeller served as a personal underwriter of the Conservation Foundation; Resources for the Future was supported by the insurance industry, the Farm Bureau, the American Petroleum Institute, and the Ford Foundation.[14] While other conservation groups were becoming involved in political battles over land preservation, these organizations focused their efforts on resource economics and the emergence of new pollution control technologies, thus helping to launch an explicitly pro-corporate approach to resource conservation.

With the rise of a new grassroots ecology movement in the 1960s and 1970s came an impressive diversity of environmental organizations, both large and small. The flowering of grassroots activism will be addressed at the beginning of Part II; this, however, is the place to briefly highlight a few of the newer organizations that helped to shape the mainstream environmental agenda. For example, today's best-known environmental law firms—Environmental Defense Fund (EDF), Natural Resources Defense Council (NRDC), and Sierra Club Legal Defense

Fund (SCLDF)—each played a role in the emerging environmental policy debates of the early 1970s. EDF and NRDC both emerged from local environmental battles in the outer suburbs of New York City—EDF from a campaign against the use of DDT in the town of Brookhaven, Long Island, and NRDC from a controversy surrounding a proposed utility pumping station known as Storm King in New York's Hudson River valley. SCLDF, which plays an important role in the Northwest forestry debates to be described in Chapter Four, was established as an independent legal arm of the Sierra Club in 1971.[15]

These three organizations helped to pioneer strategies of legal intervention in defense of the environment, each expanding from a single-issue focus to address virtually every area of environmental law and policy. They have all maintained this rather broad focus, even while developing areas of special expertise—NRDC around nuclear and food safety issues, among others, and SCLDF around forest protection. In the late 1980s, NRDC became widely known for its successful effort to ban the apple-ripening agent alar, due to the presence of a carcinogenic breakdown product.[16] Original board member Amyas Ames, chair of the executive committee of the Wall Street investment firm Kidder, Peabody, set the stage for EDF to eventually become a key advocate of market incentives as an instrument of environmental policy (see Chapter Two). The Ford Foundation played a central financial and organizational role in the founding of these groups. It helped form NRDC by introducing two Wall Street attorneys involved in opposing the Storm King pumping station to a prominent group of recent Yale Law School graduates who sought to stake out a role in the newly emerging field of environmental law. Ford established an oversight board for EDF and NRDC, consisting of five past presidents of the American Bar Association, which had to approve all cases taken on by these organizations; EDF's efforts were to be overseen by a bipartisan Litigation Review Committee as well.[17]

Several authors have traced the institutionalization of the mainstream environmental movement to a 1981 meeting of the top officers of nine of the most visible environmental organizations in Washington. The day after Ronald Reagan was inaugurated as president, Robert Allen, then vice-president of the Henry P. Kendall Foundation, summoned the nine leading environmental executives, along with representatives of three other foundations. The goal was to head off an increasingly fierce competition among national groups for funds and public visibility, while forging a more unified stand against the Reagan administration's promised attacks on the nation's public lands and environmental laws. Included were the directors of the Sierra Club, National Audubon Society, National Wildlife Federation, Wilderness Society, Izaak Walton League, NRDC, and EDF. Rounding out the group were representatives of the once-dissident Friends of the Earth—which was founded by David Brower in 1969, soon after he was forced to resign as director of the Sierra Club—and its policy offshoot, the Environmental Policy Center.[18]

In the ensuing years, the so-called Group of Ten (the National Parks and Conservation Association would become the tenth member[19]) would meet quarterly, intensify their campaign against the Reagan administration's excesses, and preside over the phenomenal growth in the size and scope of the U.S. environmental movement. At the same time, they served to reinforce the elite character of mainstream environmentalism, narrowed the movement's focus to the implementation of federal environmental laws, and became thoroughly absorbed into the policy process in Washington. In 1983, the environmental executives initiated a series of meetings with their would-be counterparts in the corporate world—the CEOs of six leading chemical companies: Du Pont, Exxon Chemical, Union Carbide, Dow, American Cyanamid, and Monsanto. The Group of Ten, in just a few years, according to Robert Gottlieb, "had effectively redefined mainstream environmentalism less as a movement and more directly as an adjunct to the policy process."[19]

The story of mainstream environmentalism is largely one of reform and compromise, but it is also a story of protracted internal struggles between conservative and activist-oriented elements in nearly every one of the leading organizations. With a changing political climate in Washington, the essential conservatism of the mainstream groups became even more entrenched. As a renewed grassroots ecology movement began to appear in the late 1980s and early '90s, activist critiques of mainstream environmentalism soon moved to center stage.

Chapter 1

Questioning Official Environmentalism

Like the original conservation movement it is emulating, today's big business conservation is not interested in preserving the earth; it is rationally reorganizing for a more efficient rape of resources ... and the production of an ever grosser national product.
—Ramparts magazine, May 1970[1]

The year 1990 was an auspicious one for environmental activists in the United States. The twentieth anniversary of the original Earth Day was on the horizon, and it appeared as though everyone wanted to be an environmentalist. The widespread popularity of environmental concerns was reflected in the rapid growth of environmental organizations, the appearance of new publications, and some of the first glossy catalogs of environmental products. Expressions of concern for the environment adorned politicians' stump speeches, both in the United States and overseas. Environmental scientists and activists widely agreed that the 1990s would be a critical decade to stem the course of environmental degradation, and political and cultural trends offered many people a renewed hope that this was indeed possible.

A *New York Times*/CBS News poll announced that people firmly supported environmental protection, despite perceptions of a growing conflict between ecology and job growth. Seventy-one percent agreed that "we must protect the environment even if it means increased govern-ment spending and higher taxes." Fifty-six percent said they would opt for environmental protection even at the expense of local job losses.[2]

Politicians of all stripes were quick to jump on board. President George Bush, a former Texas oil developer, declared himself "tough" on the environment, even though he had lobbied for oil drilling in the Arc-tic National Wildlife Refuge just weeks after the tragic 1989 Exxon Val-dez oil spill marred some 900 square miles of Alaskan coastline.[3] EPA chief William Reilly was credited with "greening the White House," even as he faced possible criminal charges in a case in which the EPA had pressured the state of North Carolina into hosting a commercial toxic waste dump. Senator Al Gore, the 1988 presidential campaign's leading Democratic hawk, began speaking out about global warming and other environmental threats. Internationally, Britain's "Iron Lady," Prime Minister Margaret Thatcher, called herself a "green," and even World Bank president Barber Conable managed to win praise from sev-eral environmental publications for voicing concerns about the Bank's role in environmental destruction.

The coming Earth Day celebrations aroused a mixture of hope and cynicism on the part of longtime activists. The hope lay in the vast num-bers of people from all walks of life who were working to make Earth Day a celebration of their own communities' concerns for the fate of the earth. The cynicism was fueled by much of the literature emanating from the official Earth Day organizations that had been established through-out the country. They had apparently decided that Earth Day was going to be a politically safe event: symbolic tree plantings, "educating our leaders," "a galaxy of celebrities," and the like. Their pronouncements included almost nothing about the institutions or the economic system responsible for ecocide, nothing about confronting corporate polluters, nothing about changing the structures of society.

The overriding message was simply, "change your lifestyle": recycle, drive less, stop wasting energy, buy better appliances, etc. And while the 1990 national Earth Day organization turned down more than $4 million in corporate donations that did not meet their quite flexible criteria, cele-brations in several major U.S. cities were supported by some of the coun-try's most notorious polluters—companies like Monsanto, Peabody

Coal, and Georgia Power, to name just a few.[4] Everyone from the nuclear power industry to the Chemical Manufacturer's Association took out full-page advertisements in newspapers and magazines proclaiming that, for them, "every day is Earth Day." The now-familiar greenwashing of Earth Day had clearly begun.

This turn of events proved disconcerting to many activists. In much of the movement's lore, Earth Day had become a symbol of the emergence of environmentalism as a social movement in its own right. Countless popular organizations traced their origin, directly or indirectly, to that auspicious day in April of 1970 when some twenty million people participated in a diverse and colorful outpouring of public concern about the natural environment.[5] Why had things changed so dramatically two decades later?

Activists began to probe the history of Earth Day, and their investigations revealed, to the surprise of many, that even the original Earth Day was largely a staged event. It was initiated by politicians like Senator Gaylord Nelson and supported, though not without controversy, by establishment institutions such as the Conservation Foundation, the corporate think tank founded in 1948 by Laurance Rockefeller.[6] Following President Nixon's rather suspect New Year's proclamation that the 1970s would be the "Environmental Decade," most anti-Vietnam War activists had come to view Earth Day as a devious attempt to divert attention from the war and from the anti-war movement's planned Spring Offensive, as well as from the common underlying causes of war, poverty, and environmental destruction. An editorial in *Ramparts*, the leading activist journal of the period, described Earth Day as "the first step in a con game that will do little more than abuse the environment even further."[7]

The Earth Day issue of *Ramparts* featured a story on "The Eco-Establishment," which focused on the corporate think tanks that were helping to shape the new environmental legislation. Following the descriptions of corporate reorganization and a "grosser national product" highlighted at the beginning of this chapter, the authors continued:

> The seeming contradictions are mind-boggling: industry is combating waste so it can afford to waste more; it is planning to produce more (smog-controlled) private autos to crowd more highways, which means even more advertising to create more "needs" to be met by

planned obsolescence. Socially, the result is disastrous. Ecologically, it could be the end.[8]

As journalist I. F. Stone wrote in his famous investigative weekly,

> Just as the Caesars once used bread and circuses so ours were at last learning to use rock-and-roll idealism and non-inflammatory social issues to turn the youth off from more urgent concerns which might really threaten the power structure.[9]

Reviewing this history intensified many activists' feelings of betrayal, and many responded by organizing more politicized local Earth Day anniversaries of their own. These events focused on local environmental struggles, inner-city issues, the nature of corporate power, and other concerns that had been largely excluded from the official Earth Day. The most ambitious of these was a demonstration in New York City called by members of the Greens and Youth Greens from throughout the Northeast, with the aid of environmental justice activists, Earth First!ers, ecofeminists, urban squatters, and many others. Early Monday morning, April 23, the day after millions had participated in polite, feel-good Earth Day commemorations all across the country, several hundred people converged on the nerve center of U.S. capitalism, the New York Stock Exchange, in an effort to obstruct the opening of trading. Juan Gonzalez, a columnist for the *New York Daily News*, decried the previous day's "embalming and fire sale of Earth Day," and told his 1.2 million readers:

> Certainly, those who sought to co-opt Earth Day into a media and marketing extravaganza, to make the public feel good while obscuring the corporate root of the Earth's pollution almost succeeded. It took angry Americans from places like Maine and Vermont to come to Wall Street on a workday and point the blame where it belongs.[10]

The Rise of Official Environmentalism

The events around Earth Day 1990—especially the blatant efforts of corporate imagemakers to identify their clients with environmental concerns—helped to provoke an unprecedented scrutiny of the habits and institutions of environmental politics in the United States.[11] Growing numbers of activists began to see the established national environmental organizations, which had long dominated media coverage, fundraising, and public visibility, as hopelessly out of step with the thousands of volunteers who largely defined the leading edge of locally based ecological activism.

Throughout the 1970s and '80s, representatives of the largest national environmental groups became an increasingly visible and entrenched part of the Washington political scene. As the appearance of success within the system grew, organizations restructured and altered their personnel so as to enhance their ability to play the insider game. The environmental movement became a stepping stone in the careers of a new generation of Washington lawyers and lobbyists, and adherents to official environmentalism came to accept the role long ago established for other public regulatory advocates: that of helping to sustain the smooth functioning of the existing political system. Environmentalism had been redefined, in the words of author and historian Robert Gottlieb, as "a kind of interest group politics tied to the maintenance of the environmental policy system.

"The activities of the mainstream groups were "defined increasingly as career training for the initiation and management of environmental policies," Gottlieb writes.[12] This shift in the character of the most nationally visible environmental groups virtually spelled the end of bold new policy initiatives on behalf of the environment. An environmental mainstream thoroughly wedded to "insider" politics proved incapable of sustaining even a moderate congressional consensus in favor of environmental protection and, ultimately, helped to prepare the stage for the anti-environmental backlash of the mid-'90s.

The institutionalization of mainstream environmentalism became entrenched with the rightward shift in the political culture of Washington, D.C. during the 1980s. With access to vast new funds, often gained through appeals to people's outrage against the Reagan administration's anti-environmentalism, the major environmental organizations assumed a conspicuously top-down corporate structure. Internal battles in organizations like the Sierra Club, Friends of the Earth, and in those years, even Greenpeace were invariably won by those advocating a more corporate style and attitude along with an avoidance of issues and tactics that might prove alienating to wealthy donors.

Prominent activists like David Brower—who faced repeated conflicts with the boards of the Sierra Club and Friends of the Earth, while amassing a record of accomplishments that made both organizations virtual household names—and Dave Foreman—who was a Wilderness Society lobbyist before achieving notoriety as a founder of Earth First!—expressed their dismay with this trend and were squeezed out of leadership roles in their respective national organizations. Foreman, who lost his position as the southwestern regional representative for the Wilderness Society in one of that organization's moves toward greater "professionalism"—wrote as early as 1984 of an intensifying "struggle between bureaucratic professionals and radical amateurs," in which the former "have a higher loyalty to the political process than to conservation." His colleagues became largely "concerned with improving their individual careers," Foreman explained several years later. "They did not want to rock the boat because they didn't want to spoil their chances of being administrative aide to a senator, or an assistant Secretary of the Interior at some point in the future."[13]

By the early 1990s, even the thoroughly mainstream former editor of *Audubon* magazine would lament over how "naturalists have been replaced by ecocrats who are more comfortable on Capitol Hill than in the woods, fields, meadows, mountains and swamps." Ironically, both Brower and Foreman would be elected to seats on the Sierra Club's board of directors in 1995 as part of a slate of candidates assembled to counter new initiatives by grassroots dissidents within the Club.[14]

Official environmentalism dramatically expanded its scope and visibility during the 1980s. The Sierra Club grew from 80,000 to 630,000 members, and the conservative National Wildlife Federation reported membership gains of up to 8,000 a month, totaling over 6 million members and supporters by 1990.[15] The World Wildlife Fund, best known for its efforts to establish national parks on the U.S. model in Third World countries, grew almost tenfold, while the Natural Resources Defense Council doubled its membership since 1985. The total budget of the ten largest environmental groups grew from less than $10 million in 1965 to $218 million in 1985, and $514 million in 1990. In 1993, journalist Mark Dowie found that of the approximately $3 billion contributed to environmental advocates each year, the twenty-five largest organizations got 70 percent, while the remaining share was divided among some 10,000 lesser-known groups.[16] Many groups became extremely dependent on direct mail, using each new environmental disaster to gain members, whether or not their organization was actively working on the issue.

Exxon's devastating 1989 oil spill in Prince William Sound, Alaska offers a striking example: environmentalists expressed outrage in the form of newspaper ads and press conferences, but they offered no forceful political response and no substantively new proposals. Everyone demanded a "proper" cleanup, along with protection for the Wildlife Refuge in the far north of Alaska, but no nationally recognized organization called for the closing of the Alaskan oil pipeline, the dismantling of Exxon, or for the limiting of new highway construction to help relieve our society's destructive dependence on fossil fuels. Still, the National Wildlife Federation gained 20,000 members in three weeks, the Sierra Club raised more than $100,000 from a *New York Times* ad (in a break from the usual practice, much of this was given to local groups in Alaska), and the Wilderness Society gained $50,000 in unsolicited contributions.[17] This was a particularly clear instance of the wholesale appropriation of a high-profile public issue for its fundraising potential, far out of proportion to the organizations' involvement in working to resolve the situation. Today, such practices have become entirely routine.

Investigating Official Environmentalism

In light of all these developments, Earth Day's twentieth anniversary came to symbolize the absorption of environmental concerns into the public relations efforts of corporate America. Activists curious about the role of the mainstream environmental groups in furthering this co-optation began to analyze them in much the same way as they had studied corporations. A perusal of the 1988 annual reports of the major environmental organizations revealed some interesting and occasionally surprising facts:

- The Sierra Club had a budget of $19 million, 64 percent of which came from member contributions. Their corporate matching gifts program, through which companies match employee contributions, brought in funds from ARCO, British Petroleum, Chemical Bank, Morgan Guaranty Trust, Pepsi, Transamerica, United Technologies, Wells Fargo, and others.

- The Audubon Society spent $38 million in 1988, with only $10 million coming from individual contributions. Corporate donors included Waste Management Incorporated, General Electric, GTE, Amoco, Chevron, Du Pont, and Morgan Guaranty Trust, with smaller donations (under $5,000) from Dow Chemical, Exxon, Ford, IBM, and Coca-Cola.
- The Wilderness Society ($9 million, 50 percent from members) also listed Morgan Guaranty and Waste Management among its corporate supporters. Its literature sought to assure readers that the federal system of designated wilderness areas, for which the group is a leading advocate, does not interfere in areas rich in oil, gas and minerals. The Society also advocates more intensive timber management in unprotected areas so that wilderness can be protected without harming the timber industry.
- The National Wildlife Federation had a 1988 budget of $63 million, with only 22 percent coming directly from members, and another 15 percent from the sale of magazine subscriptions to schoolchildren. Corporate donors included Amoco, ARCO, Coca-Cola, Dow, Duke Power, Du Pont, Exxon, General Electric, General Motors, IBM, Mobil, Monsanto, Tenneco, USX (formerly US Steel), Waste Management, Westinghouse and Weyerhaeuser. Matching grants came from Boeing, Chemical Bank, Citibank, Pepsico, the Rockefeller Group, United Technologies, and others.[18]

Shortly after these findings appeared in the February 1990 issue of *Z Magazine, Multinational Monitor* (part of Ralph Nader's unique network of organizations and publications) published a survey of the boards of directors of the leading environmental groups, and found that twenty-three directors and council members from the Audubon Society, NRDC, the Wilderness Society, the World Resources Institute, and the World Wildlife Fund were associated with nineteen corporations cited in the National Wildlife Federation's recent survey of the 500 worst industrial polluters. These companies included such recognized environmental offenders as Union Carbide, Exxon, Monsanto, Weyerhaeuser, Du Pont, and Waste Management. Furthermore, some sixty-seven individuals associated with just seven environmental groups served as CEOs, chairpersons, presidents, consultants, or directors for ninety-two major corporations.[19] This information began to be disseminated among grass-roots activists. The data on corporate contributions were distributed by the organizers of the Wall Street demonstration that followed Earth Day and were highlighted in a widely publicized open letter from leaders of the environmental justice movement questioning the racial policies of mainstream environmentalism (see Chapter Six).

The superbly well-endowed National Wildlife Federation came to be seen as the pinnacle of Washington environmentalists' accommodation to the ways of corporate America, a reputation that was illuminated by the Federation's close ties to the Bush administration. In 1982, NWF established a Corporate Conservation Council to "open dialogue" with "key industrial leaders" and further the idea that resource conservation is a essential to "economic progress." More than half of the Federation's corporate donors in the early '90s were members of the Council, which held regular seminars and conferences to promote mutually agreeable policy proposals. The National Wildlife Federation became a leading advocate for the myth of "sustainable development" in the Third World and a champion of "debt-for-nature" swaps, in which ecologically important lands in debtor countries are signed over to conservation groups in exchange for banks consenting to erase a portion of the country's debt (see Chapter Eight). "Our arguments must translate into profits, earnings, productivity, and economic incentives for industry," Federation president Jay Hair told a reporter for the *Washington Post* in 1991.[20]

In 1989, the National Wildlife Federation scandalized the emerging environmental justice movement when it offered a seat on its board of directors to Dean Buntrock, the head of Waste Management Incorporated, the world's largest processor of toxic chemical waste and the subject of numerous bribery and anti-trust convictions as well as citations for countless environmental violations. Today, Waste Management, known as WMX Technologies, cultivates a "responsible" image as a leading "environmental technology" company.

Another pivotal figure of that era was William Reilly, whose nomination by George Bush to head the EPA was widely applauded by environmentalists. Reilly's environmental credentials came from his work with the Conservation Foundation, which characteristically had become a leading proponent of "cooperation" between environmentalists and corporations. Through the Foundation's offshoot, Clean Sites, Inc., Reilly specialized in forging "compromise" solutions to environmental disputes, often at the expense of affected populations. Grassroots anti-toxics groups viewed Reilly's organization as a willing cover for corporate interests, promoting "mediated" partial cleanups of Superfund sites and helping corporations to minimize their liability for waste-site cleanups. *Environmental Action* magazine reported that the Conservation Foundation received grants of more than $50,000 from the ARCO Foundation, Du Pont, and Eastman Kodak, along with smaller grants from Exxon, General Electric, Monsanto, Shell Oil, Dow Chemical, and the Chemical Manufacturers Association, among others.[21]

In 1987 opponents of a proposed toxic waste facility in North Carolina won a strengthening of the state's wastewater discharge regulations as a means to prevent construction. The EPA intervened to block the new regulations, claiming they violated the state's responsibility under the federal Superfund Act to devise a plan for managing hazardous waste. Citizen lobbyists from North Carolina collected testimony from lawmakers showing that the state was not violating any federal laws, and Reagan's last EPA administrator, Lee Thomas, chose to back down. When Reilly took over in early 1989, he reportedly met with waste industry executives before pressing to reopen hearings challenging the North Carolina law. The story was leaked by two senior EPA officials, who filed criminal ethics charges against Reilly in the case, offering evidence of a meeting and a subsequent cover-up. The meetings between Reilly and the executives of Waste Management were initiated by none other than Jay Hair of the National Wildlife Federation, which now had Waste Management's CEO on its board. The much-touted "cooperation" between industry and environmentalists had indeed come full circle.[22]

At the time, the case was seen as a rather extreme example of collaboration between environmentalists and polluting corporations. But as mainstream environmentalists increasingly coveted their seats in Washington's policy circles, and came to identify further with those business and government interests that could bestow such access, incidents such as this became more commonplace. The history of mainstream environmentalism in the 1990s has been one of legislative compromise and capitulation, missed opportunities, and the ever persistent pursuit of "influence" in a fundamentally corrupt and anti-ecological political system. Despite consistent public support for environmental initiatives, and the rapid proliferation of environmental rhetoric and images, the actual condition of our air and water, the integrity of ecosystems, and the health of people show few signs of significant improvement.

Defenders of an "insider" approach to activism argue that access to the corridors of power enables them to work more effectively for the environment. Yet as the representatives of official environmentalism became more isolated from grassroots activists, the mainstream groups became rather comfortable in their safe and nonconfrontational stance. The politics of "acceptable risk," "flexible" regulation, and "responsible" compromise with the interests most responsible for environmental destruction has often drowned out the voices of principled opposition. These approaches have all but excluded discussion of the underlying causes of environmental destruction, while conferring added legitimacy to the interests behind the corporate greenwash.

In her 1993 book *Earth Follies*, feminist environmentalist Joni Seager highlighted the ways mainstream environmentalism is further limited by the almost uniformly white, male character of the leading organizations' professional staff and governing bodies. Women, in most mainstream groups, remain relegated to traditionally female administrative roles, and none of the thirty groups she surveyed had more than five staff members from any racial minority. The Audubon Society, Earth Island Institute, and WorldWatch Institute each had boards that were approximately 30 percent female, and none of the groups she surveyed had any more than this. Seager described the "schism" in the environmental movement as "increasingly between a mostly *male*-led professional elite and a mostly *female*-led grassroots movement."[23]

The Saga Continues

Today, analyses of the political and financial ties that have corrupted mainstream environmentalism are almost commonplace. Mainstream journalists, business schools, and even anti-environmental "wise use" organizations have published their own studies of environmental groups' finances and used the data to support their own often questionable political agendas.[24] As the largest environmental groups came to resemble the corporations they opposed, this kind of research found uses well across the political spectrum. While grassroots activists view corporate contributions as a symbol of co-optation and the dangers inherent in a strategy of working entirely within the existing political system, those seeking to discredit environmental protection see these contributions as evidence of simple corruption, greed, and a cynical response to changing public opinion. Anti-environmental advocates articulated a rather distorted theory of the decline of mainstream environmentalism, asserting despite all evidence to the contrary that the mainstream groups are bound to an "extremist" agenda that is at odds with the views of a majority of the public.[25]

In 1994, the Center for the Study of American Business at Washington University in St. Louis examined the established environmental groups' stock portfolios, ostensibly developed as a hedge against fluctuating memberships, and found that the Wilderness Society, for example, held stock in Dow Chemical, Kerr McGee and General Motors, and the NRDC in Dow, Westinghouse and General Electric. For organizations committed to protecting the environment and combating pollution to become financially dependent on the stock values of major polluters perhaps represents the ultimate corruption of ecological values. The same study confirmed that membership dues represented an ever declining share of the income of groups like the Wilderness Society and the National Audubon Society. But while the political influence wielded by these groups has fallen considerably since the early 1990s, income and membership levels have in most cases only leveled off or continued to rise at a slower rate.[26]

Though corporate contributions rarely represent a very large overall share of the budgets of the best-known environmental groups, they have conferred influence and political results well beyond their statistical measure. As Brian Lipsett, a leading researcher and editor for the environmental justice movement, has written:

> The corporations get a good return from their contributions to environmental causes.... Beyond public relations dividends and tax deductions, and even increased business opportunities, corporate sponsorship fractures internal consensus within recipient groups, di-

vides grantees from other environmental groups, blunts criticism from grantee groups, and creates openings for future influence by securing corporate representation on the groups' boards of directors.[27]

This helps to explain why corporations give to environmental organizations at nearly two and a half times the rate of overall public charitable donations to the environmental movement. Environmental giving amounts to 6 percent of corporate philanthropy, while it only accounts for 2.5 percent of all charitable donations.[28]

The 1993 and 1994 annual reports of some of the best-known environmental groups reveal a generally higher level of corporate influence than existed five years earlier. For example, the National Audubon Society, with similar budget totals and share of member contributions as in 1988, had expanded its list of corporate donors to include large gifts from Bechtel, AT&T, Citibank, Honda, Martin Marietta, Wheelabrator, Ciba-Geigy, Dow, and Scott Paper, with smaller donations (less than $5,000) from Monsanto, Mobil, and Shell Oil. The Society's major capital project, the conversion of an historic building in New York's Greenwich Village to its new headquarters—and a showcase of energy efficiency and recycled materials use—was supported by grants of over $100,000 each from WMX and Wheelabrator. The latter is a leading supplier of incinerator technologies that have been widely opposed by activists across the country due to serious environmental and public health concerns.

The World Wildlife Fund's corporate contributors are now led by the likes of the Bank of America, Kodak, and J. P. Morgan (over $250,000), with the Bank of Tokyo, Philip Morris, WMX, Du Pont and numerous others playing supporting roles. Its budget grew from $17 million in 1985 to $62 million in 1993, with roughly half of its revenues coming from individual contributions. The National Wildlife Federation's budget grew by more than 50 percent since 1988, to $96 million in 1994. Major corporate donors included Bristol Myers-Squibb, Ciba-Geigy, Du Pont, and Pennzoil, and an additional 161 companies participated in the Federation's matching gift program, in which individuals' gifts to the organization are matched by their employer. Other organizations, such as the Sierra Club, have made contributor information more difficult to obtain, but it is noteworthy that the Club's annual budget had leveled off at

$39 million, after peaking at $52 million in 1991. Membership dues had fallen to 32 percent of the Club's annual budget, half of the 1988 figure.

An interesting counterpoint to this story is the situation of Greenpeace, by far the most action-oriented of the leading national and international environmental groups. During the heady days of the late 1980s and early 1990s, Greenpeace flirted with a more respectable image and a more corporate structure. Its revenues grew rapidly, and the pool of regular contributors expanded into the millions. At the same time, its credibility among grassroots activists fell dramatically. In countless local efforts, activists accused Greenpeace of arriving in the midst of a campaign, attracting all the media attention, taking credit, raising money for Greenpeace, and leaving local activists to clean up afterward. Their image as a band of gallant, well-equipped warriors for the earth often undermined people's desire to do something about the ecological crisis. No ordinary group of citizens, it seemed, could possibly equal Greenpeace's sophistication and daring, much to the detriment of local grassroots activism.[29]

Between 1990 and 1994, Greenpeace U.S.A. lost nearly two-thirds of its members and suffered large declines in income.[30] There were major staff layoffs and their monthly magazine was forced to suspend publication. Instead of retreating into the safety of respectability and nonconfrontation, however, Greenpeace asserted its independence. It was in the forefront of environmental opposition to the Persian Gulf War. It developed closer working relationships with community activists, especially environmental justice activists in California and the South. In 1995, Greenpeace made international headlines for the first time in many years, first for preventing the dumping of an abandoned Shell Oil drilling rig off the coast of Scotland, and subsequently for its international campaign against France's sudden resumption of nuclear testing in the South Pacific. In 1996, Greenpeace took a leading role in the emerging controversy surrounding genetically engineered foods: Greenpeace activists applied a milk-based paint to a field of soybeans in Iowa that had been genetically altered by Monsanto for increased herbicide tolerance. They blocked shipments of these soybeans in the ports of Antwerp and Amsterdam, as well as at Cargill and Archer Daniels Midland's facilities in Louisiana. European consumers and food companies alike objected to the refusal of U.S. companies to separate the engineered soybeans from conventional U.S. soy exports.[31]

The Money Chase

One consistent factor in the institutionalization of official environmentalism has been the role of influential foundations in helping to frame the agendas of the leading organizations. Large foundations, like the Ford Foundation and the various Rockefeller funds, have been key players in the development of environmental organizations since the 1940s, leading some '60s activists to dismiss environmental concerns as a mere creation of corporate philanthropists.[32]

Foundations are often a controversial part of movements for social change. Organizations that wish to sustain themselves over time, initiate new projects, and offer salaries to staff members invariably need to attract large donations, and the established foundations have long been the most available source. Political scientist Joan Roelofs has demonstrated the role of foundations in the decline of '60s-era activism, arguing that grants were systematically allocated to assure "that radical energies were being channeled into safe, legalistic, bureaucratic and occasionally profit-making activities."[33] This pattern has been repeated in anti-poverty groups, women's groups, and in the African-American, Latino, and Native-American communities, as well as in the environmental movement.

In the 1990s, large donors have begun to intervene more directly to set the course of environmental activism. For example, a $275,000 grant to the Sierra Club in 1990 to support work on population issues made population advocacy the highest-funded program in the Club's budget. This raised much concern among activists who feared the effort would inadvertently support the rising wave of anti-immigration sentiment that was just beginning to sweep the country.[34]

In 1993, officers of the Pew Charitable Trusts brought together representatives from some of the leading regional and national forest protection groups in an attempt to create a unified nationwide forest campaign. While the participants initially seized the opportunity to help develop such a unified effort, they soon learned that Pew had a very particular agenda in mind.

"Pew was only interested in funding a campaign focused on legislation that would be passed by a Democratic Congress and that Clinton would sign," explains Andy Mahler of the Indiana-based Heartwood organization. Pew expressed little interest in aiding ongoing efforts at grassroots organizing, public education, or legal intervention by the member groups, suggesting to many that the potential effectiveness of the campaign was merely a secondary concern. "It was good in some ways that people were talking about uniting the movement," reports Mahler, who served as interim chair of the effort, "but it became a money chase—a search for the lowest common denominator. It put incredible stresses and strains on the forest movement that it has not recovered from to this day."[35]

Ultimately, Pew put its resources into a series of regional, rather than national, efforts. One of these was in the northeastern states, where a two-year congressional study had failed to raise sufficient political interest in protecting the endangered northern forest region. Representatives of mainstream environmental groups and leading foundations created the Northern Forest Alliance, with a stated mission of protecting the forests of northern New England and New York while promoting economic diversification. Groups in the region that depend on foundation grants were subsequently pressured to join the Alliance and mute their criticisms of its bland, noncontroversial, and piecemeal approach to the environmental health of a region that is threatened with significant short-term increases in destructive logging and commercial development.

The 1994 annual report of the Pew Charitable Trusts describes the approach that underlies these efforts. A "team of professionals," the report declares, stands behind the Trusts' environmental programs. This team, consisting of lawyers, scientists, and outside consultants, will:

> play a key role in generating many of the ideas behind the programs we support, participating with colleagues from the environmental community in defining the goals and objectives of these programs, designing their operating structures, hiring key staff and, in some cases, being directly involved in program execution.[36]

Investigative journalist Stephen Salisbury described the tactics of a growing sector of leading environmental funders when he wrote that Pew "created and funded dozens of programs and independent organizations to carry out agendas determined by the foundation and its consultants. It has promoted its own causes, pursued its own initiatives, bankrolled its own research and imposed its own order."[37]

In 1995, Northwest forest activist and journalist Jeffrey St. Clair joined with well-known columnist Alexander Cockburn to investigate the stock holdings of the three foundations that play the largest institutional role in supporting mainstream environmentalism. The three foundations, each the product of leading transnational oil fortunes, are the Pew Charitable Trusts (Sun Oil Co.), W. Alton Jones Foundation (Cities Service/CITGO), and the Rockefeller Family Fund. St. Clair and Cockburn found that the Pew endowment, with a total of $3.8 billion in holdings, is heavily invested in timber firms, mining companies, arms manufacturers, and chemical companies, as well as oil exploration. Alton Jones' timber investments include a subsidiary of the notorious Maxxam conglomerate, which is attempting to liquidate the largest single expanse of old growth redwood forest that remains in private hands (see Chapter Seven), along with Louisiana Pacific, the largest purchaser of timber from the National Forests. The foundation also holds a $1 million share in a controversial gold mining giant, the FMC Corporation. The Rockefeller Fund holds investments in no less than twenty-eight oil and gas development companies, as well as timber giants Weyerhaeuser and Boise Cascade. St. Clair and Cockburn traced a number of incidents in which environmental compromises engineered by the Clinton administration, and by groups such as the Wilderness Society, directly benefited these foundations' holdings.[38]

Confronting Corporate Power

In July 1994, four months before the Republican Party won control of Congress for the first time in forty years, the directors of the fifteen largest environmental groups, from the National Wildlife Federation to Greenpeace, sent a first-ever joint letter to their members calling for action against right-wing efforts to weaken major environmental laws.

"Even during the Reagan/[James] Watt/[Anne] Gorsuch years, we have never faced such a serious threat to our environmental laws in Congress," they wrote, despite the presence of a Democratic majority in both houses of Congress, as well as a Democrat in the White House. Their answer: Write to the White House and your representatives. There was no call for direct action or public mobilization, no unified media campaign to counter the "wise use" fraud, and no mention of corporations except for the elusive oil, timber, and mining "lobbies." Recipients were exhorted to write the president, send money to environmental groups, and trust their favorite Washington-based organization to do the rest.

In response to this well-meaning but severely limited effort, two prominent advisers to the environmental justice movement proposed an alternative. Peter Montague of the Environmental Research Foundation—and publisher of the widely quoted *RACHEL's Environment and Health Weekly*—and Richard Grossman, best known for founding Environmentalists for Full Employment during the 1970s, persuaded nearly 175 individuals and organizations—a virtual who's who of grassroots environmentalism—to sign a letter imploring the directors of the fifteen national groups to begin addressing the issue of corporate power. "We believe that it is too late to counter corporate power environmental law by environmental law, regulatory struggle by regulatory struggle. We don't have sufficient time or resources to organize chemical by chemical, forest by forest ... product by product, corporate disaster by corporate disaster," the letter pleaded, urging a coordinated strategy to address the larger issues at stake. None of the fifteen groups ever responded to their letter.

Grossman has also developed a campaign to encourage activists to challenge the myth of the inviolability of corporate charters and the fiction of legal personhood that gives "corporate leaders legal authority to make private decisions on very public issues." His research, undertaken with worker-management pioneer Frank Adams, traces the gradual but systematic erosion of the public power to regulate corporate practices in the United States.[39] Their strategy of challenging corporate charters on the state level is one important aspect of a much-needed effort to re-energize popular opposition to corporate power.

In 1995, the long-awaited twenty-fifth anniversary of Earth Day came and went with considerably less fanfare than the celebration five years earlier. Controversies over corporate contributions largely derailed plans for the biggest—and the most utterly compromised—Earth Day ever. Earth Day organizers hired a corporate public relations firm, Dorf & Stanton, to coordinate program development and communications, and established a short-lived "Earth Day Corporate Team" to actively solicit corporate participation. The organization was rocked with dissent and underwent two complete reorganizations before a revived Earth Day organization raised $6.5 million in corporate contributions.[40] The official Earth Day 1995 petition, addressed with a puzzling forthrightness to House Speaker Newt Gingrich, began with the following statement:

> With major polluters such as Texaco and Monsanto attempting to "sponsor" Earth Day, and every politician in the nation claiming to be "for the environment," it is getting hard to figure out who is really protecting the planet and who is poisoning it.[41]

The corporate co-optation of Earth Day, an idea that provoked intense controversy in 1990 and brought hundreds of people to demonstrate on Wall Street, had become 1995's conventional wisdom. One can only hope that those enlisted to circulate the petitions stopped for a moment to consider the full political significance of those words. If the lesson of corporate influence is heeded, there may be some hope for an Earth Day 2000 that will finally be worthy of its name.

Chapter 2

Trading Away the Earth

"... the IPUAIC was a creature of the smog, born of the need to give those working to produce the smog some hope of a life that was not all smog, and yet, at the same time, to celebrate its power."
—Italo Calvino, "Smog," 1958[1]

Since the beginnings of the Industrial Revolution, corporate managers have sought to obscure the social and environmental impacts of pollution. Like Calvino's bedraggled editor of a fictional trade journal improbably named *Purification*—the organ of an industry-sponsored Institute for the Purification of the Urban Atmosphere in Industrial Centers—corporate functionaries have obligingly stretched the truth to put the best possible face on their employers' destructive activities.

We have seen how extractive industries appropriated the language of conservation in the 1920s, elite think tanks took the initiative in environmental research in the 1950s, and corporations steadily increased their influence over the mainstream environmental movement during the 1980s. In the 1990s, however, these efforts have taken a bold new turn. Even as corporate lobbyists work tirelessly behind the scenes to dismantle decades' worth of environmental protections, a new generation of policy analysts and free market ideologues has successfully advanced the notion that corporations—and the capitalist market itself—are now the key to a cleaner environment. This updated version of corporate environmentalism has had a striking impact on national legislation, regulatory policies, and not surprisingly, the U.S. environmental movement.

Can the "free market" help to promote a clean environment? Can tropical forests be protected in a manner favorable to the multinational banks? Do companies have "rights" to pollute that should be tradable as a commodity? Will corporations guide themselves toward becoming "environmentally responsible"?

A decade or two ago, few environmentalists would have taken these questions seriously. But thanks to a new wave of corporate public relations, such claims have risen to the top of the agenda of several national environmental groups. At the forefront of this initiative are think tanks such as the American Enterprise Institute and the Democratic Leadership Council's Progressive Policy Institute, along with mainstream environmental groups such as the influential Environmental Defense Fund. Corporate and government officials still frequently denounce environmentalists as enemies of economic progress, but now these same officials would have the public simultaneously believe that they are the true environmentalists. The mid-1990s have seen a redoubled effort by the champions of the "free market" to co-opt the environmental movement's often not-well-defined political direction. Many mainstream environmentalists have willingly allowed themselves to be taken along for the ride, particularly as "free market" environmentalism has become an important cornerstone of the Clinton administration's environmental policies.

Glossy catalogs of "environmental products," television commercials featuring environmental themes, and appropriation of the language of environmentalism to support corporate initiatives are merely the most visible hallmarks of the greenwashing of U.S. corporations.[2] Many of the same companies that support the Republican Right's wholesale assault on environmental regulation have retained high-priced public relations firms to create an environmentally friendly public image. John Stauber and Sheldon Rampton, in their probing study of the public relations industry, sarcastically titled *Toxic Sludge Is Good for You*, estimate that corporate America spends $1 billion a year for this cynical mixture of anti-environmental lobbying and environmentally friendly imagemaking. Stauber and Rampton found that one of the leading anti-environmental PR firms, Edelman Public Relations, credited with creating the virulently anti-environmental Alliance for America, has even gotten one of its executive vice-presidents, Leslie Dach, elected to the board of the National Audubon Society.[3]

Pollution for Sale

The new corporate environmentalism goes much farther than adopting environmental language, airing television commercials, promoting "environmental products," or infiltrating high-profile environmental groups. It represents a wholesale effort to recast environmental protection based on a model of commercial transactions within the capitalist marketplace. "A new environmentalism has emerged," wrote economist Robert Stavins, who has been associated with both the Environmental Defense Fund and the Progressive Policy Institute, "that embraces ... market-oriented environmental protection policies."[4] Stavins directed a pioneering effort known as Project 88, which brought together environmentalists, academics, and government officials with representatives of Chevron, Monsanto, ARCO, and other major corporations. Its goal, back in 1988, was to propose new environmental initiatives to the administration of President-elect George Bush, featuring market incentives as a supplement to regulation. Project 88 was careful to distance itself from those who advocated "putting a price on our environment, assigning dollar values to environmental amenities or auctioning public lands to the highest bidder."[5] Despite its relatively cautious tone, however, Project 88 opened the door to a much more sweeping rejection of regulation in favor of so-called market mechanisms.

George Bush staged a significant media coup when he announced a series of proposed amendments to the federal Clean Air Act during the summer of 1989. Knowing that any positive initiative for the environment was bound to win accolades from a press corps well trained to emphasize presidential rhetoric over substance, Bush's advisers cast the proposal as a striking departure from Ronald Reagan's rabid anti-environmentalism. The plan would reduce acid rain-causing sulfur emissions, put large cities on a timetable for smog reduction, encourage the use of alternative fuels, and increase the regulation of toxic chemicals. Its most unique and far-reaching proposal would for the first time establish into U.S. law the practice of allowing companies to buy and sell the "right" to pollute.

The idea of marketable pollution rights was a cornerstone of Project 88, but it did not entirely originate with Stavins and his colleagues. The EPA had experimented with a limited program of "emissions trading" since 1974, for the benefit of corporations like Du Pont, Amoco, USX, and 3M. These were mostly individually brokered deals, in which the EPA would allow companies to offset pollution from new industrial facilities by reducing existing emissions elsewhere, or negotiating with another company to do so. This approach has been used in the Los Angeles area and other cities to broker measured reductions of particular pollutants. In a 1979 article in the *Harvard Law Review,* a Harvard law professor named Stephen Breyer, now a justice on the U.S. Supreme Court, proposed a more ambitious system of "marketable rights to pollute" as a possible alternative to both taxes and regulation (see Chapter Three).[6]

Under the Bush plan, which became law as part of the Clean Air Act reauthorization of 1990, companies that reduced emissions of sulfur dioxide or other pollutants in one location would receive credits redeemable against higher emissions elsewhere. These credits could then be sold at a profit to other companies that were not in compliance with emissions standards or wished to build new facilities. It was the first attempt to extend emissions trading to the national level, to establish allowances that could be traded freely as a commodity, and to codify such trading into law as the centerpiece of a major regulatory program. Defenders of the plan claimed that the ability to profit from pollution credits would better encourage companies to invest in new pollution control technologies than would a system of fixed standards. They predicted tremendous savings to the economy, as the most cost-effective pollution reductions would be implemented first, and more expensive ones could be postponed until new technologies became available. As pollution standards would be tightened over time, proponents argued, the credits would become more lucrative and everybody could reap higher profits while fighting pollution.

In some political circles, the idea of making pollution a tradable commodity raised considerable alarm. Would they someday be selling cancer bonds on the New York Stock Exchange, as *Village Voice* columnist James Ridgeway suggested in the aftermath of Bush's speech? Or will we follow the course envisioned by Todd Gitlin in a *New York Times* op-ed piece, where he projected that states would soon be assigned quotas for murder, rape, and armed robbery, and people would go out shopping for armed robbery credits at the end of the year so they can get their children more Christmas presents?[7]

Yet the "pollution rights" provisions now enshrined in the Clean Air Act sparked surprisingly little controversy in the mainstream environmental movement, and opponents such as the U.S. Public Interest Research Group were effectively silenced. The debate has, for the most part, been limited to technicalities, such as what kinds of pollution are sufficiently transferable from one place to another—reductions in emissions causing acid rain some distance away should be traded, some proponents argue, while local rises and falls in smog levels in different regions should not. The Environmental Defense Fund has since proposed trading programs in western water rights and offshore fishing allotments, while others are seeking to make federal mining and grazing permits tradable on the open market. The ensuing discussions have been extremely revealing of the increasing influence of pro-corporate ideology within the environmental movement.

How It Works, and Doesn't

A closer look at the scheme for nationwide emissions trading reveals a certain cleverness amid the underlying folly. For true believers in the invisible hand of the market, it may seem positively ingenious. Here is how it works: The Clean Air Act amendments were designed to halt the spread of acid rain by requiring a 50 percent reduction in the total sulfur dioxide emissions from fossil fuel-burning power plants by the year 2000. Power plants were targeted as the largest contributors to acid rain, and participation by non-utility industrial polluters remained optional. To achieve this goal, utilities were granted transferable allowances to emit sulfur dioxide in proportion to their current emissions. This would become the "free-market" alternative to mandating emissions reductions, taxing the worst polluters, or underwriting the wider use of scrubbers and other pollution controls.

Any facility that continued to pollute more than its allocated share would then have to buy allowances from someone who pollutes less. Emissions allowances were expected to begin selling for around $500 per ton of sulfur dioxide, with a theoretical ceiling of $2,000 per ton, which is the legal penalty for violating the new rules. Companies that could reduce emissions for less than the cost of the credits would be able to sell them at a profit, while those that lagged behind would have to keep buying credits at a steadily rising price. Firms could choose to purchase credits on the open market rather than implement additional pollution controls. Thus, it is argued, market forces would assure that the most cost-effective means of reducing acid rain will be implemented first, saving billions of dollars in pollution control costs and stimulating the development of new technologies.

There were numerous loopholes to entice utilities to participate in the program. A portion of the total emissions allowances were set aside to actually facilitate the construction of new projects. These were auctioned off beginning in 1993, with annual auctions of new allowances to continue indefinitely. Utilities get additional allowances for implementing an approved conservation plan. There are also many pages of rules for extensions and substitutions. The plan essentially eliminated requirements for backup systems on smokestack scrubbers and then eased the rules for estimating how much pollution is emitted when monitoring systems fail. With reduced emissions now a marketable commodity, the range of possible abuses will continue to grow, as utilities have a greater incentive than ever to cheat on reporting what comes out of their stacks.[8] "It's a bit like playing Wall Street or the Chicago Commodity Exchange," said one official of the utility industry's research arm, the Electric Power Research Institute.[9]

The comparison with more traditional forms of commodity trading came full circle in 1991, when it was announced that the entire system for trading and auctioning emissions allowances would be administered by the Chicago Board of Trade. Long famous for its ever frantic markets in everything from grain futures and pork bellies to foreign currencies, the

Board is responsible for selling and auctioning allowances, maintaining a computer bulletin board to match buyers and sellers, and even establishing a futures market, ostensibly to protect allowance holders against price fluctuations. "While a small, but significant, step toward the ultimate creation of cash and futures market trading in emission allowances, this represents a larger step toward applying free-market techniques to address societal problems," proclaimed Chicago Board of Trade Chairman William O'Connor in a January 1992 press release.[10]

But once the EPA actually began auctioning pollution credits in 1993, virtually nothing went according to their projections. The first pollution credits sold for between $122 and $310, significantly less than the agency's estimated minimum price, and by 1996 successful bids at the EPA's annual auction of sulfur dioxide allowances averaged $68 per ton of emissions.[11] Many utilities preferred to go ahead with pollution control projects, such as the installation of new scrubbers, that were planned before the credits became available. Others switched to low-sulfur coal and increased their use of natural gas in order to meet their eventual targets of 50 percent reductions in sulfur emissions.

Many companies questioned the viability of financial instruments such as pollution allowances, while others, most notably the North Carolina based utility Duke Power, are aggressively buying allowances. At the 1995 EPA auction, Duke Power alone bought 35 percent of the short-term "spot" allowances and 60 percent of the long-term allowances, which are redeemable in the years 2001 and 2002. *Forbes* magazine blamed low participation on "regulatory uncertainty": utilities were concerned that state regulators would not permit them to include the cost of sulfur dioxide allowances in their rate base and raise customers' electric bills accordingly.[12]

The outcome of the EPA's experiment in emissions trading also reveals the inherent inequalities of such a system. Seven companies, including five utilities and two brokerage firms, bought 97 percent of the short-term "spot" allowances for sulfur dioxide emissions that were auctioned in 1995 and 92 percent of the longer-term allowances. The remaining few percent were purchased by a wide variety of people and organizations, including some who sincerely wished to take pollution allowances out of circulation. Students at several law schools raised hundreds of dollars, and a group at the Glens Falls Middle School on Long Island raised $3,171 to purchase twenty-one allowances, equivalent to twenty-one tons of sulfur dioxide emissions over the course of a year. Unfortunately, this represented less than a 0.1 percent of the allowances auctioned off in 1995. By the fall of 1996, nearly $50 million in allowances had traded hands, in both public and private transactions. The Glens Falls group raised $20,000 for their 1996 effort, and were joined by six other middle and high school groups and fourteen additional nonprofit organizations, each raising much smaller amounts. These well-meaning, but ultimately naive, attempts to fight pollution by "buying" a few tons of sulfur dioxide at a time offer a curious testament to the emerging faith in market "solutions" to political problems.[13]

Where pollution credits have been traded, their effect has often run counter to the program's stated intentions. One of the first publicized deals was a sale of credits by the Long Island Lighting Company to an unidentified midwestern company, raising concerns that regions suffering from the effects of acid rain were selling "pollution rights" to companies in regions where most of the pollution that causes acid rain originates. One of the first companies to bid for additional credits, the Illinois Power Company, canceled construction of a $350 million scrubber system in Decatur, Illinois. "Our compliance plan is based almost totally on purchase of credits," an Illinois Power spokesperson told the *Wall Street Journal*.[14]

At least one company has tried to cash in on the confusion by assembling packages of "multi-year streams of pollution rights," allowing utilities to defer or supplant purchases of new pollution control technologies. "What a scrubber really is, is a decision to buy a 30-year stream of allowances," John B. Henry of Clean Air Capital Markets told the *New York Times* with impeccable capitalist logic. "If the price of allowances declines in future years," paraphrased the *Times*, "the scrubber would look like a bad buy."[15] Meanwhile, supporters of tradable allowances continue to spin improbable claims. For example, Environmental Defense Fund director Fred Krupp told a business-oriented environmental magazine in 1994, "When companies receive credit for getting rid of sulfur dioxide, they are suddenly eager to search for, find and implement

... innovative and cheaper technologies."[16] Next to such obfuscations, the cynical candor of a John B. Henry seems almost refreshing.

Other proponents are more realistic. "With a tradeable permit system, technological improvement will normally result in lower control costs and falling permit prices, rather than declining emissions levels," wrote Robert Stavins (formerly of EDF) and Bradley Whitehead (a Cleveland-based management consultant with ties to the Rockefeller Foundation) in a 1992 policy paper published by the Democratic Leadership Council's Progressive Policy Institute.[17] In contrast to environmentalists like Fred Krupp of EDF, who have to defend their devotion to the new gospel of market environmentalism, these consultants are quite ready to concede that a tradable permit system is not likely to reduce pollution. Stavins and Whitehead further acknowledge, albeit in a footnote to an appendix, that the system can quite easily be compromised by large companies' "strategic behavior." Control of 10 percent of the market, they suggest, might be enough to allow firms to engage in "price-setting behavior." To the rest of us, it should be clear that if pollution permits are like any other commodity that can be bought, sold, and traded, then the largest "players" will have substantial control over the entire "game." Emission trading thus becomes yet another way to assure that large corporate interests will remain free to threaten public health and ecological survival, often with the willing consent of official environmentalism.

A Global Casino: Offsets vs. Pollution Taxes

The Environmental Defense Fund has distinguished itself among the mainstream groups with its aggressive support for the trading of emissions allowances and the development of a futures market for pollution. EDF senior economist Daniel Dudek described the trading of acid rain emissions as a "scale model": for EDF, the "global scope [of greenhouse gas emissions] implies a much richer set of trading opportunities."[18] As a step toward what they foresee as an eventual "international system of greenhouse gas limits and trading," they have devised a plan to initiate trading of carbon dioxide emissions here in the United States. vice-president Al Gore, among others, threw his support behind this idea, endorsing it as a way to "rationalize investments" in alternatives to carbon dioxide-producing activities.[19]

The idea of offsetting new emissions in one place by reducing them elsewhere has been heavily promoted by industries seeking to clean up their environmental image. The developer of a large fossil fuel-burning power plant in Connecticut reaped considerable praise and headlines by agreeing to help fund an agroforestry project in Guatemala, and chemical companies have proposed all kinds of offset schemes to meet pollution control requirements while continuing to expand their own facilities.[20] Owners of a mothballed waste incinerator in Vermont tried unsuccessfully to get an exemption from state limits on dioxin emissions by offering to help other nearby industries reduce their dioxin output. Western European industries are trying to offset increased pollution at home by investing in pollution control measures in Poland and other former Eastern Bloc countries.

International emissions trading gained further support via a UN Conference on Trade and Development study issued in 1992. The report was coauthored by Kidder and Peabody executive managing director and Chicago Board of Trade director Richard Sandor, who told the *Wall Street Journal*, "Air and water are simply no longer the 'free goods' that economists once assumed. They must be redefined as property rights so that they can be efficiently allocated."[21]

Radical ecologists have long decried the inherent tendency of capitalism to turn everything into a commodity; here we have a rare instance in which the system fully reveals its intentions. There is little doubt that an international market in "pollution rights" would widen existing inequalities among nations and increase the dominance of those best able to shift their assets from country to country based on the daily fluctuations of financial markets. It is a highly speculative experiment with the potential for massively disruptive consequences. Even in the United States, a single large investor in pollution credits would be able to control the future development of many different industries. Expanded to an international scale, the potential for unaccountable manipulation of industrial policy would easily compound the disruptions already caused by often reckless international traders in stocks, bonds, and currencies.

How relevant are these various proposals and machinations at a time when our most basic environmental protections are under attack? Is it not better to be able to use the market to limit pollution than to have no recourse at all against the continued degradation of public health and natural ecosystems? Is the partial cooperation of powerful corporations not preferable to their unbridled hostility toward environmental agendas? The prevalence of such questions in today's environmental debates reflects the failure of vision in mainstream environmentalism, and has helped to fuel the anti-environmental backlash. Perpetuating this extremely limited view can only reinforce the power and prestige of the institutions that are ultimately responsible for the ecological crisis.

Consider, for example, the views of Robert Stavins, who helped draft the environmental chapter of *Mandate for Change*, the Progressive Policy Institute's 1992 policy blueprint for the incoming Clinton administration. The chapter, coauthored with Thomas Grumbly—then of Clean Sites, Inc. and now an assistant secretary at the Department of Energy responsible for nuclear waste management—places tradable permits, pollution taxes, and other "market solutions" in a wider political context.

Stavins and Grumbly's underlying assumption is that environmental pollution can no longer be treated as an anomaly or failure of the system. It is simply a conspicuous feature of modern industrial economies: a cost of doing business, no more, no less. The "old thinking" that condemns pollution as "a moral failing of corporate (and political) leaders" needs to be replaced by an acceptance of pollution as "a by-product of modern civilization that can be regulated and reduced, but not eliminated." Politically, this means an end to the "widespread antagonism toward corporations and a suspicion that anything supported by business [is] bad for the environment."[22]

Instead of promoting the "inefficient," "centralized," "command-and-control" regulations of the past, they write, the government should seek to control pollution largely through the use of "market mechanisms." Their language here clearly mirrors the classic rhetoric of Cold War anticommunism and the fervor surrounding capitalism's "victory." The attack on traditional technology-based standards, which were instituted by Congress as a safeguard against the widespread abuses of the Reagan-era EPA, is no less than a political crusade for pro-corporate environmentalists. Their overriding goal is to "permit the burden of pollution control to be shared more efficiently among firms" (to quote the earlier Stavins and Whitehead study), and ultimately, "to set and reach our environmental goals in ways that are smarter, cheaper, and better for economic growth."[23]

Interestingly, the "market solutions" most favored by Stavins and Grumbly—and by commentators as diverse as Justice Stephen Breyer and environmental business guru Paul Hawken—are direct charges levied against companies that pollute. Already in force in much of Western Europe, pollution charges or taxes are readily defensible in "free market" terms. Breyer has extolled pollution taxes as a way of adjusting prices to reflect the true cost of producing a product, while creating legitimate "incentives to direct behavior in a socially desirable direction," incentives that do not inherently limit "individual choice."[24] Robert Hahn of the American Enterprise Institute collaborated with Stavins on a 1991 paper advocating pollution charges and defending them in traditional microeconomic terms.[25] Paul Hawken, in his widely quoted book *The Ecology of Commerce*, takes it a step further, asserting that "Green taxes would create, perhaps for the first time since the Industrial Age began, the closest thing approximating a truly free market, with many costs now externalized fully accounted for."[26]

Unfortunately, the corporate world and its representatives in Congress have been far less friendly to the idea of a free-market utopia ushered in by pollution taxes. While tradable permits sailed through Congress with relatively little controversy in 1990, a similarly aligned Congress in 1993 dismissed Bill Clinton's early proposal for a modest energy tax, even though it was justified primarily as a deficit-cutting measure. Comprehensive pollution taxes, such as have been successfully implemented in France, the Netherlands, Italy, Germany, and the Scandinavian countries, have yet to be seriously proposed in the United States. If they were, they would certainly be condemned as an excessive and outrageous government intervention in the marketplace, and a thoughtless disincentive to business development. All the microeconomic explanations in the world are insufficient to shatter the pro-business consensus over what kinds of government "interventions" are appropriate. Oil depletion allowances, savings and loan bailouts, free trade agreements, and tradable pollution allowances are all easily rationalized for one simple reason: they enrich private interests, especially the largest corporations, at public expense. Energy and pollution taxes, however justifiable in market terms, are too "interventionist" precisely because they do not primarily serve this single-minded goal.

Saving Energy, Greening Production

Another area where the limits of a market-oriented approach to environmental issues are readily apparent is in the continuing debate over energy policy. Since the oil shortages of the 1970s, substantial economic savings and reductions in pollution have been realized by policies that divert utility investments from new power plants to energy-saving technologies. At least as much energy is now saved every year as a result of the conservation and efficiency improvements implemented since the early 1970s as is produced by burning oil.[27] In the late 1980s, with utilities again on the defensive against rising electric rates, many state utility regulators hoped to boost conservation by offering utilities additional inducements to invest in conservation. Companies were offered rate increases and other incentives for such investments, comparable to the increases that inevitably follow the construction of new power plants. Proponents of this policy, known as "demand-side management" (DSM)—most notably, the Boston-based Conservation Law Foundation—argued that as utilities profited from energy savings, customers would share in the benefits due to decreased demand, and everyone would ultimately come out ahead.

With near-term profits all but guaranteed, utilities proved quite willing to subsidize home weatherproofing, energy-saving light bulbs, and even experimental purchases of solar water heaters. Every effort was accompanied by a publicity campaign extolling the utility's commitment to conservation. Yet much of the available funds were squandered on high-profile demonstration projects, administrative costs, and specialized programs only accessible to the most affluent home owners. Sometimes, as little as a quarter of DSM expenditures actually went toward implementing energy conservation measures.[28] Many programs inadvertently served to heighten the inequities in energy expenditures between wealthier home owners and low-income people, who spend a far greater portion of their total income on electricity.

By the mid-1990s, faced with low oil prices, excess supplies of electricity—due to overbuilding of coal and nuclear plants in previous decades—and increased competition in the utility sector, many companies petitioned to opt out of their energy efficiency programs. Despite considerable windfalls from these programs, utility executives could only temporarily suppress their disdain for any activity designed to reduce sales of electricity. Conservation programs advertised as cost-conscious innovations one year were denounced a year later by the same companies as unreasonable government interventions into the marketplace. Industry analysts speculate that DSM will be an early casualty of current efforts to deregulate and restructure the utility industry.

In the heyday of demand-side management, such incentive-based approaches were seen by many environmentalists as a way of developing environmentally sound technologies throughout the industrial sector. If companies are offered incentives to implement newer, more efficient production methods, market enthusiasts still argue, they will ultimately save money and increase profit margins while helping to protect the environment. While companies may resist adopting new technologies mandated by government regulators, it is assumed that they would gladly upgrade to more efficient and less polluting technologies if offered sufficient encouragement to respond to market forces.

This approach was pioneered in the late 1970s by innovative policy analysts, led by "soft energy" wizard Amory Lovins. Lovins became a household name among safe energy advocates for his bold projections of the economic benefits and the good-sense practicality of a widespread conversion to energy efficient technologies.[29] His proposal to create a market for "negawatts"—units of energy savings, in comparison to the megawatts of electricity produced by new power plants—played a key role in popularizing demand-side management, and his earliest projections of possible energy savings were generally exceeded. Yet Lovins' gospel of efficiency, competitiveness, and leading edge technology fell far short of the ambitious goal of replacing three-quarters of U.S. oil consumption and almost 80 percent of electricity with existing energy-saving technologies, which are already far less costly than new sources.[30]

The main difficulty here is that the present economic system is oriented toward maximizing profits, not efficiency. While efficiency improvements lower the costs of production in the long run, corporations will generally accept the somewhat higher expense of sustaining production methods that have proven to keep profits growing. When companies can already reduce production costs by laying off workers, contracting out large portions of the production process, or moving entire factories overseas, the uncertain promise of lowering expenses by improving energy efficiency holds considerably less appeal. Lovins' focus on efficiency goes against the grain of a business world aggressively oriented toward growth, capital mobility, and the concentration of economic power. Even direct incentives to stockholders to encourage utility investments in energy conservation have proved insufficient to sustain long-term interest in these programs.[31]

Further, companies that supply oil, minerals, and other resources exercise considerable clout over financial markets and corporate boards of directors. Significant investments in efficiency, conservation, and pollution prevention thus run counter to the interests of the market's most influential players. Companies often prefer to hire lobbyists to press for weaker environmental regulations than to substantially invest in conservation or clean technology. This situation is unlikely to change without a far-reaching democratization of day-to-day economic decisions. Even publicly owned municipal utilities seeking to save energy are constrained by a market thoroughly dominated by large commercial utilities, which generally control the energy supply.

Similar difficulties have arisen with pollution prevention, another arena where free-market ideology and market environmentalism often conflict with political realities. Chemical companies such as Dow, Monsanto, and 3M have gained accolades from mainstream environmentalists for their highly publicized efforts to reduce waste and toxic emissions, even though these efforts are largely in response to regulatory and other political pressures. Free-market enthusiasts have proclaimed a new age of "industrial ecology," in which companies will voluntarily cooperate to reduce pollution, practice intensive materials recycling, and use each other's waste products as feedstocks for other phases of production. Management consultant Hardin Tibbs is one of the leading advocates of this approach and is acclaimed for his vision of a world of "green corporations" and an unabashedly profit-oriented corporate environmentalism:

> Our challenge now is to engineer industrial infrastructures that are good ecological citizens, so that the scale of industrial activity can continue to increase—to meet international demand without running into environmental constraints or, put another way, without resulting in a negative impact on the quality of life.[32]

Widespread changes in production methods are clearly a necessary step toward an ecologically sustainable future; however, their acceptance within a capitalist economic framework requires some scrutiny. Tibbs' most quoted example is of an industrial park in the Danish town of Kalundborg, where the power plant recycles its waste steam to heat nearby factories; an oil refinery sells excess sulfur to a chemical company and heat to a fish farm; and a leading biotechnology company, Novo Nordisk, offers high-nutrient sludge from its fermentation vats to farmers as fertilizer. Neither Tibbs nor the market-oriented environmentalists who quote him are inclined to question Novo Nordisk's production of genetically engineered enzymes for everything from detergents, cheese, and animal feeds to the "stone washing" of blue jeans.[33] Nor do they say much about the refinery's pollution and its effects on the health of nearby residents.[33] And little emphasis is placed on the Danish government's aggressive promotion of energy conservation and environmental technology, including implementation of energy efficient technologies—such as the district heating of homes linked by underground heat pipes—that are virtually unheard of in the United States.

Much of Europe has embraced increased environmental regulation, recycling requirements, and pollution taxes, and companies comply in the face of considerable public pressure to curtail the damaging effects of pollution. Ecocapitalist Paul Hawken praises the German automaker BMW for its effort to make car parts easier to disassemble and recycle, but he neglects to mention that such innovations are mandated by public policy in many parts of Europe. Norway and Sweden have national deposit-refund systems for car bodies, similar to our still hotly contested state-level "bottle bills," and companies are under considerable political pressure to adopt new recycling technologies before they are required to by law.[34] Almost as an afterthought, Hawken reveals that landfill costs in both Germany and Japan are more than ten times higher than in the United States.[35]

Industry analysts have long suggested that increased competition with European and Japanese producers will result in improved efficiency and reduced pollution. But while key environmental technologies, from photovoltaic solar cells to catalytic converters, were first developed in the United States, U.S.-based firms have been quite willing to let overseas companies improve and market their innovations.[36] U.S. companies may try to catch up, as in the market for smaller, more fuel-efficient automobiles. In other areas, such as industrial machine tools, many of the U.S. companies responsible for important innovations have long since disbanded, or have become absorbed by large conglomerates that have little lasting interest in production technologies. While corporate profits skyrocketed between 1990 and 1995, investments in new plants and equipment by *Fortune* magazine's 500 largest firms fell by 40 percent.[37]

In this time of unprecedented corporate concentration, profits from speculative financial investments increasingly outweigh profits from improved production methods. Corporate public relations departments, along with legal staffs concerned about compliance with environmental regulations, are far more engaged in the promotion of environmental technologies than those primarily concerned with the bottom line. For example, while Dow Chemical sought headlines in the early 1990s for its efforts to reduce toxic emissions, company officials traced their apparent change in philosophy to "recent anti-pollution legislation and sentencing guidelines [that] could make environmental managers the subject of criminal prosecution."[38] Procter and Gamble "significantly broadened its market share" when it added environmental claims to its labels.[39] Consulting firms specializing in "Strategic Environmental Management" are helping companies play the regulations, along with public perceptions, in pursuit of competitive advantage. Genuine environmental improvements may sometimes result, but only as long as public pressure and vigilance back up the regulatory stick.

Free Market Conservationism

Emissions trading, demand-side management, industrial ecology, and other such measures are heavily promoted by free-market enthusiasts seeking to influence environmental policy. But even their optimistic claims pale beside the arguments of those who would bring the wonders of the capitalist marketplace to the management of the United States' vast public land holdings. The most aggressive and outlandish schemes for the privatization of public lands often originate with representatives of extractive industries and the highly manipulated "wise use" property rights movement. Yet as the debate over public lands management has become more polarized, self-professed conservationists have emerged with their own "market solutions," lending further credence to the most ardent privatizers.

One simple fact has driven many environmentalists to consider market-based alternatives to the present system of public lands management: much of the unsustainable resource extraction currently taking place on federally managed lands is heavily subsidized. Logging in the National Forests is supported by federally funded road construction, surveying, administration, and aid to county governments, as well as by the government's long-standing policy of offering timber contracts to private companies at well below cost. Grazing and mining on federal lands are governed by archaic laws dating back to the 19th century, laws that set fees at astoundingly low rates. Ranchers still pay $2 a month to graze livestock on public land; mining companies can still stake their claims for a few dollars an acre and pay no royalties whatsoever into the federal coffers. Modest proposals advanced by Interior Secretary Bruce Babbitt to update these laws were scuttled early in the Clinton administration due to pressure from powerful ranching and mining interests. This was one of the first examples of Clinton's capitulation to pressure from the Right, a telling incident that failed to adequately warn environmentalists who believed Clinton was firmly on their side.

When the Republicans took control of Congress in 1995, it became clear that sensible reforms of logging, mining, and grazing policies were not on the immediate horizon. Even though such reforms would advance the oft-repeated goal of balancing the federal budget, they had lit-

tle chance of passage in a Congress so blatantly beholden to moneyed interests. So environmentalists began to look elsewhere for ways to curb
the abuse of public lands, and some, perhaps inevitably, heard the siren
call of market-based solutions.

An early proponent of this approach, Oregon-based economist Randal O'Toole's careful studies of the U.S. Forest Service and other agencies
revealed losses in the range of $100 million a year in the timber sector
alone.[40] He proposed the implementation of fees for all forest uses, including recreation and freshwater resources along with timber and mining, a plan that gained the support of environmental organizations such
as the prestigious Washington, D.C.-based WorldWatch Institute.[41] Since
beneficial uses of the forests are inherently more valuable than extractive
ones, O'Toole argued, such a plan would ensure that the proper management of the forests would pay for itself. Proponents of user fees assume that "fair market values" for various amenities will outweigh the
dubious benefits of current patterns of exploitation.

In recent years, O'Toole has become a born-again advocate of a more
vehemently anti-government, pro-business approach to environmental
issues, an approach that has isolated him from most—though not all—
environmentalists and endeared him to supporters of the libertarian
Right. "Nearly all environmental problems are rooted in society's failure
to adequately define property rights for some resource," O'Toole has
written, advocating "property rights for owls and salmon" to "protect
them from pollution."[42] Whenever there is a conflict between marketed
and nonmarketed resources—for example, between timber sales and
scenic beauty—he has argued that the solution is to assign the latter a
market value to create an incentive for protection. O'Toole would divide
the National Forest system into individual units, each governed by its
users and operated on a for-profit basis, with a portion of user fees allocated for such needs as protection of biological diversity.

Other "free-market environmentalists" offer even more fanciful pre-
scriptions for protecting natural areas through the beneficence of private
ownership and economic exchange, and they have captured the attention of conservationists with their appropriation of the language of democracy, decentralization, and localism. One of these is Karl Hess, Jr., a
widely quoted advocate of tradable grazing permits, open bidding, and

even more overt forms of privatization. Hess wants those who seek to protect the beauty and integrity of western lands to place their faith in a fiction he calls the "deep market," defined as "the social arena ... where economy and society assume a manageable scale and where the concerns of political economy meld with those of the economy of nature."[43] This is nothing less than an idealized image of the precapitalist marketplace, where social and commercial interactions would presumably coalesce in an atmosphere of "mutual aid and cooperation." Hess overlooks the ways in which traditional village-based societies, which have in many instances survived for millennia precisely because they do *not* function like capitalist "free markets," are being rapidly dismantled by the overwhelming pressures of today's corporate-dominated global marketplace.[44]

Hess' solution to the destruction of forests is simply "opening up the sale process and letting groups who want to preserve forest integrity bid against those who want to harvest it." Ranchers, environmental groups, and civic associations can learn to be good neighbors, creating a "sea of little commons ... that would be neither public nor private, but simply self-governing land communities."[45] Of course, such imagery evaporates quickly when the eccentric, but good-hearted rancher-next-door is replaced by a giant multinational timber company like Weyerhaeuser, or a holding company specializing in corporate buyouts and liquidation of assets, such as the notorious Maxxam corporation, with its vast holdings of redwood forests in northern California. The middle school students on Long Island, with their $20,000 in sulfur dioxide credits, might see themselves in a relatively advantageous position compared to small landowners left drowning in such a "sea" of corporate landholdings.

While the current system is clearly failing, due to the staggering influence of corporations over our existing political institutions as well as the inefficiencies of centralized management, decision-making in the public sphere at least offers the promise of accountability and the ideal of "one person, one vote." To relegate environmental policies to the private sphere is to enter a realm where every dollar has a vote, and where thoroughly unaccountable outside interests can easily overwhelm local institutions with their economic power. In the private sector, important decisions are generally made entirely in secret and solely for the short-term benefit of those with the most economic leverage. This is rarely compatible with environmental protection, public health, or the long-term integrity of affected communities of people. Advocates of privatization thus completely surrender the possibility of an ecologically or socially responsible solution to the present crisis in public lands management.

Even the most moderate proposals to adopt economic incentives as a management tool raise serious conceptual problems. The key assumption for proponents of various incentive schemes is that markets can meaningfully assign dollar values to noneconomic goods, such as clean air, intact natural ecosystems, or an undisturbed scenic view. The question of how to adequately value economic "intangibles" has preoccupied resource economists and policy analysts for nearly two decades.

Lacking an objective basis for quantifying such noneconomic values, their efforts rely on various sociological methods, market analyses, and psychological studies. People are asked how much they would pay for a given environmental amenity, and their answers are compared with the actual prices of everything from wilderness expeditions to vacation homes. Researchers ask how much people would pay to protect a resource, and also how much money they would accept to do without it. Discount rates are calculated to correct for the effects of future decisions as compared to present-day ones. The results vary widely depending on how questions are asked, how knowledgeable respondents are, and what assumptions are made in the analysis.[46]

Still, proponents of this approach continue to insist that complex, multidimensional, and highly subjective qualities can and should be reducible to a market price. The morality of such an approach is highly questionable, too, as in the case of a study commissioned by the industry-supported think tank Resources for the Future to determine an appropriate discount rate for human lives lost from exposures to toxic pollution in the future compared to the present. Based on 1,000 telephone interviews, they concluded that one life saved in the present is equivalent to six lives saved twenty-five years in the future and forty-four lives 100 years in the future.[47] A recent cost-benefit study on the consequences global climate change valued the lives of people living in northern industrial countries at a rate ten times higher than the lives of people in China, India, and Africa.[48] The idealized market scenarios of a Karl Hess or a Randal O'Toole—with their deep markets and property rights for salmon—rapidly break down in the face of such stark and troubling realities.

The free-market approach assumes that everyone is equally capable of exercising their preferences in the marketplace, an assumption thoroughly contradicted by even a cursory look at present-day economic life. Environmentalists are not in a position to compete with multinational corporations for land rights, mining claims, or air pollution permits, if these are to be treated simply as commodities in the marketplace. The market in pollution allowances—in which a few companies are buying the vast majority of available credits and environmentalists are left with the crumbs—offers a clear indication of how this is likely to play itself out in less controlled settings.

These examples illustrate a fundamental underlying conflict and raise numerous important questions. Can the market and its institutions be made compatible with the long-range health of communities and ecosystems, or does an ecological outlook require us to envision a very different kind of economy? Can the features of the market that are least conducive to environmental protection be altered or reformed? What kind of economic system might be more compatible with long-term ecological integrity? We will return to these questions in the closing chapters of this book. First, it is necessary to take a closer look at the complex and politically contentious world of environmental regulation.

Chapter 3

The Limits of Regulation

There was nothing natural about laissez faire; free markets could never have come into being merely by allowing things to take their course. Just as cotton manufactures—the leading free trade industry—were created by the help of protective tariffs, export bounties and indirect wage subsidies, laissez faire itself was enforced by the state.

—Karl Polanyi
The Great Transformation, 1944[1]

Today's fractious debates over environmental policy invariably center on the highly contentious issue of regulation. Corporate interests and their supporters in Congress have launched a ruthless attack on the framework of environmental regulations established since the early 1970s, even as they seek to co-opt the language of environmentalism. Mainstream environmentalists, ever hesitant to address the wider political implications of environmental policy, rush to defend the regulatory system in its own rather limited terms. As a result, public health debates are often reduced to questions of how many parts per million of a given chemical is truly dangerous, and struggles over public lands become lost in a bureaucratic maze of timber harvest plans, environmental impact assessments, and the like.

While these approaches may be justified as steps toward establishing a firmer scientific basis for policy decisions, they also further the illusion that the future of our communities and the earth's ecosystems is best left to those lawyers, administrators, and technicians responsible for implementing a highly compromised body of regulations. A broader historical outlook on the development of the regulatory system is necessary if activists are to reach beyond limited, technical debates, and regain the initiative on behalf of public health and ecological integrity. These explorations will attempt to cast a different light on the Clinton administration's many environmental compromises, as well as on recent efforts to dismantle the regulatory system.

The various myths and misunderstandings that often drive the present debate are rooted in the origins of the regulatory system. Listening to today's most vocal crusaders against environmental regulation, one might believe that modern regulations are merely a brief interruption in a long, triumphant history of unbridled free-market practices. From corporate consultants to the Republican leadership of Congress, free-market ideologues describe regulations as a disruptive bureaucratic interference with an economic system that is best left to its own devices.

A look at the early history of the so-called "free-market system" reveals that nothing could be further from the truth. Polanyi and other economic historians have demonstrated how the myth of a self-regulating marketplace emerged in late 18th and early 19th century Europe, at a time of massive social dislocation. While preaching the gospel of a self-regulating market, early capitalists relied on the institutions of the nation-state to enshrine the conditions that make a market economy possible. Traditional village economies were destroyed by land enclosures and the abolition of legal protections for the poor, casting people adrift to sell their labor power in the nominally "free" marketplace. Communal ties to the land were replaced by commercial relationships enforceable by law, and a wide variety of regulations were established to create a setting amenable to the rapid expansion of commerce and investment.[2]

From the 19th century to the present, business interests have called upon the nation-state to stabilize currencies, provide economic stimulus, and, in the mid-20th century, codify labor and environmental regulations to encourage a more predictable business climate. Whether the government is buying dollars on the international market to conserve the currency's value or sending the president on another international trade mission, it is acting in a manner quite consistent with historical precedent, one that extends to environmental regulation as well.

While regulation of business practices is far from the unprecedented intrusion it is claimed to be by corporate leaders, neither is it a sufficient means to effectively constrain corporate abuses. Regulations are, in fact, highly mutable, subject as any other laws to changes in the political climate. Enforcement is often selective and, as we will see, officials can easily bend the rules on behalf of powerful economic interests. Regulations designed to protect the public from various abuses are generally enforced in a manner that places the heaviest burden on individuals and small companies, while large corporations are skillfully guided through the loopholes. Unfortunately, those at the receiving end of the government's selective enforcement have proven to be easy prey for anti-regulatory advocates. People justifiably distrustful of bureaucracy have been mobilized against regulation and toward false "free market" solutions that ultimately put everyone at greater risk.

Like most political measures, regulations can only facilitate positive change when they are backed by an active citizenry willing to confront challenges to public health and ecological integrity. This often means pressuring public officials to take actions they might otherwise resist. No amount of behind-the-scenes lobbying, or careful crafting of rules, can take the place of effective public mobilization and genuine grassroots activism. A brief review of the development of environmental regulations in the United States reveals the origins of the present anti-regulatory backlash and the urgency of an effective citizen response.

* * *

Today's most prominent environmental regulations originated during a period of widespread public alarm about the effects of pollution. Suffocating smog in the nation's largest cities, rivers such as Ohio's Cuyahoga catching fire due to high levels of flammable industrial wastes, public beaches fouled by massive oil spills, and natural habitats poisoned by pesticides and other industrial chemicals: these were some of the compelling environmental concerns that first gained attention in the 1960s. States and municipalities responded by implementing their own, sometimes far-reaching programs of environmental monitoring and enforcement. Early environmental lawsuits established important and even unanticipated precedents, extending the right of citizens to sue to protect ecological values and facilitating judicial review of the actions of government agencies.[3]

The environmental outcry of the 1960s—and the lawsuits that followed—proved costly for business, and corporate interests saw federal intervention as a possible solution. "[T]he elite of business leadership," reported *Fortune* magazine on the eve of the first Earth Day, "strongly desire the federal government to step in, set the standards, regulate all activities pertaining to the environment, and help finance the job with tax incentives."[4] Far from an interference with business prerogatives, environmental regulation was seen as a way to allay public concerns while offering corporate America a menu of uniform and relatively predictable environmental rules. The alarm over environmental issues, from dying rivers to the spread of urban blight, was so widely shared that well over 80 percent of the executives polled by *Fortune* in 1970 favored environmental protection, even if it meant restrictions on new products, constraints on the pace of production, or even decreases in profits. While laws passed in the aftermath of Earth Day funded necessary public works projects, such as the construction of sewage treatment plants throughout the country, and offered some protection of public health and the natural environment, they also routinized and made consistent the permitting processes for vast categories of highly polluting industrial facilities. In many instances, federal rules also preempted states and localities from enforcing regulations more stringent than those codified at the national level.

But no sooner did the EPA and other agencies begin enforcing these protections than the agency's practices fell under attack. The 1970s turned out to be an unexpectedly difficult period for U.S. corporations: worldwide economic growth slowed significantly, and the once uncontested dominance of U.S.-based industrial and financial capital faced heightened competition from Europe and the Far East. A rising corporate backlash against all forms of regulation set the stage for a comprehensive 1979 review of the federal regulatory apparatus. This study, by Harvard law professor Stephen Breyer, examined everything from environmental regulations to controls over financial markets and airline rates, and also proposed a system of "marketable rights to pollute," as we have seen in the previous chapter. Breyer's study offered an articulate reassertion of the discredited myth of the self-regulating market.

While regulations sometimes meet an "important public objective," Breyer argued, their only defensible function was to "replicate the price and output results of a hypothetically competitive world." Regulations should therefore only be implemented in the most unusual of circumstances: "one must believe the market is working very badly before advocating regulation as a cure."[5] Though Breyer acknowledged that the public requires legal protection from the abuses of a less-regulated market, he believed that anti-trust laws would offer sufficient protection. He could not have predicted the wholesale abandonment of antitrust enforcement that has, since the 1980s, brought us a world of leveraged buyouts, corporate megamergers, and capitalist monopolies on a global scale.

The administration of President Jimmy Carter was the first to attempt to "streamline" federal regulations, establishing a regulatory council to coordinate the activities of various federal agencies. A 1980 General Accounting Office study defended the system on the grounds that regulations—compared to pollution taxes or incentives—are the only way to minimize "uncertainty about the level of a clean-up that will be achieved." A regulatory system based on the now-disputed concept of the "best available control technology" was generally viewed as the most reliable way to protect public health and assure that anti-pollution rules would apply equally, even to "large firms with significant market power."[6]

These measured assessments of the workings of the regulatory system would prove short-lived, however. Ronald Reagan captured the White House in 1980 by riding a wave of anti-regulatory rhetoric, and soon bestowed the character of a grand public crusade upon a blatantly deregulatory agenda. Reagan's EPA became famous for its backroom deals with industry officials, in which favored companies were promised lax enforcement and greatly reduced fines. EPA administrator Anne

Gorsuch Burford resigned after two years in office, facing charges of contempt of Congress, and her special assistant, Rita Lavelle, was jailed for lying to Congress. Burford had replaced the agency's senior staff with officials from companies like General Motors and Exxon and had slashed its budget mercilessly. Even more notorious was Reagan's Interior Secretary, James Watt, who came to the administration from a "property rights" law firm in Colorado that advocated massive sell-offs of federal lands. In the words of former *New York Times* reporter Philip Shabecoff, Watt "introduced policies aimed at transferring control of public lands and resources to private entrepreneurs at a rate that had not been seen since the great giveaways of the nineteenth century."[7]

Even after the high-profile environmental scandals of the early Reagan years had passed, the EPA and Occupational Safety and Health Administration (OSHA) continued to face severe budget cuts, especially in the area of enforcement. Environmental groups discovered that the only way to assure enforcement of rules shunned by polluting industries was to file suit against federal agencies for failing to implement their own regulations. This practice has become a central activity of groups such as the Sierra Club Legal Defense Fund, the Environmental Defense Fund, and others. The persistent demands of activists for greater, more reliable environmental protection were often diffused by important, but inherently limited, legal battles for proper regulatory enforcement.

The Reagan administration also introduced cost-benefit analysis as a requirement for regulatory action, beginning a long debate that has gained increasing prominence in the 1990s. Further behind the scenes, Vice-President George Bush created a Task Force on Regulatory Relief, which was credited with sabotaging occupational health standards, delaying requirements to phase out leaded gasoline and put airbags in automobiles, and other dubious achievements. The Bush task force helped to establish the practice of White House interference with the regulatory process, which would come to fruition during his own presidency.

The Bush Years: Regulatory Sabotage

The Bush years may best be remembered for the collapse of the Soviet bloc in eastern Europe, but the late 1980s and early '90s were also a time of social malaise and depressed economies worldwide. Profits were falling, U.S. government deficits continued to rise, and the tab for the Reagan era's financial debaucheries was rapidly coming due. With the much heralded "historic victory" of capitalism, the growth of ecological awareness in the industrialized countries was seen by architects of Bush's "New World Order" as one of the few remaining obstacles to the final hegemony of the transnational corporate system. From this setting emerged a renewed effort to accommodate corporate interests by dismantling regulations to protect the environment, public health, and the rights of consumers. By the time profits began to rise again during the early Clinton years, the crusade against regulation had become established as a central theme within the wider corporate agenda.

Many of today's anti-regulatory initiatives had their origins in the Bush White House, and proponents gained important positions in Congress and the regulatory agencies during this period. "Free-market" environmentalists often led the call for "flexible" regulations, tradable pollution credits, and similar measures. These changes were defended as "realistic," even as the cutting edge of environmental policy. Their advocates began to cultivate influence and prestige in the halls of government, while sometimes unwittingly supporting the Bush administration's agenda of regulatory sabotage, an agenda as vicious as Reagan's, but considerably more sophisticated.

The Bush era's anti-regulatory initiatives developed at a time when the costs of environmental regulation, which had been steadily rising since the early 1970s, were in fact beginning to level off. A 1990 EPA study attempted to calculate the total cost to the U.S. economy of all types of pollution control measures. Pollution controls cost some $26 billion in 1972 (less than 1 percent of the GNP), $80 billion in 1986 (1.9 percent of the GNP), and were projected to increase to $132 billion (2.6 percent of the GNP) by the mid-'90s. Yet the rate of increase had fallen dramatically, from 14 percent per year in the early '70s to a projected 3 percent in the late '90s, and capital expenditures for pollution control equipment had remained at a relatively stable 2.5 to 3 percent of total investments since the early '70s. Government outlays for pollution controls amounted to only 4 percent of the total cost, with 61 percent borne by the private sector, 29 percent by local governments, and the remainder by state governments.[8] The relatively modest cost, however, has never inhibited the ideological fervor of those committed to curtailing regulations.

The personification of Bush's anti-regulatory agenda was his awkward and often laughably inept vice-president, Dan Quayle. Unfortunately, despite the endless rounds of jokes that enveloped Quayle's tenure, his legacy has yet to be reversed. An extremely secretive agency operated out of Vice-President Quayle's office, one that worked tirelessly behind the scenes to alter and delay regulations for the administration's corporate benefactors.

The Council on Competitiveness, as it was called, was empowered to interrupt regulations at the most vulnerable time, when agencies are crafting detailed implementation plans and procedures from newly passed laws. The White House Office of Management and Budget (OMB) had assumed oversight of this phase of regulation in the early years of the Carter administration. Under Bush and Quayle, however, the Council on Competitiveness became the designated agent of OMB, with the power to sabotage actions by any federal agency that might conflict with the administration's pro-business agenda. Laws that had already cleared the hurdles of Congress and a presidential signature were often altered or delayed at their final rulemaking stage.[9]

The Council on Competitiveness first fell under the scrutiny of the news media in 1991, when it offered more than 100 proposed changes to the EPA's rules for administering the newly amended Clean Air Act. Many of the proposals were taken verbatim from industry documents, and they offered important new loopholes for utilities to evade compliance with the Act. These measures were credited to council director and Quayle deputy chief of staff Allan Hubbard, a major utility investor and part owner of a chemical company in his and Quayle's home state of Indiana.[10] Faced with increasing congressional scrutiny, Hubbard eventually resigned and was replaced with David McIntosh, a former special legal assistant to Ronald Reagan and his attorney general, Ed Meese.

McIntosh was subsequently elected to Congress from Indiana in 1994, where he became known as one of the most vocal and unscrupulous of the notorious first-term Republicans of the right-wing-dominated 104th Congress.

Independent investigators from the Washington-based OMB Watch and Congress Watch documented numerous cases of the Council on Competitiveness' interrupting the final implementation of already agreed upon regulations.[11] Most often, a corporate ally of the administration would complain about a new regulation and the Council would intervene at the last minute, while the technical details of implementation were being worked out. Discussions between the Council and regulatory officials were held in secret, and regulations were upheld by OMB until officials complied with the Council's demands.

According to various media accounts, and a detailed study by OMB Watch and Congress Watch, the Council on Competitiveness was responsible for a long list of little-known and quite unseemly achievements. Some were implemented with little public scrutiny, while others were revived as legislative initiatives once the Republican Party gained control of Congress. For example, the Council initiated efforts[12] to:

- redefine wetlands so as to remove federal protections in twenty-nine states, including the Florida Everglades, much of the Chesapeake Bay region, and parts of the fragile New Jersey Pine Barrens;
- amend Clean Air Act rules to allow utilities to freely revise their own air emissions permits;
- eliminate a proposed ban on the incineration of lead batteries, and abolish a popular requirement that new incinerators recycle 25 percent of incoming garbage before burning (despite support for recycling across the political spectrum, and the knowledge that incineration had become the leading source of airborne lead pollution);
- accelerate the Food and Drug Administration (FDA) approval process for new drugs, dismiss new quality control standards for medical laboratories, and promote the use of private contractors to perform clinical trials of new medicines;

- and dismantle an eight-year attempt by federal agencies to coordinate rules for regulating biotechnology. The FDA was ordered to begin approving genetically engineered drug and food products without any consideration of the special risks and uncertainties of gene manipulation, initiating the deregulation of biotechnology that has continued during the Clinton administration.

George Bush's EPA administrator, William Reilly, also supported regulatory changes promoted through the Council. He caved in to industry pressure on many important measures, such as recertifying previously banned agricultural chemicals, relaxing rules governing dioxin emissions, and facilitating the siting of hazardous waste plants. Meanwhile, Quayle became the administration's voice against mandated increases in the fuel economy of automobiles and in favor of limiting the legal rights of victims of corporate practices. Citing a rise in "frivolous" lawsuits, the Council proposed limiting damage awards, restricting access to corporate documents, and requiring losers of damage suits to pay the defendant's legal costs. These proposals remain the basis of corporate efforts to weaken federal liability laws under the guise of "tort reform."

Finally, the Bush administration threw its weight behind a then little-known movement to challenge environmental regulations on the grounds that they interfere with private property rights. In the early 1990s, federal courts began to hear cases involving claims of the illegal taking of property due to federal laws mandating toxic cleanups, regulating water rights, restricting mining in wilderness areas, and limiting development on wetlands.[13] The U.S. Claims Court, which heard many of these cases, had been established specifically to hear property cases not involving injury claims, and was already dominated by right-wing judges appointed during the 1980s. Early judgments in favor of companies wishing to build on wetlands and expand coal and limestone mining opened the door for a landmark 1992 Supreme Court decision mandating compensation for a would-be beachfront developer in South Carolina. The legal and rhetorical war against regulation reached a fever pitch once the Republicans took control of Congress.

Clinton and Gore: An Environmental Presidency?

Despite his overwhelming support for anti-environmental initiatives, George Bush still sought to cultivate a reputation as "the environmental president," based largely on his efforts around the Clean Air Act. The absurdity of this claim became clearer during the 1992 presidential campaign, as Bush became an increasingly strident spokesperson for the right-wing, anti-environmental activists who had by then gained considerable influence over the Republican Party.

So it was with great hope and anticipation that many environmental activists followed Bill Clinton's ascendance to the presidency. Many of the prominent national environmental groups—including the Sierra Club, which had previously eschewed involvement in presidential politics—endorsed the Clinton-Gore ticket in 1992, and the most self-consciously moderate lawyer-lobbyist groups, such as the Environmental Defense Fund and the Natural Resources Defense Council, were granted unprecedented access to Clinton's transition team. Prominent mainstream environmentalists such as James Gustave Speth of the World Resources Institute and George Frampton of the Wilderness Society were offered high-profile positions in the new administration, at the United Nations and the Interior Department, respectively, and former Wilderness Society staff member Alice Rivlin became Clinton's director of the OMB. Mainstream environmental leaders boasted openly about their new-found "access" to the White House and various executive agencies.

One important factor behind mainstream environmentalists' hopes for the Clinton administration was the presence of Al Gore in the vice-president's office. Gore's 1992 book, *Earth in the Balance*, was generally praised for its comprehensive overview of the scientific, historical, cultural, ethical, and psychological implications of the ecological crisis. The "rescue of the environment," Gore wrote, needs to be made "the central organizing principle for civilization," even if it means going up against "nothing less than the current logic of world civilization."[14] Such statements affirmed the popular view that a Clinton-Gore administration would support strong measures in defense of the natural environment.

What many commentators on Gore's book ignored, however, was its consistent deference to both corporate interests and the myth of American superiority. The book asserts, despite overwhelming evidence to the contrary, that corporations will play a positive role in cleaning up the environment, and that the "American spirit" that "won" the Cold War— what Gore repeatedly terms "the stunning victory of free-market economics over communism in the global war of ideas"—will usher in a new era of environmental awareness. The nuclear arms race and other atrocities are bypassed as "mistakes" along the way to this triumphant end. Gore's approach to the spiritual and psychological aspects of the ecological crisis is precisely the kind of environmental philosophy that allows many corporate managers and politicians to celebrate their "inner ecology" (Gore's phrase) while denying their complicity in the destruction of the earth and its peoples. Gore's proposal for a "Global Marshall Plan" to heal the earth is described as a way "to remove the bottlenecks presently inhibiting the healthy functioning of the global economy," with only a rhetorical acknowledgment of the system's repeated assaults on the health of communities and ecosystems.[15]

In its earliest weeks, the Clinton administration sought to demonstrate its environmental commitment in a number of largely symbolic ways. Bush and Quayle's Council on Competitiveness was quickly eliminated, and a White House Office on Environmental Policy was established in its place. In his first State of the Union speech, Clinton proposed a modest but comprehensive tax on fossil fuel consumption, and the elimination of the Energy Department's inflated nuclear reactor research budget. He pledged to reform archaic mining and grazing laws that encourage commercial exploitation of public lands at bargain basement prices, and held a much publicized "Forest Summit" in Portland, Oregon to discuss possible solutions to the long-standing political deadlock over the future of the Pacific Northwest's endangered forests.

Within a few short months, however, another side of Clinton's approach to environmental issues became apparent. As with so many other areas of policy—from welfare and crime prevention to civil rights enforcement, military spending, and health care—Clinton's desire to "have it both ways" around environmental issues led to a series of contradictory policies and attempted compromises that hardly anyone could enthusiastically support. Energy taxes and other such innovations were early casualties of budget negotiations and backroom deals. While

Washington's official environmentalists continued to support the administration's highly compromised policies, anti-environmental extremists dug in their heels, thus sustaining the illusion that a true compromise position might lie far closer to their own.

One early point of capitulation was around a controversial toxic waste incinerator in a densely populated district of East Liverpool, Ohio, northwest of Pittsburgh, which had been cited by Al Gore during the presidential campaign as a key symbol of how a Clinton administration would stand up for the environment. Once in office, though, Clinton refused to take any action against the incinerator's operating permits. In May of 1993, East Liverpool residents and numerous grassroots supporters demonstrated outside the White House, many brandishing copies of Al Gore's book. More than fifty people were arrested, some chained to a twenty-four-foot Greenpeace truck that had been decorated as an incinerator.[16] The next day, EPA officials announced an eighteen-month moratorium on new hazardous waste incinerators that, due to varying state-level permitting rules, only applied to a handful of states, not including Ohio. The Liverpool incinerator was rushed into operation by EPA officials amid lingering questions about its ability to meet regulatory requirements.[17]

Another issue that arose early in the administration concerned the future of the Delaney Clause, which was passed in 1958 to prohibit cancer-causing additives in food. Ignoring a 1993 court order to comply with the clause, EPA administrator Carol Browner instead opted to continue the Bush administration's policy of allowing pesticide residues in food in cases where the agency could statistically demonstrate a "negligible risk" to consumers.[18] The administration pledged to adopt the findings of a new National Academy of Sciences study documenting the heightened effects of pesticide residues on children.[19] The Natural Resources Defense Council, which had sued the EPA in 1990 to enforce the ban on carcinogens in food, moved toward supporting the administration in seeking "comprehensive reform" legislation. The battle for Delaney soon became enmeshed in the wider struggle around Republican efforts to redesign the entire federal regulatory apparatus.

Efforts to reach a bipartisan compromise on food safety suddenly bore fruit during the months leading up to the 1996 presidential election.

A bill passed unanimously by the House of Representatives, and subsequently signed by President Clinton, repealed the long-standing Delaney Clause, replacing it with a statistical standard of "reasonable certainty of no harm." Suppliers of both raw and processed food now had to demonstrate a cancer risk of less than one in a million from pesticide residues (Delaney applied only to ingredients used in processed food), though this restriction could be waived where there might be "significant disruption" to the food supply. States were prohibited from enacting more stringent food safety standards. Groups such as NRDC, the National Audubon Society, and the World Wildlife Fund united with food industry trade associations in backing the proposal, citing its applicability to raw foods and the administration's promise to protect children. The U.S. Public Research Group joined with grassroots anti-pesticide groups, such as Food & Water and the National Coalition Against the Misuse of Pesticides, in condemning the new law's reliance on a readily manipulated statistical standard to replace the long-standing prohibition on cancer-causing chemicals.[20]

Clinton and Gore celebrated their first Earth Day in the White House by announcing their administration's endorsement of the international agreements on global climate change and the protection of biological diversity that were approved at the 1992 UN environmental summit in Rio de Janeiro, Brazil. George Bush faced considerable ridicule and international protest for his refusal to sign the biodiversity convention in Rio. But while Bush tried to dismiss the issues raised at Rio, Clinton sought to mollify his corporate backers through manipulation of the details. For example, while most industrialized nations had pledged to cap climate-altering carbon dioxide emissions at 1990 levels by the year 2000 and work to reduce them from there, Clinton only agreed to reduce emissions to 1990 levels by 2000. What would happen after that date was left conspicuously vague.

To address the biotechnology industry's concerns over the biodiversity convention, Vice-President Gore arranged a meeting with representatives from the World Wildlife Fund, the World Resources Institute, and something called the Environmental and Energy Study Institute, together with officials from three key pharmaceutical companies: Merck, Genentech, and Shaman Pharmaceuticals. The first is a major international chemical supplier, the second is the largest independent biotechnology company, and the third is an emerging player in the discovery and marketing of new drugs from the tropics. The result of this meeting was an "interpretive statement" that exempted private corporations from the biodiversity agreement's commitment to share new technologies and research findings with indigenous communities. Under this agreement, biotechnology companies seeking to profit from the botanical knowledge of these communities would no longer be bound by government obligations. According to Vandana Shiva, a prominent activist from India, the Clinton administration's actions decisively "shift the focus of the Biodiversity Convention from protection of the earth's living diversity to protection of corporate demands for monopoly control of life forms."[21]

Andrew Kimbrell, who helped frame many of the past decade's most important lawsuits against the biotechnology industry, described the Clinton administration's role here as "deceptive and destructive," undercutting international efforts to regulate genetic engineering. "This administration is more difficult to deal with than Reagan and Bush," said Kimbrell. "With Watt, Gorsuch, and the like, it was straight warfare. Now we have to deal with Clinton's friendly face."[22]

Another issue that graphically highlighted the Clinton administration's subservience to corporate interests—and the willingness of the official voices of environmentalism to follow in lockstep—was that of international trade, particularly the North American Free Trade Agreement (NAFTA) and the General Agreement on Tariffs and Trade (GATT). During the Bush years, virtually all of the major environmental groups lined up in opposition to these "free trade" deals, arguing that the agreements would target local, state, and even national environmental protections for sanctions and eventual repeal as "nontariff barriers" to trade. Environmental opposition to the trade deals came to a head in 1991 when GATT officials challenged the U.S. Marine Mammal Protection Act, in support of a Mexican claim that the act unfairly harmed Mexican tuna fishing by imposing strict standards against the accidental trapping of dolphins by tuna nets.[23]

NAFTA and GATT came to be seen by many grassroots environmental and economic justice advocates as important new steps toward the consolidation of transnational corporate control over the world economy. These agreements would enshrine the supremacy of trade and capital mobility over and above all other political and economic considerations, while providing a means for challenging specific environmental laws.[24] In May of 1993, six other groups joined the already pro-NAFTA National Wildlife Federation in offering a compromise plan for NAFTA side agreements with Canada and Mexico on environmental protection. They were the Natural Resources Defense Council, the Environmental Defense Fund, World Wildlife Fund, National Audubon Society, Nature Conservancy, and Defenders of Wildlife. The seven organizations agreed to drop their remaining objections to NAFTA if their plan for a cross-border environmental commission was adopted.[25] While the Sierra Club, Friends of the Earth, and hundreds of grassroots environmental groups actively opposed NAFTA, eco-activists seeking to build alliances with organized labor and other constituencies against the agreement often found themselves upstaged by the larger groups' persistent pro-NAFTA efforts, including full-page advertisements in several major urban dailies.

Mainstream environmentalists did, however, hold their ground when it came to the far more sweeping GATT. Activists worldwide agreed that the new World Trade Organization called for by the revised agreement would seriously constrain the ability of countries to protect the environment and the health of their populations from the excesses of the global marketplace.[26] In a 1994 report, Friends of the Earth outlined a number of specific U.S. environmental laws that officials of the European Union pledged to challenge as trade barriers, including fuel economy standards for automobiles, nutritional labeling of foods, curbs on driftnet fishing, and California's requirement that products be labeled to identify ingredients known to cause birth defects or impair reproductive functions.[27] These objections proved insufficient to restrain the Clinton administration's aggressive promotion of GATT in both domestic and international forums.

Controversies over toxic waste, food safety, free trade, and international environmental policy continued throughout the first Clinton administration. Presidential rhetoric in support of environmental initiatives was often coupled with backhanded favors to anti-environmental interests. This pattern led David Brower, now director of the San Francisco-based Earth Island Institute, to conclude in 1996 that "President Clinton has done more to harm the environment and to weaken environmental regulations in three years than Presidents Bush and Reagan did in twelve years."[28] Clinton's rather measured response to anti-environmental initiatives by members of Congress often helped legitimate those initiatives; only the 1996 election campaign brought a significant change in tone. The *New York Times* described his policies as an attempt at "building at least a rhetorical record" on the environment.[29] The event that most set the stage for the anti-environmental backlash of the Republican-controlled 104th Congress, however, was Clinton's early capitulation to mineral and ranching interests on the issues of mining and grazing reform.

The administration's 1994 budget proposal included a plan to raise revenue by reforming policies that promote unsustainable resource extraction on public lands in the West. Long advocated by western environmentalists and strongly supported by Interior Secretary Bruce Babbitt, the plan would have ended federal subsidies for timber sales in the National Forests, raised federal livestock grazing fees well above the long-standing $2 per cow per month, and revised the archaic 1872 law that permanently fixed the rates for mining claims on public land. Under pressure from western senators closely allied with ranching and mining interests, these reforms were bargained away rather quickly in the president's effort to win Senate votes for an ill-fated economic stimulus package.[30] While various modified proposals to reform public land policies continued to be advanced by Babbitt, this early acquiescence contributed more than any other single event to Clinton's reputation as a president willing to concede matters of principle in the face of pressure from powerful moneyed interests. It fueled the perception of Clinton's weakness that Republicans in Congress maneuvered to exploit to their advantage. In the next chapter, we will see how this pattern was reinforced in the battle over of the ancient forests of the Pacific Northwest.

The New Anti-Regulatory Agenda

The 1994 Republican congressional victory brought a new breed of elected officials to Washington, unabashed in their right-wing extremism and staunchly opposed to environmental regulation. While the Republican newcomers to the 104th Congress trumpeted their hostility to anything originating in Washington, their specific policy proposals were often products of the leading right-wing policy think tanks that gained prominence in the capital during the Reagan years. These include the Heritage Foundation, with an annual budget of $20 million, the American Enterprise Institute, and the Right-libertarian Cato Institute. Each of these organizations boasts large staffs of researchers, writers, lawyers, and policy analysts. And each has tirelessly advanced proposals to reduce or eliminate government regulation of business activities—proposals that were generally dismissed as absurd in the 1970s, raised eyebrows in the '80s, and gained the status of serious policy options in the '90s.

Leading the charge for anti-regulatory advocates was the so-called "wise use" property rights movement, which got its name at a landmark 1988 conference that brought together industry associations such as the American Petroleum Institute and the American Mining Congress, anti-environmental law firms such as James Watt's Mountain States Legal Foundation, and corporations including Exxon and Du Pont.[31] The conference was organized by a group of right-wing fundraisers and publicists who set out to cultivate a grassroots constituency for anti-environmental initiatives. "In an activist society like ours, the only way to defeat a social movement is with another social movement," "wise use" cofounder Ron Arnold told journalist David Helvarg. "So now we had a nonprofit mechanism [the Center for the Defense of Free Enterprise] to work with and told industry, let us help you to organize our constituencies."[32] The "wise use" movement combined crisp, inflammatory rhetoric, well-funded media campaigns, and mobilizations of angry blue-collar workers to arouse grassroots support for corporate agendas, including stepped-up resource extraction from public lands, transference of federal lands and water rights to the states, and the abolition of wilderness protections.[33]

By the mid-'90s, various "wise use" groups were ready to provide the shock troops for Republican efforts to dismantle the country's environmental laws. Most of the landmark environmental laws of the 1970s had built-in provisions requiring that they be reauthorized after twenty years. Reauthorization of key measures, such as the Clean Water and Endangered Species Acts, as well as the Superfund for toxic waste cleanups, has been held hostage by lawmakers seeking to use the process to advance the interests of polluting industries. Even before the Republican Party's victory in the 1994 congressional elections, three major themes came to dominate their anti-regulatory proposals: unfunded mandates, regulatory takings, and risk assessment. Each still carries serious implications for the future of environmental protection.

"Unfunded mandates" are regulations that state and local governments are required by federal law to follow, but that are not entirely supported by federal tax dollars. They include everything from workplace health and safety rules to requirements for sewage treatment plants. As state and local governments have had an increasingly difficult time raising tax revenues to maintain essential services—largely because of the sweeping reductions in income tax rates for the wealthy during the 1980s—reducing the burden of federal regulations has become a popular cry for politicians seeking re-election. One of the first measures passed by the new Republican-led Congress, and immediately signed into law by President Clinton, was a bill limiting the federal government's right to impose such mandates.

A report issued by OMB Watch and endorsed by a large coalition of labor, public health, and consumer groups outlined the implications of this law. A government commission empowered to map out its enforcement recommended the significant weakening of the Clean Air, Safe Drinking Water, and Endangered Species Acts, as well as the repeal of federal laws protecting occupational health and safety, fair labor standards and other rights, as well as the Family and Medical Leave Act. Federal involvement in these areas would be limited to providing research and technical advice, even where there is a documented history of noncompliance at the state level, or where inaction could impact neighboring states and regions. The coalition assembled by OMB Watch perceived a calculated attempt to pit various groups against each other (for example, labor activists vs. environmentalists), and asserted the need for a coordinated, broad-based response.[34]

"Takings" is a once-obscure legal concept that dates back to the U.S. Constitution's provision against taking private property for public use "without just compensation." Property rights advocates have relentlessly pursued this concept in the courts over the past several years, seeking monetary damages for clients subjected to the enforcement of federal laws mandating cleanups of toxic waste, regulation of water rights, restrictions on mining in wilderness areas, and limits on development in wetlands, to name just a few. In the Southwest, property rights advocates aligned themselves with the militia movement's claim that only county governments and their sheriffs hold jurisdiction over public lands. Angry landowners reopened roads closed by the Forest Service, refused to pay federal grazing fees, and in several incidents threatened Forest Service officials at gunpoint.[35] Ironically, the property rights to be protected from takings were to include such "rights" as federally subsidized water for irrigation, upon which ranching and mining activities in the arid West are entirely dependent. The expectation of a sustained flow of government-subsidized amenities—from water to logging roads to mining royalties fixed at 19th-century rates—is a powerful contradiction in the arguments of many property rights advocates.

The property rights movement seeks to channel people's healthy distrust of bureaucracy toward a rejection of any public role in land use decisions. The movement was bolstered by a 1992 Supreme Court decision requiring compensation for an owner of beachfront land in South Carolina who faced development restrictions for the sake of shoreline protection, and a 1994 ruling in favor of an Oregon store owner who refused to allow a public bicycle path to cross his land.[36] Property rights advocates in many states have spread numerous unsettling tales of landowners whose rights have allegedly been violated by officials seeking to enforce various environmental laws. But a closer investigation has revealed that many alleged victims of regulatory takings are, in reality, united by a rather blatant disregard for the rights of their neighbors, as well as for the natural environment.[37]

Proposals debated by the 104th Congress and passed by the House of Representatives would have required cash payments by the government to anyone whose property value decreased 10 percent or more due to regulatory actions. This would have constituted a virtually unlimited, budget-breaking subsidy to polluting industries and those engaged in speculative real estate investments; each would have become entitled to substantial government payments to refrain from polluting activities. Voters in both Arizona and Washington State rejected takings measures that had been placed on their statewide ballots in 1995. Twenty-seven state legislatures considered takings bills in 1996, but only two—both modified to emphasize mediation and study—were enacted by mid-year, in Maine and Michigan.[38] Critics asked why compensation for takings should not be balanced with taxation of landowners for public amenities that disproportionately increase the value of their holdings.[39] But despite such contradictions well-financed support from the real estate and construction industries, among others, make it unlikely that the takings issue will soon go away.

Controversies over risk assessment and cost-benefit analysis in environmental regulation have occupied economists and public officials for as long as such regulations have existed in the United States. The "risks" from environmental pollution are a complex mix of profoundly interdependent factors, few of which have been adequately quantified. In Chapter Two, we saw how efforts to quantify intangible qualities—from the value of human lives to a scenic view—are ridden with uncertainties and implicit value judgments. Former EPA administrator William Ruckleshaus, now CEO of the waste disposal giant BFI, described risk assessment as "a kind of pretense: to avoid paralysis of protective action that would result from waiting for 'definitive' data, we assume that we have greater knowledge than scientists actually possess and make decisions based on those assumptions."[40] Risk assessors choose among a variety of plausible statistical models, often in anticipation of a desired outcome and generally in disregard of the biological effects of chemicals that are not easily modeled.[41]

Some see an even more devious agenda. "Risk assessment is basically a fraud," said Peter Montague of the Washington, D.C.-based Environmental Research Foundation in an interview. "It's a process, the goal of which is to obtain permission to kill people and to destroy the environment.... The whole thing is unconscionable, it's immoral, it's a form of premeditated murder."[42] In September of 1993, Clinton quietly signed Executive Order 12866, officially designating risk assessment as part of the federal government's "philosophy of regulation."[43]

Bills debated in Congress in 1995 would have required detailed risk assessments for all future regulatory measures and embedded these risk assessments in an unprecedented bureaucratic maze of technical criteria, administrative reviews, economic impact analyses, and judicial appeals. Many analysts saw the proposed risk assessment provisions as nothing less than an attempt to strangle both existing and future regulations, rendering environmental and public safety laws virtually unenforceable without actually repealing any existing laws.[44]

"By adding layers of bureaucratic red tape to the rule-making process, the proposed legislation will render unenforceable many of our most important health and safety laws and cripple the ability of agencies to implement and enforce those laws," according to an analysis developed by Ralph Nader's Public Citizen organization.[45] Coming from a political movement that has based its entire public appeal on the call to "get the government off our backs," this legislation represented a rather cynical attempt to smother environmental protections in extraneous bureaucratic requirements. Besides subjecting regulations to unending appeals and administrative reviews, the House proposal would have made it illegal to exclude individuals with clear conflicts of interest from participating in the technical panels appointed to evaluate risk assessments.[46]

The 1995-96 congressional session was also noted for its unprecedented use of industry lobbyists in the drafting of legislation. While moneyed interests have long enjoyed an insider role in legislative proceedings, lobbyist involvement in the drafting of laws during this session was too blatant for even the mainstream press to ignore. For example, a reauthorization of the Clean Water Act passed by the House of Representatives in May of 1995, with notable bipartisan support, would have ended protection for most wetlands, virtually abolished controls on nonpoint source pollution, and prevented states from passing water standards more stringent than federal rules, to mention just a few changes. Lobbyists from the chemical, paper, food processing, petroleum, mining, and metal finishing industries proposed numerous waivers, exemptions, and changes in enforcement procedures, nearly all of which were inserted unchanged into the final bill.[47] Clinton's threatened veto of this bill helped embolden a number of moderate Republican representatives whose constituents would clearly not have condoned support for such a measure.

Anti-environmental advocates in Congress also used legislative riders to advance controversial proposals unlikely to be approved on their own merits. "Riders" are items attached to important appropriations bills and other measures most likely to be passed into law. Influential members of Congress have often used riders to further the interests of powerful constituents, but the 104th Congress saw their use in an unprecedented variety of ways. The Natural Resources Defense Council listed more than sixty riders to various key appropriations bills during the months-long budget battles between the Congress and the Clinton administration.[48] They included moratoria on the listing of new endangered species and Superfund sites, measures to increase logging and oil drilling in Alaska, suspension of appliance efficiency standards, automatic renewal of grazing and mining permits, fast-track development of a nuclear waste repository in the California desert, and numerous remissions of specific EPA rulemaking efforts. Most notorious of all was the so-called timber salvage rider, which was attached to a 1995 budget bill, and unleashed a new era of widespread clearcut logging in western and southern states. We will return to the saga of salvage logging in the following chapter.

The Future of Regulation

What are the lessons of this problematic and sometimes obscure history of regulatory action and inaction? First, it is clear that the processes of environmental regulation are, and always have been, highly political. Despite the pretense of scientific objectivity and legal due process, regulations continue to be subject to political horse trading, administrative sabotage, and sometimes outright repeal. Even judicial decisions are rarely immune from political pressures. As the continuing debate over risk assessment shows, even the scientific findings that are supposed to form the basis for regulatory standards are inherently uncertain and open to interpretation.

Uncertainty is the only constant in the world of scientific research, and this is especially true in fields such as ecology and public health, where the ideal of a controlled laboratory experiment is generally impossible to achieve. When the overwhelming weight of scientific evidence argues in favor of curbs on carbon dioxide emissions, the protection of endangered ecosystems, or other such measures, hostile politicians have defunded the scientific studies upon which regulations depend. In 1995, budget-cutting enthusiasts worked to slash funding for research efforts at the EPA and the National Oceanic and Atmospheric Administration, and tried to abolish the Interior Department's National Biological Survey.[49]

Second, environmental regulation has been repeatedly compromised by politicians of both major political parties. Whether they are seeking specific favors for industries that support their electoral campaigns or promoting sweeping efforts to "streamline" or "reinvent" government regulation, both Democrats and Republicans have demonstrated time and again that deference to corporate interests supersedes the public interest in the world of Washington politics. While Clinton rushed to take credit for the defeat of some of the most strident anti-environmental measures proposed by the Republican leadership of the 104th Congress, his own environmental initiatives consistently emphasize rhetoric over substance, with an oft-demonstrated willingness to defer to moneyed interests when the course becomes difficult.

In August of 1995, the *New York Times*, itself no consistent defender of environmental integrity, described Clinton in a lead editorial as "a President who can lay no serious claim to environmental leadership."[50] Only after Clinton's pollsters demonstrated that public support for environmental protection would be a factor in the 1996 presidential election—and grassroots pressure began to call the president to task for signing a bill permitting unregulated "salvage" logging on public lands—did Clinton begin to dig in his heels against Republican anti-environmental measures.[51] The displeasure of moderate Republican voters toward their party's anti-environmental agenda may have done more to neutralize it than the Clinton administration's threatened vetoes, however. "If this party is to resuscitate its reputation in this important area, we cannot be seen as using the budget crisis as an excuse to emasculate [*sic*] environmental protection," proclaimed a letter circulated by some thirty pro-environment Republican Congress members in January of 1996.[52] The majority-Republican New Jersey delegation united to press for full funding of the Superfund program for cleaning up toxic waste sites.

Third, public support for greater environmental protection continues to grow, despite increasingly strident anti-environmental rhetoric and an environmental PR machine fueled by more than $1 billion a year.[53] "Professional grassroots lobbying" has become an $800 million-a-year industry in the United States, influencing economic and social as well as environmental policies. This innovation in public relations involves the creation of corporate-funded "volunteer" organizations to support industry initiatives and emulate the workings of grassroots groups. "Technology makes building volunteer organizations as simple as writing a check," reports author Ron Faucheaux, who has described how consultants are hired to identify key supporters of a bill, mobilize employees of affected companies, and maximize personal contact between elected officials and influential constituents. This approach has been used by interests as diverse as the insurance industry, nurses' and teachers' organizations, and the National Rifle Association and numerous industry associations, as well as by companies such as General Motors, Exxon, and McDonalds.[54] Despite these well-funded efforts, a majority of citizens consistently tell pollsters that environmental laws need to be strengthened rather than modified or repealed.[55]

The discrepancy between public relations and public opinion has become eminently clear in recent debates over western land policies. While efforts to protect public lands are attacked with noisy displays of populist rhetoric and paeans to "Old West" individualism, the vast majority of people, East or West, North or South, urban or rural, consistently express support for more protection. A 1995 regional survey from the University of Idaho revealed overwhelming support for the protection of watersheds, wilderness ecosystems, fish and wildlife habitat, and endangered species, as compared to logging, mining, and grazing. When western senators advanced a spurious "wilderness" bill that would have allowed the construction of roads, reservoirs, and power lines in a vastly reduced wilderness reserve in Utah, 70 percent of more than 22,000 public comments favored alternative proposals for a greatly expanded, fully protected wilderness area.[56] In Arizona, where militant property rights advocates have been especially vocal, a poll demonstrated strong bipartisan support for a 1995 injunction barring logging on National Forests in the state and in neighboring New Mexico. Support for the logging ban among Arizonans between the ages of eighteen and twenty-four was by a nearly eight to one margin.[57]

Still, the defense of environmental protections remains an uphill battle in an era of sometimes overwhelming corporate dominance. Unless activists can develop an agenda to challenge corporate power, it is unclear how the minimal protections that communities and ecosystems now depend on can be maintained. Corporate lobbyists have learned how to manipulate regulatory proposals so that their clients will be able to readily pass costs and legal obligations on to less powerful actors in the economic arena. For example, when the Clean Air Act was amended to require more stringent controls on automobile pollution, the onus was placed on gas station owners rather than automobile manufacturers. Instead of requiring the industry to implement existing technologies to reduce emissions, state regulators have been forced into divisive battles over gas pump design, new gasoline formulas, and other measures in order to keep abreast of new federal guidelines.[58]

Enforcement practices that favor powerful interests extend to land use policies as well. Individual landowners often face the same legal and permitting requirements as major commercial and industrial developers. While large corporations have teams of lawyers and consultants to skillfully guide them through state and local permit processes, homeowners and small businesspeople often become frustrated trying to play by the rules, making them more susceptible to anti-regulatory rhetoric. The myth of corporate personhood makes it possible for companies to seek "civil rights" protections, leaving advocates of more stringent rules for the most damaging projects vulnerable to accusations of "discrimination" and to charges of violating due process for corporations.[59]

While current regulations protecting the environment and public health need to be preserved and strengthened, activists should not harbor the illusion that government regulation is a panacea. Many regulatory programs simply codify the terms by which corporations are granted permits to pollute. There is a long history of regulatory agencies supporting corporate cover-ups and interfering with the public's right to know what hazards they are facing. For example, activists fighting the opening of an incinerator to burn dioxin-contaminated soil from the toxic ghost town of Times Beach, Missouri recently discovered that the EPA concealed for over twenty years information that documents high concentrations of PCBs in samples from Times Beach. Working to expose this finding, anti-toxics activists found themselves in an uncomfortable alliance with anti-regulatory politicians who sought to discredit the EPA altogether.[60] While timber interests and their political allies rail against federal ownership of National Forest lands, forest activists have exposed the U.S. Forest Service's relentless promotion of logging on public lands, along with the numerous amenities the Forest Service provides the timber industry at public expense.

Regulatory agencies clearly cannot be relied upon to protect the public interest when powerful economic interests are at stake. One recent survey found that fewer than 1 percent of the cases filed by the U.S. Department of Justice involve environmental crimes or related consumer safety and occupational health claims, and that fewer than a quarter of these are ever prosecuted.[61] Mainstream environmentalists who limit their efforts to the regulatory and legislative arenas are willfully overlooking these realities and perhaps ultimately forestalling efforts to establish wider democratic control over important political and economic decisions.

In recent years, scholars and activists have proposed a series of innovations and preventive measures that could help reinforce society's ability to protect people and ecosystems from the effects of environmental pollution. The International Joint Commission, a U.S.-Canadian body that assesses threats to water quality in the Great Lakes, has proposed the total elimination of any chemical that is proved to be persistent or bioaccumulative—that is, either its half-life in air, water, or soil is greater than eight weeks or its concentration increases as it moves through the food chain. University of Maryland economist Robert Costanza has proposed that companies seeking to introduce a new chemical or technology be required to post an "assurance bond" equal to the cost of the greatest possible harm that may result.[62] Greenpeace and other international organizations have proposed banning the use of synthetic organic chemicals containing chlorine, due to the large number of uniquely toxic by-products of organochlorine chemistry. To implement such innovations will obviously require a significant shift in the social balance of power from corporations to ordinary citizens.

Proposals to strengthen environmental regulations raise additional questions of political principle. How is the desire for stronger regulation of corporate polluters to be reconciled with a green agenda supporting the decentralization of political and economic activity? This has become a serious dilemma for many activists, as right-wing politicians have adopted the rhetoric of a libertarian rejection of bureaucratic control. But while politicians have become adept at manipulating the language of individual rights and freedoms to further anti-regulatory initiatives, their rhetoric carefully disguises an agenda far more threatening to basic freedoms. Corporations are by far the most powerful, secretive, publicly unaccountable, and inherently authoritarian institutions exercising control over people's lives today. Some fifty corporations control more wealth than the vast majority of countries in the world, and the revenues of the 500 largest corporations in the United States are equal to nearly two-thirds of the gross domestic product, while contributing an ever shrinking share of federal tax dollars.[63] Thus it is thoroughly disingenuous to condemn excessive government power without also addressing the overwhelming economic and political power of corporations.

The real choice is not between government regulation and personal freedom. The question is, how can we control excesses of power, whether they emanate from the halls of government or the board rooms of the largest corporations? How can communities of people unite to create a vital public sphere in which everyone has a real choice in decisions that affect their lives? Only an active and politically engaged citizenry can make institutions accountable and can resist undemocratic concentrations of power. While advocates of corporate environmentalism, such as President Clinton's business-dominated Council on Sustainable Development, call for more "collaboration and consensus," those unable to buy influence in Washington are left to create more effective ways to exert meaningful political pressure.[64]

What are we to do in the near term? Bureaucratic government power cannot ultimately advance public accountability for political and economic decisions, any more than environmental lobbyists loyal to the maintenance of the status quo can adequately defend the land and our health from continuing corporate attacks. It would be foolish to undermine the very minimal protections that are currently in place. Yet the inability of existing institutions to protect people and ecosystems from the continuing assaults of centralized power heightens the need for a more fundamental political transformation. Subsequent chapters will profile some of the organizations and movements that are creating new models of popular organization in these generally apolitical times. But first, we will take a closer look at how politics-as-usual, and the behind-the-scenes manipulations of the Clinton administration have increased the peril faced by some of this continent's most endangered ecosystems.

Chapter 4

Activist Dilemmas:
Insider Politics vs. the Forests

"On this Earth Day, let me pledge we will not allow lobbyists to re-write our environmental laws in ways that benefit polluters and hurt our families, our children and our future."
—Bill Clinton, April 1995[1]

"Rarely if ever has a new government promised so much for one of its core constituencies and delivered so little."
—Michael Silverstein
environmental economist and business advocate[2]

"The danger of Clinton's consensus approach is that it will push the environmental community just enough to fracture our resolve, but not enough to unite us in opposition."
—Sam Hitt, New Mexico forest activist[3]

"His moral compass is swinging so widely that it is impossible to know where the Administration will end up."
—Carl Pope, executive director, Sierra Club[4]

The vast ancient forests of the Pacific Northwest are a place of over-whelming power and mystery. From the 1,000-year-old redwoods of northern California to the Douglas fir and hemlock forests of Oregon and Washington to the giant red cedars and Sitka spruce of British Columbia and coastal Alaska, the region's forests inspire a profound sense of awe and reverence. To forest ecologists, they are also among the most biologically productive forests on earth. Thousands of species of plants and animals depend on intact old growth forests for their survival, including some 150 varieties of Pacific salmon and the much celebrated northern spotted owl. Snow-capped mountains feed wild, raging rivers that provide fresh water, as well as fish, to the vast coastal region, while the forests help to maintain soil fertility and protect gravelly hillsides from erosion and flooding.

Environmentalists of varying political perspectives have become enmeshed in a complex series of political struggles over the future of this region's forests. These struggles offer what may be the most striking example of Bill Clinton's often underhanded approach to environmental compromise, along with unsettling tales of the capitulation of mainstream environmentalists to his administration's political maneuvers. The persistent "timber wars" of the Northwest highlight the conflict between mainstream, Washington, D.C.-based environmental groups and their regional representatives, on the one hand, and the numerous smaller organizations more closely tied to grassroots initiatives, on the other. The 1995 arrival of large-scale "salvage" logging in the region sparked a revival of grassroots activism and nonviolent action in defense of the forests; the expanded logging infuriated and also invigorated grassroots environmentalists all across the country.

Timber interests have long characterized the forests of the Northwest as "decadent" and "overgrown," indoctrinating many generations of loggers with this view. Widespread logging in the Northwest began over a century ago, and speeded up dramatically in the 1980s. Anyone who has hiked the Cascades or the Olympic Mountains, or seen the dramatic aerial photographs made available in recent years, is likely to be stunned by the checkerboard of clearcut devastation. Steep mountainsides are routinely cleared to stumps, and exposed soils are washed away by heavy rains, silting up the rivers and threatening fish populations. Today, less than 5 percent of the original old growth forest remains, most of which is in the region's National Parks, National Forests, and other federal and state holdings. Satellite photographs released by NASA during the 1992 UN Earth Summit revealed destruction and fragmentation in the American Northwest far more advanced than the destruction of the Amazon rainforest in Brazil.[5]

As the pace of logging in the Northwest has increased, timber industry employment has declined steadily. Each increase in the rate of logging appears to have brought a statistically equivalent *decrease* in the workforce, mainly due to timber exports and increased mechanization.[6] About half of the region's annual timber harvest is exported. The region's lumber mills, once a leading source of employment, are moving to Mexico and other low-wage countries, further depressing employment in timber-dependent communities. Whole, unprocessed logs are shipped to Japan, China, and elsewhere, along with wood chips and pulp. In 1992, for example, nearly a third of the twelve billion board-feet of softwood that left West Coast ports was in the form of pulp, 29 percent was raw logs, 23 percent was wood chips, and only 16 percent was classified as processed lumber.[7]

Of the major multinational timber companies based in the United States, Weyerhaeuser is by far the most active in exporting logs from both public and private lands in the Northwest. Other major players in the region include Georgia Pacific, International Paper, ITT-Rayonier, and several smaller but regionally powerful companies, such as Plumb Creek, Willamette Industries, and Young and Morgan. These companies and the politicians they lavishly support have succeeded in painting the intensely polarized struggle over the region's future as a choice between jobs and the environment. Timber communities, encouraged by well-financed "wise use" organizers, have fallen prey to industry claims that environmentalists are to blame for their economic woes. Meanwhile, environmental activists in the region have worked hard to illustrate how the timber industry is treating its workers as expendable commodities, just like the forests.

While the ensuing war of conflicting cultures and economic realities often overshadows debates about environmental policy, the fact is, the region has become embroiled in congressional power politics, as well as in heated clashes between grassroots activists and the leading Washington-based environmental groups. Heavily manipulated media images of angry loggers in the Northwest venting their frustrations against eco-activists, government regulations, and spotted owls reinforce the view that the main conflict is between environmental protection and "jobs." Environmentalists and loggers alike have made the endangered northern spotted owl the best-known symbol of the highly charged character of this debate.

For the area's environmentalists, the so-called spotted owl controversy is more accurately seen as a struggle for the future ecological integrity of the entire region. The problem lies far beyond the protection of any single species. Since ecosystems as a whole have no legal standing, however, endangered species like the northern spotted owl have become the centerpiece of legal strategies to protect endangered regions. Species such as the spotted owl and marbled murrelet—a rare seabird that nests inland on the mossy limbs of old growth trees—are completely dependent on old growth forests for their survival, and hence have become important scientific, as well as legal, indicators of the health of the entire forest.

In 1992, a dozen regional and national environmental groups filed suit in federal district court in Seattle to block further sales of timber harvested on federal lands in the region. Their argument hinged largely on a provision of the 1976 National Forest Management Act that requires timber companies operating in the National Forests to protect the long-range and widely distributed viability of forest-dependent species. Judge William Dwyer issued an injunction charging "repeated and systematic" violations of environmental laws, and the release of new federal acreage for logging came to a halt. Timber cutting on privately owned land, however, continued unabated.

Bill Clinton campaigned and gained significant support in the Northwest as a voice of balance and compromise, promising a timely resolution to the controversy that produced the Dwyer injunction. Soon after taking office, Clinton held a much publicized "Forest Summit" in Portland, Oregon that brought together a considerable spectrum of forest advocates and industry representatives. He pledged to develop a plan that would consider the long-term health of both the forests and the timber communities, preserving endangered ecosystems while also maintaining a "predictable and sustainable level of timber sales and non-timber resources."[8]

Grassroots activists in the region hoped for the best. "Everyone was expecting that Clinton would give us a good plan," explained Jeffrey St. Clair, a longtime activist, journalist, and editor of the Portland-based *Wild Forest Review*, "at least one that would end logging of old growth in the National Forests."[9] If logging in the National Forests were banned outright, it would risk about a quarter of Northwest timber industry jobs (some 33,000 overall), which, some local activists argued, pales in comparison to the jobs that are lost due to timber exports—or to recent layoffs by Boeing and other manufacturing companies in the region. While politicians continued to play the jobs card, Oregon, the region's leading timber producing state, would soon report the lowest unemployment rate in nearly twenty years, with high-technology jobs now exceeding those in timber.[10]

In April of 1994, after a contentious year of backroom deals, political arm-twisting, and viciously polarized debate, the Clinton administration released its long-awaited plan for the future of these embattled forests. Like most of Clinton's high-profile "compromises," the plan pleased virtually no one. The timber companies complained that too much forest land was being locked up in wildlife reserves, while environmentalists in the region pointed out that the plan's limited reserves—which would continue to be open to some forms of logging—were insufficient to ensure the future of species dependent on intact old growth forests. But while timber interests appeared united in outrage, mainstream environmentalists were generally circumspect, unwilling to openly criticize their friends in the administration.

Mainstream activists argued for a strategy of prudence and pragmatism; others in the Northwest viewed the mainstream groups' steps toward accommodation as signs of co-optation and of the inherent limits of "insider" politics. Media reports consistently depicted the Clinton plan as weighted in favor of the environmentalists, and so administration officials sought further concessions from forest advocates to try to make the plan more "salable" to the timber industry. The story of this plan reveals a great deal about the nature of the continuing conflict between local activists and the leading national environmental groups.

The Clinton Forest Plan

On the heels of the 1993 Forest Summit, the Clinton administration commissioned the U.S. Forest Service to come up with a series of options for resuming National Forest timber sales in accordance with Judge Dwyer's ruling. The study team was headed by Jack Ward Thomas, a senior research ecologist at the Forest Service who would soon be appointed by Clinton to head the agency. Thomas was the author of a pioneering text on wildlife management, and architect of a 1990 "conservation strategy" for the northern spotted owl that was widely quoted by environmentalists as a scientific demonstration of the need for more forest land to be set aside for owl habitat.[11] Activists in the Northwest, however, were also critical of Thomas for bending to political expediency, proposing that as many as half the owls be sacrificed in the short term in hopes of stabilizing the population in 100 years. The plan advanced by the Clinton administration would echo this approach, allowing some of the last remaining ancient forests to be cut in the near term in exchange for the promise of a more regulated forest in the future.

Thomas' team came up with eight scenarios, allowing nearly a billion board feet (approximately 20,000 acres) of National Forest timber to be cut every year for a decade, about a quarter of the typical 1980s rate. Each scenario was evaluated for its projected effect on the survival of key forest species (owls, murrelets, salmon, and over 1,000 others) into the next century.[12] But the White House rejected these eight options, ordering the development of an additional scenario that would permit more logging, and perhaps better satisfy the timber industry's friends in Congress. This alternative came to be known as "Option 9."

Like many Clinton initiatives, Option 9 borrows much of the language of more progressive alternatives, in this case, watershed-based ecosystem management. It promised limitations on future logging, reserves for spotted owls, and buffer zones along important river watersheds. Funds were pledged for job-creating watershed restoration programs to protect salmon runs. But there were also countless exceptions, conditions, and loopholes that would ultimately give the timber industry free reign over about 40 percent of the remaining old growth forest.[13] Thinning and "salvage" logging would be allowed even in the reserves set aside for the spotted owl, and logging would be stepped up on the arid eastern slopes of the Cascades to compensate for losses in timber revenue on the more closely watched western side. The plan would relax limits on logging on privately owned land, a precedent widely noted in northern California, where most of the remaining unprotected redwoods are owned by the infamous Maxxam conglomerate. Forest-dependent species would continue to disappear, even according to the plan's calculations, and the neglectful practices of the timber companies would continue to dominate the ecology and the economy of the region long into the future.[14]

Having advanced a plan that only began to address the desire of most environmentalists to protect the remaining ancient forests, the Clinton administration sought to lock them into supporting its implementation. As soon as the first draft of Option 9 was released, Interior Secretary Bruce Babbitt was dispatched to sell the plan to timber interests with a promise that thousands of acres of land would immediately be released from the 1992 injunction. This could only happen with the consent of the twelve groups that brought the original lawsuit. The carrot offered to environmentalists was a promise—quite attractive to the more mainstream groups among them—that they would have a greater role in refining the forest plan before it was submitted to Judge Dwyer in support of the lifting of his injunction.

The stick came in the form of a threat by the administration to join with Democratic House Speaker Tom Foley, a long-time supporter of the timber industry, to attach a rider to the 1994 Interior Department appropriations bill to make future timber sales essentially immune from legal action.[15] As conservationists had become increasingly dependent on federal lawsuits and administrative challenges of timber sales in order to save particular patches of forest from the chainsaws, the threat of so-called "sufficiency" legislation was enough to bring the twelve original plaintiffs to the bargaining table. Under such a provision, whatever the government chooses to do is deemed sufficient to meet legal requirements, and further legal challenges or appeals are prohibited. With the passage of the 1995 "salvage" logging rider, the full consequences of sufficiency would soon become horrifyingly clear.

By November of 1993, the twelve plaintiff groups had agreed to release some eighty-three million board feet (over 2,000 acres) of forest
from the Dwyer injunction. The Sierra Club's independent legal arm, the
Sierra Club Legal Defense Fund (SCLDF), was reported to have pressured reluctant activists to stay in the game.[16] More mainstream activists
viewed this as a legitimate trade off of forests that would soon be cut
anyway—what Andy Stahl of SCLDF termed "stands of sales on death
row"—for more ecologically important areas that the plan would place
inside reserves.[17] It was also described as a vote of confidence for the environmental movement's well-placed friends in Washington. "[T]he
plaintiffs did not capitulate; we negotiated," insisted Oregon Natural Resources Council Conservation Director Andy Kerr, one of the region's
most respected activist lawyers.[18]

To many grassroots activists and smaller regional environmental
groups, however, this was an outrageous power play that had put
groups like the Sierra Club and Audubon Society firmly in the administration's pocket. While representatives of the twelve plaintiff groups
were searching their maps for patches of forest to release for cutting, the
White House announced that this was only the beginning, and that vast
additional acreage would soon follow. According to Jeffrey St. Clair,

> The point was never about the amount of timber released... but to
> turn key environmentalists from defenders of ancient forests to de-
> signers and defenders of timber sales in ancient forests. The point was
> about building a relationship of power and control, not goodwill, co-
> operation and trust.[19]

The "access" to high levels of the Clinton administration once boasted
by the leaders of the prominent national environmental groups had been
transformed into what Mark Dowie has termed "reverse access"—the
administration could now freely exploit its ties to movement insiders,
play upon well-known internal divisions, and compel the mainstream
groups to do the president's bidding. "The Clinton team has been a
nightmare for us," St. Clair explained. "They've given us a plan that
could have been produced during the Reagan-Bush years, and environmentalists are unwilling to criticize their former leaders who are now in

Washington. People act as if they expect a stealth revolution from within the administration, but it's not coming."[20]

It took a last-minute intervention by four small Oregon-based environmental groups to temporarily save these forests. The grassroots coalition Save the West, the Eugene-based Native Forest Council—which has led a campaign to halt all logging in the National Forests—the southwestern Oregon (Kalmiopsis) chapter of the Audubon Society, and the Friends of the Breitenbush Cascades filed a legal brief against the release of timber sales that temporarily held up the deal. All four groups were founded by individuals who had worked their way up through the ranks of the major regional environmental groups, only to become disillusioned and depart to form smaller, less compromising organizations of their own.

Meanwhile, the Washington, D.C.-based Western Ancient Forest Campaign (WAFC), which itself began as a coalition of Northwest groups under the supervision of the Pew Charitable Trusts, organized a door-to-door canvass in the region that produced a record 80,000 public comments criticizing Clinton's original draft plan.[21] This delayed the release of a final plan for several months, as interagency battles raged and more last-minute deals were struck. When the final Environmental Impact Statement elaborating Option 9 was released, it reduced the annual timber cut by 10 percent and strengthened some watershed conservation measures. Yet, it also exempted private—i.e., corporate—lands from the Endangered Species Act's prohibition against "incidental takings" of endangered species by destroying their habitat. None of the hoped for limitations on "salvage" logging in prime spotted owl habitat or logging on the eastern slopes of the Cascades were considered, and activists in the region saw the plan's watershed protections as insufficient to significantly raise endangered species' chances of survival.[22] The Clinton plan also reduced the acreage set aside for the protection of the endangered marbled murrelet. Jim Owens of WAFC correctly predicted that the Clinton administration would "continue to try to split hairs in an attempt to meet the requirements of Judge William Dwyer."[23]

In late April of 1994, all but one of the twelve plaintiff groups announced that they would not oppose the lifting of the 1992 logging injunction in response to the administration's final plan. By June, Judge

Dwyer had little choice but to lift his injunction, given the acquiescence of the lead plaintiffs.[24] In December, he ruled that the revised Option 9 met the minimum requirements of the law, based on government projections of the future recovery of populations of salmon and spotted owls.[25] The Native Forest Council and two other groups filed appeals against the resumption of timber concessions, but these were quickly denied. Various groups, including the Native Forest Council and the Oregon Natural Resources Council, pledged comprehensive new lawsuits seeking greater protection for salmon and other species, as well as a ban on log exports. Meanwhile, the timber industry pursued its own legal actions, along with a high-profile public campaign rejecting all limitations on logging in the National Forests.[26] Weyerhaeuser appeared to be the plan's only willing supporter, surprising everyone with an endorsement in April of 1994. With huge private holdings throughout the region, Weyerhaeuser was poised to benefit from restrictions on public lands logging and exemptions for large landholders from provisions of the Endangered Species Act.[27]

The Salvage Rider

In the summer of 1995, the ongoing controversy over the Clinton forest plan was superseded by a far more immediate threat to forests throughout the country: an unprecedented increase in so-called "salvage" logging, accompanied by a comprehensive sufficiency provision exempting such logging from environmental enforcement and appeals. The new salvage provision was enacted into law as a rider on the 1995 budget recissions bill—the bill that was to implement the 104th Congress' reductions in the previously approved 1995 federal budget. President Clinton vetoed the first version of this bill that came across his desk, partly in response to well over 50,000 messages to the White House from people opposed to the rider. This outpouring of opposition was the result of a wide-ranging effort by both regional and national groups, most notably the Washington-based Save America's Forests. Many of the better-known national environmental groups bought ads in the national press thanking Clinton for his veto.

But Congress soon returned with a modified version of the recissions bill that restored funding for a few programs favored by Clinton—particularly the AmeriCorps national service program—and shortened the time limit for expanded "salvage" logging. Clinton intervened to halt a Democratic filibuster of the new bill in the Senate and signed it into law at the end of July. By September of 1995, hundreds of acres of previously protected Northwest forest began to fall to the chainsaws, along with vast acreages in the northern Rockies, the Midwest and the South. The Forest Service predicted a sixfold increase in logging under the provisions of the rider.[28]

What was so unique about the "salvage rider," and why did it have such a devastating impact on forests all across the country? The rider was based on the powerful myth, conceived by the timber industry and aggressively marketed by its most vocal supporters in Congress, of a widespread crisis in forest health. The only cure to this fictitious forest health emergency was said to be a massive salvage program—an effort to remove dead and dying trees from all of the nation's forests as soon as possible. "Dead and dying" was broadly defined to include any forest containing trees that were diseased, charred by fire, or simply too old to still be growing rapidly.

Virtually every healthy forest contains such trees, if the terms are defined loosely enough, which is exactly what the Forest Service had been doing since 1992. Numerous allotments of National Forest timber once considered "green" had been reclassified as salvage sales.[29] Since the 1995 salvage rider exempted salvage sales from environmental enforcement, legal challenges, or citizen appeals, the reclassification of timber sales as "salvage" became a license for the wanton destruction of healthy forests, and the advance of logging crews into formerly roadless areas. Even where glutted markets meant a shortage of bids for salvaged timber, the Forest Service was ordered to sustain its inflated timber quotas at all costs.[30] The final reward for timber companies in the Northwest was a provision mandating the immediate release of some 180 older timber stands in Oregon and Washington, mostly in prime old growth habitat, where logging had been held up by legal appeals.[31]

Environmentalists presented a great deal of evidence challenging the need for a new salvage program. The most widely quoted testimony was by Dr. Arthur Partridge of the University of Idaho, who compiled 30 years of data on the inland Pacific Northwest region, the area most severely affected by the salvage program. "In general, our tests show that, during the last four years, we detected the lowest levels of disease and insect activity in 28 years," Partridge reported in February of 1995.[32] Partridge and others went on to describe the numerous ecological functions of dead and diseased trees, including providing nesting sites and shelter for wildlife, biomass for sustained forest growth, and the culling of genetically weak and ecologically unsuitable trees from the forest. In December, Senator Slade Gorton (R-WA), who first introduced the salvage rider in the Senate, was quoted by the Associated Press, saying, "The salvage legislation is about one thing and one thing only, and that is jobs."[33]

The response of grassroots forest activists, especially in the Northwest and South, was swift and determined. More than 200 people were arrested trying to block the logging of a long-contested old growth stand in southern Oregon. Logging of the site required what eyewitnesses described as a "military-style closure" covering some thirty-five square miles.[34] Some 250 people tried to block the logging of 300-year-old trees in Washington's Olympic National Forest, and a year-long encampment was established in Oregon's Willamette National Forest on land released by a judge for "salvage" logging, even though fire damage was attributed to arson.[35] In the spring of 1996, nearly 1,000 people gathered to protest the logging of a Native-American sacred site on Oregon's Mount Hood. In Montana, hundreds attended rallies and public hearings and hiked deep into the forest to witness the effects of salvage logging.[36] Oregon's Andy Kerr, a leading voice for compromise during the battles over Option 9, sat in with Earth First! co-founder Mike Roselle at Senator Mark Hatfield's Portland office and launched a new political action arm of the Oregon Natural Resources Council.[37]

On the legislative front, regional groups, such as the Alliance for the Wild Rockies, and Washington-based groups most closely allied with grassroots activists, such as Save America's Forests, pressed for the immediate repeal of the salvage rider. But the better-known national groups scrambled for a more "realistic" compromise. Throughout 1996, as trees were falling from Oregon to Alabama, environmentalists sought to narrow the scope of the salvage program, while the timber industry advanced proposals to make its temporary provisions more permanent. Some environmental lobbyists expressed a willingness to trade a partial resumption of environmental enforcement over salvage sales for a permanent extension of the salvage program.[38]

In response to public pressure, however, the Clinton administration intervened against Republican efforts to attach a more permanent salvage rider to the 1996 federal budget. The administration also made efforts to restrain some of the most egregious excesses of the salvage program, including the overly broad criteria for designating forests as unhealthy or fire prone, and the classification of stands of mostly live trees as salvage. Even though a few of the most publicly contested salvage sales in roadless areas of Oregon, Montana, and elsewhere were spared due to these efforts, logging continued at a pace that had not been seen since the Reagan years.[39] While the Clinton administration halted the listing of new salvage sales two weeks before the December 31 deadline, logging of forests already relegated to salvage would continue for a long time to come. In a September 1996 interview with David Frost, Al Gore described the salvage rider as the "biggest mistake we have made" in the administration's first four years.[40]

Endangering Species

While the continuing struggles over the forests of the Northwest remained a focus of public attention, Interior Secretary Babbitt and others in the Clinton administration were busily reneging on other promises they had made to environmentalists. Efforts to reform grazing and mining laws remained at a virtual standstill, and Babbitt tried to demonstrate the "flexibility" of the Endangered Species Act by striking numerous deals with developers and timber interests. Bureau of Land Management Director Jim Baca and several lower-level officials were forced to resign, reportedly due to their outspoken support for mining and grazing reform. Emboldened by Babbitt's and Clinton's rhetoric of reform, these officials appeared to have been purged simply for trying to enforce the law.[41]

The Endangered Species Act, which was originally scheduled to be reauthorized by Congress in 1991, remains the symbolic centerpiece of right-wing efforts to dismantle U.S. environmental laws. To soften opposition to endangered species protection, Babbitt highlighted efforts to permit several high-profile projects in endangered habitat in exchange for negotiated concessions by the developers. Housing developments in California, a Wal-Mart store in Florida, and a commercial logging operation in the deep South, among others, were granted exemptions from the Act's more comprehensive provisions in exchange for long-term Habitat Conservation Plans (HCPs) and negotiated agreements to set aside protected zones for endangered species.[42] Habitat Conservation Plans were first implemented as a measure of "flexibility" in endangered species protection during the Reagan administration, but the Forest Service has long insisted that the plans be modified if found to jeopardize the survival or recovery of endangered animals and plants. In 1994, the Clinton administration adopted a policy of limiting such modifications. In an effort to shield landowners from unanticipated changes to HCPs, plan revisions would heretofore only be imposed under "extraordinary circumstances," and would require the voluntary approval of the landowner.[43]

These modifications are defended as ways to assuage the concerns of political opponents of the Endangered Species Act, but most often they merely legitimate and embolden such opposition. Skeptics point out that efforts to make endangered species enforcement more flexible ultimately increase the fragmentation and isolation of endangered habitat, and threaten species' long-term survival. This may be the case even where the most biologically significant patches of land—for example, known nesting sites for endangered birds—are designated for immediate protection.[44] The use of Habitat Conservation Plans has allowed the administration to co-opt conservationists' calls for ecosystem-wide protections, while actively promoting the piecemeal development of endangered ecosystems.

The legislative battle over endangered species escalated in the aftermath of a 1995 Supreme Court decision affirming that comprehensive habitat protections, including limits on development of private lands, were a legally valid means to protect endangered species.[45] The decision was in response to a timber industry lawsuit challenging Clinton's Northwest forest plan. Opponents of the Endangered Species Act proposed numerous revisions to the act in the ensuing months. Lobbyists for the timber and paper industries attempted to replace existing enforcement provisions with an entirely voluntary program seeking landowners' cooperation in the protection of endangered animals and plants. Monetary incentives to landowners would be paid for through more sales of public land to private interests. Another proposal would have simply deferred implementation to the states. Each of these proposals would require compensation to landowners for financial losses that could be attributed to endangered species protection.[46]

One "compromise" bill, which would have delayed enforcement provisions and based endangered species listings on cost-benefit analyses, carried the endorsements of the National Audubon Society, Environmental Defense Fund, National Wildlife Federation, and Defenders of Wildlife. Republicans in Congress attached a moratorium on new endangered species listings to a defense appropriations bill that the president had already pledged to sign. While congressional liberals maneuvered to draft less sweeping proposals that still fundamentally weakened the Act, property rights advocates and lobbyists for extractive industries advanced progressively more extreme measures.[47]

The debate over reauthorization of the Endangered Species Act took shape amid considerable scientific controversy over the Act's efficacy. Critics charged that it had only saved a minimal number of species after more than twenty years on the books. More species may have been removed from the list due to extinction or administrative error than because they ceased to be endangered.[48] A wide spectrum of environmentalists responded, citing high-profile comebacks by charismatic species such as the bald eagle, eastern timber wolf, and peregrine falcon, along with numerous lesser-known species whose populations had just begun to stabilize under endangered species protections. Being added to the endangered species list is essentially a protection of last resort for species on the edge of extinction. In many cases, species are "listed so late they couldn't ever be recovered no matter what," the Nature Conservancy's director of natural heritage programs told *Science* magazine. A 1995 National Academy of Science report cast the issue in clearly political terms:

Many of the conflicts and disagreements about the ESA do not appear to be based on scientific issues. Instead, they appear to result because the act—in the committee's opinion designed as a safety net or act of last resort—is called into play when other policies and management strategies or their failures, or human activities in general, have led to the endangerment of species and populations.[49]

The activities most responsible for endangering species are often heavily subsidized by the federal government, especially dam building, dredging, grazing, logging, and mining. A 1995 study revealed that more than two-thirds of endangered and threatened species are at risk, in part, due to resource extraction, and a quarter are endangered by recreational activities, particularly off-road vehicle use.[50]

While Bill Clinton and congressional Democrats continued to trumpet their commitment to protecting endangered species, the administration's actions tell a different story. Not only has the Interior Department continued to grant waivers to developers in return for filing Habitat Conservation Plans, but the mechanisms for enforcing the Act have been compromised in a number of ways. According to David Hogan of the Southwest Center for Biological Diversity, changes in endangered species enforcement emerged from a deal between the head of the Fish and Wildlife Service and House Speaker Newt Gingrich. Gingrich reportedly agreed to delay a congressional vote on reauthorizing the Act—a vote environmentalists would likely have regretted—in exchange for an administrative exemption for developments under five acres, the elimination of Fish and Wildlife's "watch lists" of vulnerable species requiring further research, and the transfer of much of the agency's role in species listings to more pro-development branches of the Interior Department.[51]

While the president took credit for ending the year-long moratorium on adding new species to the endangered list as part of the 1996 budget deal, regional and grassroots activists pointed out that the Justice and Interior Departments persisted in challenging petitions for new listings in court.[52] Once again, Clinton was able to claim a symbolic legislative victory on a high-profile issue while his administration undercut the substance of the victory from behind the scenes.

In March 1996, activists in the broad-based national Endangered Species Coalition discovered that three members of their steering committee were negotiating in secret with timber and real estate interests to advance yet another "compromise" solution to the Endangered Species Act reauthorization. The new plan, endorsed by the Environmental Defense Fund, World Wildlife Fund, and Center for Marine Conservation—along with the Nature Conservancy, which was not part of the coalition—would have overturned the Supreme Court's ruling in support of habitat protection on private land, while limiting lawsuits and authorizing states to negotiate conservation plans, among other controversial provisions. Rather than passively accepting this move, as so many broad environmental coalitions have in the past, the Endangered Species Coalition voted to expel the unrepentant Environmental Defense Fund from its ranks and reassert the Coalition's commitment to strengthening the Endangered Species Act.[53]

The Limits of Compromise

In recent years, numerous regional controversies over land preservation have heightened the conflict between the national mainstream environmental groups and local grassroots activists. While mainstream groups often set their sights on rather limited policy victories that advance their reputations in Washington, local and regional activists are far more focused on protecting the natural places they know best. One important controversy during the first Clinton administration concerned a bill ostensibly designed to protect wilderness in Montana. The so-called Montana Wilderness Bill would have designated 1.7 million acres for protection; in exchange, an additional four million acres of undisturbed roadless forest in Montana would permanently be excluded from future consideration. Activists in Montana and throughout the northern Rockies were outraged when the national office of the Sierra Club announced its support for the bill.

Regional activists were already rallying behind what they viewed as a more comprehensive ecological alternative. Their proposal aimed to protect enough land throughout the northern Rockies region to permanently sustain a full historical complement of native species—from grizzly bears, elk, and caribou to bald eagles and 1,000-year-old cedars. They would designate some sixteen million acres as wilderness, with core wilderness areas connected to each other by a web of migration corridors to significantly enhance the genetic diversity—and, hence, the survival potential—of once isolated populations of wildlife. In contrast, much of the land to be protected by the so-called Wilderness Bill consisted of high-elevation rocks and ice, of little interest to extractive industries and rather impoverished in ecological terms as well. Millions of acres of intact forest would have been released for logging, mining, and other destructive activities, while a far smaller share of roadless forest would be meaningfully protected.[54]

"By assessing our victories in terms of legislative and litigative milestones, we have lost sight of the real issue—the health and abundance of natural ecosystems," stated a letter of protest to Sierra Club members signed by a dozen prominent Club members from across the country.[55] While passage of a comprehensive Northern Rockies Ecosystem Protection Act remains a long-range goal of groups throughout the region, the 1994 Montana Wilderness Bill went down to what many activists viewed as a well-deserved defeat. The struggle over these proposals within the Sierra Club helped to solidify support among Club members for a membership referendum calling for an end to commercial logging in all National Forests (see Chapter Seven).

In Maine, a compromise supported by the state chapter of the Audubon Society contributed to the defeat in 1996 of a grassroots campaign to ban the practice of clearcut logging. Several months after forest activists and Green Party members in Maine collected 58,000 signatures to place an anti-clearcutting referendum on the statewide ballot, polls demonstrated 70 percent support for the measure.[56] With the active support of Maine's governor, Angus King, officials of the Maine Audubon Society began meeting in private with industry representatives and some of the state's largest landowners to draft a compromise measure. Other environmental groups were reportedly pressured to join this effort, in exchange for continued access to behind-the-scenes policy deliberations on forest issues.[57]

Here, the Sierra Club staked its position in favor of the proposal to ban clearcutting outright, whereas the Wilderness Society declined to take a stand, even though its public statements expressed support for the deliberations between environmentalists and industry representatives.

The governor declared that a clearcutting ban would destroy the state's economy, and the timber industry spent nearly $6 million in support of the competing compromise measure.[58] Many people in Maine believed that the real purpose of the so-called Compact for Maine's Forests was simply to draw votes away from the proposal to ban clearcutting. When the ballots were counted, 29 percent had voted for the anti-clearcutting initiative, 47 percent for the compact, and 23 percent for neither. Under Maine law, a majority vote is necessary to pass a statewide referendum, leaving the legislature to decide if any further action would be taken.

Even if the bill had passed, it is unlikely that it would have helped to spare the Maine forests from timber industry abuses. While supporters of the proposed compromise highlighted its provision to limit the size of clearcuts, others believed that it would merely enshrine current unsustainable forestry practices into law. Some saw a hidden incentive to encourage clearcuts nearer to the upper limit of the proposed maximum acreage.[59] The compact would have also restricted the ability of towns to enact more stringent forestry ordinances. Though some landowners pledged to voluntarily adopt aspects of the compact, most observers predicted that further action against clearcutting would be delayed at least a year.

As the 1996 election approached, mainstream groups rallied behind President Clinton's efforts to recast himself as an environmentalist. Two high-profile pre-election announcements revealed a disturbing new trend in environmental policy, undertaken with the tacit approval of official environmentalism. First, Clinton announced that the U.S. subsidiary of the Canadian mining conglomerate Noranda would be offered nearly $65 million in federal property to withdraw its proposal for a massive gold mining operation just north of Yellowstone National Park. Secondly, 1.7 million acres in Utah would be declared a national monument, while a Dutch mining consortium would be offered an unspecified amount of federal land if it would refrain from mining coal in this area. Instead of simply denying permits for these mining projects, or fulfilling his long-standing pledge to revise federal mining laws that had barely been amended since the 1870s, Clinton chose to handsomely reward these two companies for not exercising their "property rights." In the case of the Utah monument, administration spokespeople refused to state conclusively whether or not mining could still proceed in the designated region.[60]

The emergence of land swaps as a central federal land preservation strategy has encouraged both mainstream environmental groups, such as the Nature Conservancy, as well as commercial real estate speculators to come forward as brokers and intermediaries for these deals. Meanwhile, over $10 billion in federal funds designated for land purchases remain largely unspent, and instead are being used to help balance the budget.[61] The government has offered trades of federal land with a combined value of several hundred million dollars to mining companies in Arizona, timber companies in the Northwest, and the Houston-based conglomerate Maxxam, in exchange for the protection of a portion of their California redwood forest holdings. In the aftermath of these announcements, the Sierra Club offered its enthusiastic support for Clinton's re-election effort—"Bill Clinton has redeemed our faith in his administration," said Club president Adam Werbach—and the Environmental Defense Fund described tradeoffs of federal land as the best "source of revenue on the horizon that is going to enable us to protect these sensitive areas as quickly as we have to."[62]

Representatives of mainstream groups continue to argue for compromise and acceptance of the status quo, despite the repeated disappointments of the Clinton years. They have acquiesced to lowered expectations for environmental protection in the face of right-wing attacks, and thus surrendered the initiative for continued environmental progress. Idealistic, well-meaning activists often enter the political fray in good faith, hoping that the facts will hold sway, only to discover that "insider" politics has its own set of rules. Those who enter the system to try to change it are more often changed by it, or else they find themselves unable to fully play the game. Either they accept the view of forests as "timber sales," old growth trees as "board feet," and nature as a "renewable resource," surrendering the rhetorical high ground to the charlatans of the property rights movement, or they are soon pushed aside by those who will. "America's flagship environmental groups are still top-heavy bureaucracies in which self-perpetuation has replaced environmental protection as the primary goal," wrote Karyn Strickler, former director of the Endangered Species Coalition.[63]

But grassroots activists all across the country are standing up for their principles, even when it brings them into open conflict with their much better-funded counterparts in Washington. There are definite signs that the environmental opportunism of the Clinton White House and the anti-environmental fervor of the Republican-led Congress are shifting the balance in the environmental movement away from Washington and back to the grassroots. In the following chapters, we will visit many of the emerging ecological movements that are working to make such a shift possible.

PART II

NEW ECOLOGICAL MOVEMENTS

Chapter 5

Ecology and Revolution

The mainstream media often paint a rather grim picture of the state of the environmental movement. While the voices of greenwash would have us believe that "responsible" corporations are taking care of environmental problems for us, they also seek to highlight the declining influence of the leading national environmental groups. This has spurred numerous premature assessments of the movement's overall demise. On the eve of the twenty-fifth anniversary of Earth Day in 1995, the *New York Times* described the environmental movement as "endangered."[1] Investigative journalist Mark Dowie made his colleagues stand up and take notice when he accurately described mainstream environmentalism as "a movement courting irrelevance."[2] Even the rhetorical emergence of the environment as a campaign issue in 1996 brought a curious mixture of exultation and skepticism. "The environmental issue in American politics is a character issue," Sierra Club Executive Director Carl Pope told a Washington audience a month before the election, not a political one. The belief that the United States is making steady "civic progress" toward cleaning up the environment has seriously clouded the public's assessment of specific environmental policy matters, he suggested.[3]

This perception of environmental progress depends, to a large extent, on where one chooses to look. Many statistical measures suggest that there has been a steady, though modest, improvement in recent decades.

Emissions of the best-known air pollutants, such as sulfur dioxide and carbon monoxide, generally peaked in the early 1970s, and have since gradually declined to pre-1960s levels.[4] For the most part, cities have ended the routine disposal of raw sewage and untreated industrial waste into nearby waterways. Numerous species of endangered animals and plants have returned from the brink of extinction. Continued public concern and vigilance over these issues and many others has made it difficult for twenty-five years of moderate regulatory measures to be overturned in recent years, as corporate lobbyists, and more than a few elected officials, might have liked.

But a very different story emerges if you ask people in the Mississippi Delta region of Louisiana, where a dense concentration of oil refineries, chemical plants, and plastics factories contributes to the highest cancer rate in the United States; or in southern Appalachia, where pulp and paper processors are decimating the region's forests and their mills' toxic emissions are poisoning entire communities; or in northern California, where some of the last remaining intact redwood forests are threatened with liquidation merely for the sake of corporate greed. You will get a very different assessment of environmental "progress" if you ask the members of any of the hundreds of breast cancer support groups that have emerged in recent years, as women of all social backgrounds confront the consequences of the continued poisoning of our air, water, and food.

As the voices of mainstream environmentalism have found themselves increasingly on the defensive in the courtrooms and legislative chambers of Washington, D.C., a renewed grassroots ecological activism has emerged in small towns, urban neighborhoods, and the vast forested regions of North America, as well as around the world. Activists are confronting persistent environmental challenges with new insights, strategies, and accomplishments. People carrying the banner of environmental justice are reawakening their neighbors to the understanding that environmental health is inseparable from social and economic justice. Forest activists from Maine to California, from Alabama to British Columbia, are confronting the corporations responsible for the destruction of ecosystems worldwide. Innovative ecological approaches are being articulated by Third World and indigenous communities challenging

unsustainable models of economic development. Experiments in ecological living, community design, and grassroots political organizing are
flourishing in urban and rural communities alike.

With the emergence of new movements and new political strategies
has come a more developed social and ethical vision as well. Movements
for environmental justice, the protection of endangered ecosystems, and
the creation of ecological alternatives draw upon two central aspects of
ecological activism that more mainstream organizations often overlook:
a firm rootedness in community, and the goal of a more harmonious relationship between human communities and the natural world. Environmental advocates and policymakers generally view the environment
as something separate—a view, a landscape, an endangered ecosystem—which can be abstracted as an object for contemplation, scientific
study, or bureaucratic management. The most socially engaged forms of
grassroots ecological activism take a much different approach. "To people in the environmental justice movement, the environment is where
we live, where we work and where we play," Richard Moore of the
Southwest Network for Environmental and Economic Justice points
out.[5]

For Native Americans and other indigenous peoples throughout the
world, the very notion of an "environment" as something external and
separate from oneself can be a violation of the most sacred principles.
"We are shown that our life exists with the tree life, that our well-being
depends on the well-being of the vegetable life, that we are close relatives of the four-legged beings," explained a spokesperson for the Six
Nations of the Haudenosaunee, or Iroquois Confederacy, at one of the
first UN conferences to specifically address the concerns of native peoples.[6] Environmental activists of European descent have also moved toward such views in recent years. Australian rainforest activist John Seed,
for example, suggests that a marked change in perspective can accom-
pany persistent work in defense of living ecosystems. In geological time,
he explains, people are "a species only recently emerged from the rainforest," and many people today have seen their outlook transformed
from "I am protecting the rainforest" to "I am part of the rainforest protecting myself."[7]

While many people remain justifiably skeptical of this confluence of pragmatic and spiritual imperatives, outlooks such as these are motivated by a firm refusal to see people as separate from the earth. And this perspective is fundamentally in conflict with the dominant world view that sees every being on earth, human and nonhuman alike, as a mere resource, as an object to be owned, manipulated, and controlled. The views of environmental justice advocates, the indigenous defenders of the land, and the people of all nations who have risen up in defense of their land and traditional livelihood, are also supported by the latest findings in ecological science. Ecologists know that every inhabitant of an ecosystem depends on the entire web of relationships that define that ecosystem's integrity.[8] The ancient earth-centered wisdom of many indigenous cultures illuminates and personalizes this most fundamental biological reality.

Industrial capitalist civilization, on the other hand, promotes a radical separation from fundamental ecological realities, furthering myths of domination and control in lieu of an acceptance and celebration of the ecological relationships that sustain us.[9] People concerned about the future of human civilization and the survival of life on earth have thus been driven to a profound questioning of the nature of contemporary society, and the social and economic system that supports it. The simple desire for life to continue to survive and flourish compels us to challenge the underlying assumptions and daily realities of a social and economic system committed to the fantasy that human beings exist outside of nature. The exaggerated fascination with technological artifice that periodically shapes our national culture is only one aspect of this mentality, which aspires to control—and ultimately replace—the natural world with its manufactured tools and its manufactured dreams.

The origins of the social and ethical perspectives that often underpin the various new ecological movements can be found in the same 19th-century world that helped to set the stage for our discussion in Part One. The radical romanticism, precise observations of the natural world, and pointed social criticism of Thoreau and Muir; the movements of farmers and urban dwellers against the excesses of the new industrial order; the rise of the labor movement and the birth of agrarian populism: all of these early currents contributed to the emergence of a wide range of radical perspectives on the nature of political power, as well as the relationship between people and the natural world.

The Anglo-American roots of conservationism lie, for the most part, in the legal and political doctrines of "natural rights" that to this day motivate many traditional environmentalists.[10] Yet close observation of the patterns of nature and society has inspired a flowering of social criticism and social action that encompasses many different traditions. As vast concentrations of private wealth were beginning to transform society in the 19th century, the inherent irrationality of the entire social system was clear to those with a critical eye. Perhaps the most famous of these were the English workers of the early 1800s who roamed the countryside destroying the machinery that was being deployed by businessmen seeking to control wages, working conditions, and the quality of rural life at the dawn of the Industrial Revolution. The so-called Luddites, writes historian David Noble, "were not against technology *per se* but rather against the social changes that the new technology reflected and reinforced." The late British scholar and activist E. P. Thompson demonstrated how the bread riots that swept the English countryside nearly a century earlier represented a concerted attempt to preserve the "moral economy" of traditional village life against the early intrusions of capitalist inequalities.[11]

One of the most articulate precursors of a radical ecological vision was the Russian naturalist and geographer Peter Kropotkin, who renounced the prevailing interpretation of Charles Darwin's principle of evolution as a relentless "struggle for existence," and set out to examine cooperation and mutual aid as factors in both natural and social evolution.[12] Kropotkin also examined the irrationalities of mass industry in a detailed study that offered ample evidence to support his anarchistic social philosophy. The abolition of authoritarian state power, he wrote, would create the basis for a cooperative society in which confederated, village-based economies combined agriculture and industry, and enhanced human creativity by reconciling mental and manual work.[13]

Kropotkin's contemporary, the pioneering French geographer Elisée Reclus, sought an even more thoroughgoing reharmonization of nature and culture. He envisioned a humanity that would re-emerge as full participants in, as well as astute observers of, nature's beauty and nourishment. In an 1866 essay, "The Feeling for Nature in Modern Society," he wrote:

> Humanity's development is most intimately connected with the nature that surrounds it...In places where the land has been defaced, where all poetry has disappeared from the countryside, the imagination is extinguished, the mind becomes impoverished, and routine and servility seize the soul . . .[14]

In the social realm, Reclus was dedicated to the principle of "complete and absolute liberty." Individuals have the right to act as they please, he argued, and individual freedom is expanded, rather than limited, by joining with others in "collective endeavors."[15]

The revolutionary movements of the early 20th century, however, did not initially develop along the lines of these naturalist philosophies. In an age of social upheaval and world war, people for the most part embraced an idealized vision of technological progress as the expression of human creativity that would someday defeat oppression and totalitarianism. Many political radicals inherited the Marxist belief in the "human conquest of nature," accepting such a goal as an historic fulfillment of human nature or, in more critical times, as an unfortunate but necessary consequence of the struggle to develop civilization.[16] Not until the 1960s did large numbers of activists begin to question these views.

Subversive Ecology

By the 1960s, ecology had become established as a scientific discipline, one that extended the insights of 20th-century biology beyond the study of cells, organisms, and individual species to a fuller understanding of how species interact with one another in living ecosystems. Ecology came into its own at a time of profound questioning of contemporary life, especially the alienated, high-consumption ways that had emerged in the United States after World War II. Pollution, resource depletion, and the loss of ecosystems were not yet front-page stories, but a new environmental awareness was clearly on the horizon.

The effects of nuclear fallout from weapons testing had been a volatile public issue since the 1950s, and activists made the connection between the continuing development of nuclear weapons and the "peaceful" nuclear power plants that were beginning to mar the countryside. The publication of Rachel Carson's *Silent Spring* in 1962 shocked millions of people into an awareness of the effects of DDT and other toxic pesticides. The postwar boom of consumerism and massive industrial development also alerted corporate America to the threat of future shortages of basic raw materials, and as we have seen, elite think tanks such as the Conservation Foundation and Resources for the Future were commissioned to study ways to mitigate resource shortages, population growth, and pollution without impeding the engines of economic growth.

While a new moderate conservationist consensus was emerging among the leading shapers of public opinion, a growing number of people realized that much larger issues were at stake. Despite Carson's determined avoidance of politics, the chemical industry spent a quarter of a million dollars trying to discredit her book.[17] In 1964, an ecologist named Paul Sears published an article entitled "Ecology—A Subversive Subject" in the journal of the American Institute of Biological Sciences.[18] Concerned about the censorship of a study on the effects of pesticides by another leading scientific magazine, Sears asked whether ecology, "if taken seriously as an instrument for the long run welfare of mankind [*sic*], would... endanger the assumptions and practices accepted by modern societies."

Sears' most immediate concern was whether ecology would find its proper place in the biology curricula of public schools, but more universal matters were clearly on his agenda. "By its very nature, ecology affords a continuing critique of man's [*sic*] operations within the ecosystem," he wrote. Sears also anticipated an ecological critique of the uncontrolled growth that plagues all so-called developed societies. He first compared uncontrolled population growth to "the spread of cancer cells within an organism," but then went on to address the central problem of a growth-oriented economics:

> Growth, in all biological experience, is a determinate process. Out of control, say by pituitary imbalance, it becomes pathological gigantism and by no means the same thing as health. With the concept of a healthy economy there can be no quarrel, but to equate this with an ever-expanding, ever-rising spiral is to relapse into the folly of perpet-

ual motion, long since discredited by a sane understanding of energetics.[19]

Writing in the same issue of *BioScience*, the pioneering ecologist Eugene Odum challenged the prevailing notion that the simplification of ecosystems was a desideratum, making the world easier to control for human purposes. "Nature's theory, if the reader will pardon the teleology, seems to hold that diversification results in greater biological control and stabilization of the environment," Odum wrote, anticipating today's awareness of the central role of biological diversity as an indicator of ecosystem health.[20]

It was the political philosopher and activist Murray Bookchin who first articulated the full political implications of such views. Bookchin had been writing about chemical pollution and opposition to nuclear power since the 1950s. His first widely available book, *Our Synthetic Environment*, was published the same year as *Silent Spring*, and offered a comprehensive overview of the hazards of urban concentration, chemical agriculture, and the rise of chronic, environmentally related disease.[21] In 1965, in a small, underground newsletter based in New York City, Bookchin first published the essay "Ecology and Revolutionary Thought," which posited a new, radical ecological activism for the 1960s and beyond:

> The explosive implications of an ecological approach arise not only because ecology is intrinsically a critical science—critical on a scale that the most radical systems of political economy have failed to attain—but also because it is an integrative and reconstructive science. This integrative, reconstructive aspect of ecology, carried through to all its implications, leads directly into anarchic areas of social thought. For, in the final analysis, it is impossible to achieve a harmonization of man [sic] and nature without creating a human community that lives in a lasting balance with its natural environment.[22]

For Bookchin, only a stateless society based on face-to-face democracy, humanistic technologies, and a profound decentralization of social and economic power could relieve the destructive imbalances imposed by modern society on the natural world, and also express the reconstructive aspects of ecological science. The anarchist imperative of decentralization, as articulated by Kropotkin and others, would serve as the social expression of the ecological principles of organic differentiation and diversity.

In his later writings, Bookchin would draw an emphatic distinction between ecology as an integrative world view—encompassing a critical understanding of the relationship between society and nature, as well as the scientific analysis of interspecies relationships—and environmentalism, which he has described as "a very crude form of natural engineering," and "a mechanistic, instrumental outlook that sees nature as a passive habitat composed of 'objects'... that must merely be rendered more serviceable for human use."[23] The scope of Bookchin's social ecology has evolved over three decades to encompass an uncompromising political analysis of the institutional roots of the ecological crisis, an historical understanding of the specifically social origins of the myth of the domination of nature, and an ethical philosophy that views the potential for human freedom as an emergent property of the dialectic of natural evolution.[24]

The past decade has seen an impressive flowering of philosophical and ethical approaches to ecological problems. Diverse ecological philosophies have inspired people to devote their lives to defending wilderness areas, protecting communities from pollution, and creating political and cultural alternatives to the life-denying practices of industrial capitalist society. In Chapter Nine, we will review the contributions of ecofeminism, bioregionalism, deep ecology, and other emerging perspectives on ecological activism. Social ecology, however, remains the richest, most coherent expression of ecological radicalism, and an approach uniquely suited to confronting the challenges of the next century. Former *New York Times* correspondent Philip Shabecoff offered a surprising testimony to the staying power of social ecology when he wrote,

> [I]f one were to ask mainstream environmentalists to pause in their hectic daily efforts to influence legislation, ban toxic chemicals, save a particular piece of land, or elect sympathetic politicians, and think of the kind of world they are working for, many of them would probably respond with goals similar to those proposed by the social ecologists.[25]

Revolutionary Movements

While today's mainstream environmentalists are most comfortable working behind the scenes in the legislative, legal, and policy arenas, the ecological activism of in the 1960s often reflected the confrontative, revolutionary tenor of the times. Two of the landmark events of the 1960s New Left, the 1968 sit-ins at Columbia University and the creation of People's Park in Berkeley in 1969, were responses to the aggressive expansion plans of major universities and their impact on the land and people of surrounding neighborhoods. People's Park became a national symbol of confrontation between countercultural activists and the state when California Governor Ronald Reagan called in the National Guard, resulting in the tear gassing of a dense residential and commercial neighborhood, and the death of a young man who was watching the unfolding events from a nearby rooftop. Groups such as Ecology Action and the Revolutionary Garden Party on the West Coast and Ecology Action East in New York reflected an exuberant, irreverent, and life-affirming ecological politics defined in sharp opposition to the system that was waging an ecocidal, as well as genocidal, war in Vietnam.

With the dissolution of the New Left in the early 1970s, activists continued to express their ecological commitments in myriad new ways. Many fled the cities, seeking to establish models of communal living in harmony with the earth in rural areas throughout the country. Others carried their commitments deeper into their urban communities, founding food coops, recycling centers, community gardens, and other experiments in ecological urban living. The political commitments that continued to underlie these choices also shaped the ways in which they were carried out.

In the early 1970s, people recycled not only because it was the responsible thing to do, but because they knew that an economic system based on profit was incapable of properly handling its wastes. They grew organic food to affirm the joys of living close to the soil, and because corporations were poisoning people daily with toxic pesticides and additives; a few large companies would soon become interested in healthy food, but only when it could be packaged as a luxury item for the privileged few. People built solar collectors, greenhouses, and wind power generators to help free society from a suicidal dependence on fossil fuels and nuclear power, and from the utilities, oil companies, and government agencies that thrive on that dependence. People accepted the rigors, and often the emotional turmoil, of communal living because they knew that even their most intimate relationships were tainted by the influences of a competitive, patriarchal society that had to be overturned in the name of human liberation. "Utopias are relative," wrote the editors of *Ramparts* magazine on the eve of the first Earth Day in 1970. "More utopian by far than revolution is the idea that the present society, dominated by business, can create lasting, meaningful reforms sufficient... to permit mankind [*sic*] to survive the century."[26]

For most mainstream commentators, the 1970s were the "Me Decade," a period when the revolutionary, communitarian impulses of the 1960s were diverted into the pursuit of self-improvement, hedonistic pleasures, and a new "hip" consumerism that would set the stage for the high-consumption excesses of the 1980s. Environmental responsibility for many became a personal lifestyle choice of "voluntary simplicity," which ultimately became quite removed from the critical outlook of the 1960s' movements. But amid the unabashedly promoted abandonment of 1960s' ideals, a new movement emerged that not only embraced a utopian ecological vision, but also tried to learn from many of the organizational and interpersonal failings of the New Left, finally catalyzing important and unanticipated changes in policy.

The grassroots movement against nuclear power demonstrated the potential for radical ecological politics to change the lives of people engaged in it, as well as society itself. In the mid-1970s, government and utility industry officials announced that they would build hundreds of nuclear power plants throughout the United States before the end of the century. These facilities, they insisted, would help assure continued growth in energy consumption in the coming decades, and also offer protection against the "foreign" control of U.S. energy resources, as symbolized by the Organization of Petroleum Exporting Countries (OPEC). Rural communities all across the country were chosen as sites for nuclear reactors, and local activists, armed with technical reports and legal briefs, began working tirelessly to oppose these plans.

The politics of nuclear power in the United States changed dramatically on April 30, 1977, when over 2,000 demonstrators, prepared for nonviolent civil disobedience, converged on the construction site of a nuclear power plant in the coastal town of Seabrook, New Hampshire. They were people of all ages, rural and urban, seasoned activists and those coming to their first demonstration. Local supporters and participants included long-established New Hampshire residents as well as more recent arrivals, who had fled the cities to live closer to the land and escape the alienation of urban life. They were united in their determination that the Public Service Company of New Hampshire was not going to force the residents of this popular seacoast town to accept the overwhelming health and safety hazards of nuclear power.

Over the next several days, 1,414 people were arrested by the New Hampshire State Police for refusing to leave the construction site. Most declined to pay bail or otherwise cooperate with the authorities, and were incarcerated for two weeks in National Guard armories scattered throughout southern New Hampshire. A new kind of anti-nuclear organization was born in the armories, a model that spread like wildfire all across the country. The Clamshell Alliance—named in honor of the clams that inhabit the vast salt marshes where this nuclear plant was to be built—was committed not only to the abolition of nuclear power, but to nonviolent direct action, a principle of "life before property," and an internal organization that further embodied ecological and decentralist ideals.[27]

The basic unit of organization was the affinity group. Affinity groups, or in Spanish, *grupos de afinidad*, were the decentralized foundation of the Iberian Anarchist Federation (FAI) of pre-civil war Spain. In the 1930s, affinity groups in Spain helped free large stretches of countryside, as well as much of industrial Barcelona, from the control of powerful interests, instituting a system of direct citizen management of communities, factories, and farms.[28] The concept was brought to the United States by Murray Bookchin, who in 1969 compared the Spanish *grupos* to the countercultural collectives that were beginning to appear in U.S. cities. "The affinity group could easily be regarded as a new type of extended family," Bookchin wrote, "in which kinship ties are replaced by deeply empathetic human relationships—relationships nourished by common revolutionary ideas and practice."[29] Psychologist and social critic Joel Kovel describes the potential of affinity groups as "a force of transcendent quality and strength, a force radical in scope and empowering in practice."[30]

Affinity groups were first tried in the United States at a huge anti-war sit-in in Washington, D.C. in 1971, where people were encouraged to form small groups to offer mutual support and security in the face of an overwhelming police presence. Police efforts to sow confusion among demonstrators would be foiled by a structure that encouraged people to work together and strengthen personal bonds. In Clamshell, affinity groups were formed at nonviolence training sessions to foster solidarity and intimacy at Seabrook, but they soon took on a much wider organizational role. Many groups returned to their communities and became a local core of anti-nuclear organizers, seeking creative ways to involve their neighbors in the movement; several affinity groups that were formed to go to Seabrook survived well into the 1990s. Affinity groups were organized into local and regional chapters, and spokespeople from these chapters met in a New England-wide Coordinating Committee where all decisions were to be made by consensus.[31] By the time of the devastating nuclear accident at Three Mile Island in Pennsylvania in 1979, grassroots anti-nuclear alliances all over the United States had created a political climate in which cover-up was impossible. Not a single new nuclear plant would be ordered in the United States from that time on.

The anti-nuclear power movement demonstrated the utopian potential of ecological politics. Discussions within the movement often focused on visions of a cooperative, decentralized society powered by community-controlled alternative energy sources, such as solar and wind power. Publications popular with anti-nuclear activists, such as the Oregon-based *Rain* magazine, featured ongoing coverage of the movement; practical hands-on information about solar energy and other alternative technologies; and essays by the leading utopian thinkers of the time. Handbooks published to help people prepare for upcoming direct action campaigns regularly ran articles on feminist politics and the philosophy of nonviolence and direct action, and listed resources for affinity groups seeking to transform personal relationships in their communities by addressing racism, sexism, and other forms of oppression.

Writing about the role of anarchist-feminist activists in the California-based anti-nuclear Abalone Alliance, feminist historian Barbara Epstein explained:

> The anarchists were able to articulate what was central to Abalone as a whole: the experience of total engagement, of politics merged with personal life, that came with dedication to visionary politics and with the attempt to build a prefigurative community. The quality of human relationships and the attempt to realize shared goals in the practice of the movement itself gave old and new Abalones alike the energy to keep going, rather than fear of nuclear power plants or the desire to replace them with something safer... [It was] a movement that was fundamentally about social, communal and personal transformation.[32]

Internal tensions, changes in the political climate, and an inability to reap the fruits of their own successes led to the dissolution of many of the anti-nuclear alliances during the early 1980s. Perennial debates over leadership and accountability, group structure, the efficacy of consensus, and the nature of nonviolence often overshadowed activists' shared ecological visions. Yet the activist style, the attention to group process and interpersonal relationships, and the creative utopian orientation of the anti-nuclear movement greatly aided future campaigns for nuclear disarmament and against U.S. military intervention in Central America, as well as the new ecological movements we will visit in the following chapters. While nuclear power ceased to be a central activist focus in much of the United States, the prefigurative politics of the anti-nuclear movement—with its struggles to build visions of a future ecological society into the movement's internal workings—kept many people engaged in activism through the Reagan years and beyond. This is a crucial lesson for activists seeking to sustain and strengthen grassroots ecological movements into the 21st century.

An ecological approach to social transformation speaks to the urgent need for hope in this period of despair. Such hope emerges from a personal identification with the cycles of the natural world and the potential for a more earth-centered way of life, one in which people contemplate and celebrate nature, while actively engaging in its sustenance. In the political sphere, an ecological view is often linked to models of decentralized, participatory power; to cooperative, community control of basic social decisions; and to confederative forms of democratic political organization from the ground up. While there is no simple blueprint for realizing such a vision, the daily practices of grassroots ecological movements offer renewed confidence that such a vision can be realized, even as we deepen our awareness of the many obstacles we face.

The 1980s and 1990s have spawned a rich diversity of radical ecological paths to social transformation. Some have emerged from communities of people struggling to protect their health and livelihood from the toxic assaults of an economic system that knows no bounds. Others are inspired by a positive, reconstructive vision of an ecological society and the urge to create a liberatory, earth-centered politics and culture. The following chapters will focus on three of the most striking developments: the environmental justice movement, the new forest activism, and ecological movements in the so-called developing world. We will briefly survey the unique aspects of each of these movements, their problematic relationships to mainstream environmentalism, and the insights they offer for the development of a far-reaching social vision. Chapter Nine will address a variety of theoretical and practical approaches to realizing a more cohesive ecological movement, focusing on Green politics, bioregionalism, ecofeminism, social and deep ecology, and the prospects for an ecological economics. In conclusion, we will assess the potential for a renewed ecological activism to reinvigorate democracy and community in these often distressing times.

Chapter 6

Environmental Justice

In the fall of 1982, one of the boldest and most persistent civil rights campaigns since the early 1960s unfolded in North Carolina's rural Warren County. The issue was not voting rights, segregated facilities, or any of the other landmark issues of that earlier era. What brought hundreds of citizens—both black and white—and their ministers, as well as the state highway patrol and the national guard, to the highways of Warren County's Shocco Township was the planned importation of more than 7,000 truckloads of soil, heavily contaminated with PCBs, to be dumped in a local landfill. Every day for six weeks, as many as 300 people gathered to meet the toxic shipments. Many lay down across the road in front of the oncoming trucks. Overall, more than 500 people were arrested attempting to block these shipments of toxic soil.[1]

Though the people of Warren County were ultimately unable to halt these particular shipments of PCB waste, they permanently transformed the political debate over toxic waste in North Carolina and across the country. They foiled the state's plans to make their landfill, in a poor unincorporated township whose population is 75 percent black, a major regional depot for continuing hazardous waste shipments, and they won a two-year statewide moratorium on permits for new landfills.[2] They also demonstrated for the first time that hazardous waste dumping was an issue that could unite black and white residents in communities that had long been divided along racial lines. The events in Warren County were the harbinger of a new grassroots movement that would soon become known as "environmental justice."

Toxic waste had been very much in the news across the United States since the dramatic events at Love Canal, a residential neighborhood in Niagara Falls, New York. In 1978, Love Canal residents discovered that the Hooker Chemical Company, a subsidiary of Occidental Petroleum, had buried 20,000 tons of toxic chemical sludge more than two decades earlier right where their neighborhood now stood. The local school stood alongside the hidden toxic waste dump, resulting in a high incidence of rare childhood diseases in the community. The mothers of Love Canal got organized, and were soon able to put sufficient pressure on state and federal officials, all the way up to President Jimmy Carter, to win the evacuation and relocation of hundreds of affected families.[3]

Lois Gibbs, who initiated the mothers' campaign at Love Canal with the simple, brave act of knocking on her neighbors' doors, began to hear from people all across the country who were facing similar predicaments. She founded the Citizens Clearinghouse for Hazardous Wastes, which has since grown into a loose network of some 8,000 local groups that have won hundreds of campaigns against chemical industries, landfills, incinerators, and other sources of toxic hazards all across the United States. The Clearinghouse provides technical and legal assistance, moral and emotional support, and an impressive network of once-isolated people who have joined together to confront toxic threats to their health and their communities.

Initially, the concerns of people opposing toxic hazards were dismissed by the media as selfish, irresponsible, and unscientific. State and local officials across the country joined the chorus, belittling the importance of "NIMBYs" (Not In My Back Yarders) and their "LULUs" (Locally Undesirable Land Uses). Participants in these campaigns were, for the most part, ordinary citizens with no previous political organizing experience. Many became involved in struggles against toxic pollution as mothers and homemakers, or as workers in toxic industries, motivated by an overarching concern for their health and the health of their families. Organizing often happened around kitchen tables, rather than in traditional public settings, and the emerging anti-toxics groups had little patience for the compromises and short-term payoffs they were consistently offered by public officials. They often perceived a compelling need to look beyond their own backyards and back alleys to seek allies in other affected communities, and to understand the root causes of toxic pollution. According to sociologist Dorceta Taylor:

> These people looked directly at the relationships among class, race, political power, and the exposure to environmental hazards. They thus rejected conventional [middle-class] NIMBYism... They refused to say "not in my backyard" without questioning or caring about whose backyard the problem ended up in.[4]

Many anti-toxics groups found it difficult to sustain their organizing focus once the issue that initially brought them together was finally won or lost. But as the anti-toxics movement matured, and the economic and racial dimensions of the toxic waste issue became a central focus for organizing, activists across the country came to see how the immediate effects of toxic exposure were closely related to the other forms of oppression they faced in their daily lives.

"There's more than just one problem in these communities," explains Lois Gibbs. "Once they get involved, they realize everything is connected and can see the bigger picture that includes their health, their schools, the economy, and everything else."[5] The linking of environmental, social, and economic concerns aroused a furor that proved difficult for officials to ignore, especially when communities of color became organized around these issues. "Activists of color were more experientially equipped to perceive the injustice in the distribution of environmental hazards and envision a world where these burdens would be eliminated, reduced, or, where unavoidable, distributed equitably in the future," Taylor explains.

Diverse Communities, Diverse Strategies

Some of the most persistent struggles against toxic contamination have been in communities that are highly dependent on polluting industries for their economic survival. In refinery towns such as Richmond, California and chemical industry strongholds like Institute, West Virginia, people have come to understand that their jobs are compromising their health and the health of their children. Community groups have pressed for full disclosure of the hazards they face in the workplace and for better emergency planning. They have controlled the expansion of toxic industries and, in some cases, worked with other environmentalists to press for changes in production processes to minimize toxic exposure. Some community groups have joined with unionized workers to pressure companies into signing legally binding agreements to upgrade their facilities and grant affected populations the right to periodically review plant operations.[6]

Indeed, the involvement of organized labor in the environmental justice movement has been a pivotal factor in its development. In central California, a carefully nurtured coalition of labor and community activists has revealed the toxic hazards that plague the region's high-technology industries. While the myth of "clean" high-tech industry has led to fierce competition among communities throughout the United States to attract new microelectronics plants, the people of California's Silicon Valley tell a different story. Their groundwater is contaminated with cyanides, arsenic, heavy metals, and toxic chlorinated solvents. The rate of occupational illness, including chronic nervous system and reproductive disorders, is among the highest for all manufacturing industries. As the microelectronics industry has spread across the country, the Silicon Valley Toxics Coalition has helped groups in other regions expose the persistent myths of the economic and environmental benefits of high technology.[7]

Coordinated anti-corporate campaigns by labor and environmental justice activists also helped to build community resistance to a five-and-a-half-year lockout of BASF chemical workers in Louisiana. When 370 active members of the Oil, Chemical and Atomic Workers (OCAW)—long at the forefront of occupational health and safety activism—were locked out of the Geismar, Louisiana plant in 1984, organizers developed alliances with a wide spectrum of community groups concerned about the company's dismal environmental record. Five years later, many of the original workers were reinstated, and a new model of labor/environmental cooperation was born.[8]

More recently, steelworkers in Louisiana collected information on companies' environmental and worker safety violations to help energize their campaign against anti-union initiatives in the steel and lead smelting industries. The steelworkers have intervened to help activists in other areas of the country, and internationally as well, expose environmental abuses by some of the most consistently anti-union companies.[9] A newer activist network, Communities Concerned about Corporations, is linking activists in various parts of the United States who are confronting the practices of some of the most notorious transnational polluters, including Union Carbide, Du Pont, and ARCO.[10] "The modern multinational corporation is the connection between job insecurity and pollution," explains OCAW's Les Leopold, who is also the director of the Labor Institute, an organization seeking to join labor activists and environmentalists in support of a "just transition" from toxic chemical use. Their proposals include a new "Superfund" that would provide monetary benefits, training, and relocation assistance for displaced chemical workers.[11]

The incineration of municipal waste is another issue that has united people in every region of the country against toxic pollution. In the mid-1980s, when hundreds of cities and towns were moving to build incinerators to burn municipal waste, activists uncovered the health and environmental hazards of these facilities, noting that they are among the most persistent sources of dioxin emissions, among other toxics. With little national media attention or support from the mainstream environmental groups, grassroots community activists defeated more than three-quarters of over 280 proposed incinerators.[12] One of the most notable of these was a thirteen-acre incineration facility planned for South Central Los Angeles in the mid-1980s; a broad, multiracial coalition of community residents, aided by organizers from Greenpeace and local members of the Green Party, defeated this proposal. Robin Cannon, a founder of the group Mothers of East L.A., told activist and political scientist Cynthia Hamilton,

> This fight has really turned me around, things are intertwined in ways I hadn't realized... All these social issues as well as political and economic issues are really intertwined. Before, I was concerned only about health and then I began to get into the politics, decision making, and so many things.[13]

Numerous national and regional networks have emerged since the 1980s, along with the Citizens Clearinghouse, to address toxics issues, unite local groups, and bring anti-toxics organizers into discussions of wider political issues. For ten years, the Boston-based National Toxics Campaign developed its own network of local activists, issued in-depth investigative reports on national issues, and brought a grassroots citizen voice into national policy debates around toxics.[14] The Highlander Center, a long-renowned activist research and education center with roots in the civil rights movement, convened frequent gatherings and strategy sessions for anti-toxics activists, and in 1992 sent a grassroots delegation of people who had personally faced the effects of toxic pollution in the United States to the UN Earth Summit in Rio de Janeiro, Brazil.[15] These local activists, mostly from the South, helped to reveal an underside of life in the United States that is generally well hidden from people in other countries.

Across the South, two important regional networks have emerged in the 1990s: the Southern Organizing Committee, based in Atlanta, Georgia, and the Southwest Network for Environmental and Economic Justice, based in Albuquerque, New Mexico. They have drawn upon the energies of African-American churches, Latino community and youth groups, labor, students, and numerous others to create a broad-based, multiracial movement. The newer environmental justice networks reach well beyond immediate local issues toward a vision of interracial solidarity and community empowerment. The Southwest Network has also joined people from six Southwestern states with their counterparts in Mexico to address the dismal environmental conditions created by the *maquiladora* industries that line the U.S.-Mexican border, a condition that has steadily worsened since the passage of NAFTA, despite official claims to the contrary.[16] According to its mission statement, the network:

> recognizes the direct link between economic and environmental issues. As people of color, we recognize that the demand for a safe, clean environment and workplace can only be achieved by building a multiracial, multicultural and international movement that promotes environmental and economic justice.[17]

Confronting Environmental Racism

This interracial dimension of anti-toxics organizing has a much longer history than is generally acknowledged. In the late 1960s, the United Farm Workers (UFW) in California called attention to the toxic effects of DDT and other pesticides in their organizing drives, consumer boycott campaigns, and legal strategies.[18] By the mid-1980s, the pesticide issue had become a central one for UFW organizers, who sought to alleviate farmworker exposure to a new generation of toxic pesticides by reviving their popular boycott of California grapes. Ecofeminist activist Ellen O'Loughlin described this revived boycott campaign as "a movement that not only addresses the various exploitations involved in farm labor but also has an expanded vision that confronts the many ways the capitalist agribusiness structure oppresses people throughout the system."[19]

Some of the first scientific studies of the effects of long-term radiation exposure focused on Native American uranium miners in New Mexico. These studies were also among the first to demonstrate that the combined effect of exposure to several carcinogens—radiation and cigarette smoke, in this instance—is far greater than the sum of the individual effects.[20] This remains one of the central arguments against risk assessments that treat each exposure as an isolated event. When a massive spill of radioactive uranium tailings contaminated the Rio Puerco in northern New Mexico in 1979, destroying the water supply of numerous Navajo communities, anti-nuclear activists across the country strengthened their focus on the hazards of uranium mining and milling, and the disproportionate effect of those practices on native peoples from New Mexico to Canada.[21] Workplace hazards, inner-city lead poisoning, and numerous other problems disproportionately affecting people of color have long highlighted the need to broaden ecological movements to fully embrace urban concerns.[22]

One of the landmark events in the transformation of the anti-toxics movement into a broad-based movement for environmental justice was the publication in 1987 of a comprehensive study, *Toxic Wastes and Race in the United States,* by the Commission for Racial Justice of the United Church of Christ. The Reverend Benjamin Chavis, who had participated in the events in Warren County, was then the deputy director of the

Commission. *Toxic Wastes and Race* compared the racial and socioeconomic makeup of every U.S. community with one or more commercial hazardous waste facility or landfill. The researchers found that race was the single most important factor associated with the siting of toxic facilities, outweighing household income, property values, and other social and economic indicators.[23] Three out of five African Americans were found to live in communities with abandoned toxic waste sites. This confirmed earlier research by Robert Bullard of the University of California, who first demonstrated that both poor and middle-class African-American communities in Texas and other states are disproportionately subjected to incinerators, landfills, and toxic industries.[24]

A 1994 update, *Toxic Wastes and Race Revisited*, revealed that these inequities have not been alleviated, despite increasing media attention and numerous rhetorical gestures by the Clinton administration. According to the revised study, the average proportion of people of color in the twenty-two communities with three or more commercial hazardous waste facilities, an incinerator, or one of the nation's largest landfills had increased from under 40 percent to over 45 percent, compared to an average 25 percent population of color in areas with no such facilities. Overall, people of color were found to be 47 percent more likely than European Americans to live near hazardous facilities. In contrast, the proportion of people living in poverty was only 17 percent higher in the most exposed communities.[25]

These statistics are far less remote to the people facing toxic hazards in their everyday lives, and sometimes their experiences are brought home to a wider community of people. One such example was a University of Southern California study of 100 inner-city youths in Los Angeles who had died from nonmedical causes—everything from accidents to urban violence. Researchers found that 80 percent had notable abnormalities in their lung tissue and more than a quarter had severe lesions on their lungs. For antipollution activists in Los Angeles, this was an important signal that it was time to "de-emphasize unproductive maneuvering with legislative and regulatory bodies and to create new models for direct action to change corporate policy," in the words of Eric Mann of Los Angeles' Labor/Community Strategy Center.[26]

Challenging the Nationals

The relationship between urban-centered environmental justice organizers and the well-known national environmental groups has often been a rocky one. Initially, the nationals kept their distance from toxics issues. Some dismissed anti-toxics activists as too parochial in their focus and others approached these determined, but inexperienced—and entirely unprofessional—new groups in an unmistakably patronizing manner. Once Love Canal made national headlines, however, the larger groups began to take more of an interest in toxics and ultimately came to play a role in suing toxic polluters, pressing for better enforcement, and strengthening the 1980 Superfund law.

But tensions remained high. Various consulting firms emerged to help develop toxic cleanup strategies, often leaving the most affected populations entirely out of the discussion. The most noted of these was Clean Sites, Inc., an offshoot of William Reilly's Conservation Foundation, which generally preferred to mediate between industry and government agencies without the involvement of affected communities. Organizations such as EDF and NRDC rarely hesitated to jump into the fray, sometimes seeking to represent victims of toxic exposure and their neighbors in such proceedings, often without the knowledge or consent, much less the participation, of those with the greatest stake in the outcome.

One experience that came to symbolize the antagonism between grassroots anti-toxics activists and the national groups was the campaign against the use of styrofoam that was launched in the Northeast in the late 1980s. While manufacturers quickly substituted pentane gas for the ozone-destroying CFCs that were originally used to inflate styrofoam cups and containers, activists continued their efforts, noting that these products are still manufactured from highly toxic, petroleum-derived compounds, a likely source of styrene residues in human fat tissue as well as a serious disposal problem.

In 1987, high school students in Vermont, New Jersey, and several other states launched a boycott of McDonald's, seeking to highlight that company's responsibility for large volumes of styrofoam waste. The Citizens Clearinghouse for Hazardous Wastes and its local affiliates offered organizational support for this effort. When the youthful activists refused to be pacified by the company's disingenuous effort to collect styrofoam packaging for recycling—styrofoam cannot truly be recycled; at best, it is ground up and hidden in other plastic products—McDonald's hired the Environmental Defense Fund to help it devise a better plan. Three years later, McDonald's switched to a plastic-coated paper wrapping (also not recyclable), and the company joined with EDF to proclaim this as a landmark case of cooperation between industry and environmentalists. McDonald's advertised itself as a beacon of environmental responsibility, and EDF proclaimed another milestone in its campaign to promote its pro-business "free-market" approach to environmentalism.[27]

The emergence of an explicit environmental justice focus made the conflict between local activists and the national environmental groups more readily apparent. In 1990, during the lead-up to the high-profile twentieth anniversary Earth Day celebrations, Richard Moore of the Southwest Organizing Project (and later a founder of the Southwest Network) wrote a letter to the heads of eight prominent national environmental organizations. The letter, which was signed by more than 100 community-based activists, highlighted the disturbing lack of people of color on the boards and staff of the major environmental groups, as well as these groups' growing reliance on corporate funding.[28] Attracting significant national media attention, the letter also decried the mainstream groups' systematic isolation from impoverished communities of color that are clearly the main victims of pollution.

Predictably, the responses varied widely. Some groups initiated new environmental justice projects and, at least temporarily, added more people of color to their staffs. Greenpeace, most notably, began to devote substantial organizing resources to issues affecting communities of color, including the groundbreaking anti-incinerator battle in the inner city of Los Angeles. They also invited Anishinabe activist Winona LaDuke, a vocal critic of Greenpeace's anti-fur trapping campaigns and their impact on the livelihood of native peoples in the Arctic, to join the organization's board. More mainstream groups initiated legal actions, often using civil rights law to block the siting of new hazardous facilities; these victories sparked a series of new studies, many designed to discredit the concept of environmental racism.[29] The EPA established an Office of Environmental Equity in 1992, and in 1994 Bill Clinton issued an executive order requiring federal agencies to address racial and economic disparities in environmental enforcement.[30]

Yet the fundamental structural problems still remain. As Robert Bullard has written:

> The crux of the problem is that the mainstream environmental movement has not sufficiently addressed the fact that social inequality and imbalances of power are at the heart of environmental degradation, resource depletion, pollution and even overpopulation. The environmental crisis can simply not be solved effectively without social justice.[31]

Thus, the inability of mainstream environmentalism to adequately address environmental racism continues to reflect these groups' willing blindness to the inherent links between environmental and social ills, and to the underlying nature of social and political power.

The relative independence of the environmental justice movement from the machinations and compromises of mainstream environmentalism has encouraged a great diversity of activist styles and organizational approaches. A variety of new and promising alliances have emerged from efforts to address issues of immediate local concern, within the wider context of environmental justice.

Native-American activists have formed an Indigenous Environmental Network to resist the targeting of their lands for the dumping of toxic chemical and radioactive waste. State and federal officials have cynically co-opted native peoples' demands for tribal sovereignty by declaring reservation lands exempt from environmental enforcement, often with the cooperation of compliant tribal officials. For example, the Mescalero Apache in southern New Mexico attempted to resist the siting of a utility-financed repository for highly radioactive spent nuclear fuel rods on their land. After the community voted against the siting of the facility, tribal officials launched a drive for a re-vote, reportedly pressuring many residents to change their minds. While the second vote tipped in favor of the nuclear depot, continuing controversy on the reservation and calls for an investigation by state officials have pushed several utilities to back out of the project.[32]

In the upper Midwest, Chippewa activists have joined with members of the Wisconsin and Minnesota Greens to resist a return of copper and zinc mining to their region. The alliance between native activists and Greens began with a campaign of nonviolent action in defense of the Chippewa's traditional spearfishing practices. Racist groups in northern Wisconsin had taken to disrupting the traditional fishing season, mobilizing a threatening presence at boat landing sites, and accusing the Chippewa of depleting fish populations and endangering tourism. Green activists from throughout Wisconsin organized a Witness for Nonviolence to serve as a human buffer between the native people and the assembled angry crowds, as well as to defend native treaty rights. After several years, the Chippewa were able to obtain a court injunction against physical interference with their fishing and, ultimately, joined with the Greens in a long-range effort to reshape the economy of the region along the lines of a shared vision of ecological sustainability.[33]

Meanwhile, multinational mining companies—including Exxon, Rio Tinto Zinc, and Kennecott Copper—resumed explorations of the region that they had begun in the 1970s. Some activists suspected that these companies had played a role in inciting anti-Chippewa agitation in the region, since native/environmentalist alliances had helped to defeat earlier mining proposals.[34] In 1994, the *New York Times* described the ongoing struggle against Exxon's plans to mine copper and zinc near the Sokaogon Chippewa reservation as "one of the country's fiercest environmental face-offs."[35] At a national environmental justice gathering in 1996, Indigenous Environmental Network spokesperson Tom Goldtooth explained that indigenous peoples are the human equivalent of an indicator species for the effects of environmental toxins: not only are hazardous facilities disproportionately sited on native lands, but subsistence hunting and fishing peoples are especially vulnerable to the effects of dioxins and other toxic chemicals that have been found to accumulate in the tissues of fish and wildlife.[36]

An alliance between environmental justice organizers and Green political activists also initiated an inspiring effort at community renewal in the inner city of Detroit. In 1992, Greens from across the country helped local activists to launch Detroit Summer, a campaign to bring young people to the city each summer to work with neighborhood organizations involved in urban gardening, rehabilitating homes, building parks, and marching against violence. For several years now, Detroit Summer has offered a model, in the words of Detroit Green activist Paul Stark, of how to "rebuild our cities house by house, street by street, neighborhood by neighborhood with the spirit of community self-reliance, cooperation, compassion and a celebration of cultural diversity."[37] Campaigns such as this bring an important reconstructive dimension to an environmental justice movement best known for its often desperate battles against toxic contamination.

Uniting Against Dioxin

How can a movement such as environmental justice, made up of small, beleaguered local groups with very limited resources, begin to address wider issues, from the causes of pollution to the toxic nature of present-day industrial and economic systems? One issue that has brought people together from all of the leading national, regional, and issue-oriented environmental justice groups is exposure to dioxin, a potent carcinogen even in the most minute doses. Recent studies have revealed that dioxin, along with a large family of related chemicals, has damaging effects on the reproductive, immune, and nervous systems. It accumulates in the fatty tissues of people and animals alike, and is now found in meat, dairy products, and fish worldwide, largely due to incinerator emissions and the atmospheric dispersal of dioxin-contaminated dust.[38] Dioxin is the single most toxic ingredient in emissions from incinerators, pulp and paper mills, plastics manufacturing, and pesticides.

In 1991, paper manufacturers and other industries pressured the EPA to undertake a systematic reassessment of the toxicity of dioxin and other chlorinated organic compounds, confident that the scientific data would justify a weakening of dioxin-based regulations. Instead, the agency's investigations brought wider attention to dioxin's myriad biological effects.[39] Dioxins, PCBs, dibenzofurans, and a class of chemically related pesticides are now generally recognized as "environmental hormones," which mimic the actions of vital molecular messengers in living cells and send misleading and highly disruptive chemical messages to every cell in every organ system of the body. At doses already found in the bodies of people all over the world, these chemicals appear to alter levels of sex hormones, disturb fetal development, reduce sperm counts, increase the likelihood of learning disabilities, and impair immune system functioning. "Chemical AIDS" is the name given to dioxin in some quarters.

In 1996, in the heart of Louisiana's notorious Cancer Alley—an eighty-five-mile industrial corridor near the mouth of the Mississippi River where residents are plagued with the highest cancer rate in the United States—nearly 600 activists gathered to coordinate a national strategy against dioxin and related chemical threats. People whose communities had survived long-term battles against toxic industries, waste dumps, and incinerators—and those still desperately seeking evacuation from toxic hazards—joined with Greenpeace and Native Forest Network activists, Vietnam veterans, Native-American activists, and supportive scientists and health workers. It was one of the most inspiring, diverse, and unified environmental gatherings in many years. "Everybody is affected by dioxins and endocrine disrupters, no matter what campaign they are working on," explained Gary Cohen, a member of the conference organizing committee and former director of the National Toxics Campaign Fund, "so there is a way of uniting people around the health impacts and the worst corporate actors that gets beyond the old turf issues."[40]

Discussions ranged from new scientific findings and international political developments regarding dioxin to the experiences of communities facing dioxin hazards, the nature of environmental racism, ways to ally with chemical workers, and the development of economic as well as technological alternatives. Participants developed strategies to end the use of chlorine for bleaching paper, PVC (vinyl) in its many industrial and household uses, and incineration as a form of waste disposal, among other key sources of dioxin exposure.[41] The imperative of economic democracy was a central theme, and calls to directly challenge corporate power consistently received the most enthusiastic response.

"We're trying to create a worldview in which activists can wage long-term campaigns which embody environmental justice, economic justice, a clear analysis of corporate power, and an understanding of the international dimensions of this issue as well," said Cohen. "We are seeing the development of a politicized, educated mass movement." The Baton Rouge gathering—which ended on an exuberant note with a spirited and energetic march against a local Shoney's restaurant that had refused to serve members of a North Carolina Cherokee delegation to the conference—demonstrated the growing sophistication and deepening political commitment of environmental justice activists in the late 1990s.

The gathering also offered renewed hope for uniting environmental justice activists and other environmental activists around an explicitly anti-corporate agenda. "It's time to target the welfare folk, the real welfare recipients: IBM, Dow Chemical," and so on, exclaimed Mildred McClain, a mother and community organizer from Savannah, Georgia. Peter Montague of the Environmental Research Foundation, and publisher of the acclaimed *RACHEL's Environment and Health Weekly*, explained that legal limits on liability for damages amount to a virtual guarantee of sociopathic behavior by corporations. "When you can't feel the consequences of your actions, when you can't feel pain, you inevitably end up acting like a bully," Montague said, proposing a campaign to revoke corporate charters as well as free speech and civil rights protections for commercial activities by fictional corporate "persons." "If it doesn't breathe, it doesn't deserve free speech," he suggested.

"Most of the people in the environmental justice movement are people who came to the movement because they felt that they'd been wronged," Lois Gibbs told the editor of a leading journal for forest activists in the Northeast. "This is different than folks who are traditionally environmentalists or think of themselves as environmentalists."[42] Her solution: a unified movement that can bring people together to "rebuild democracy." Activist and scholar Cynthia Hamilton echoes this call for democracy, criticizing mainstream environmentalists' narrow focus on "rules, bureaucracy and administration." "What's needed instead," she writes, "is the creation of an 'economic democracy' that institutionalizes decentralized, local and regional approaches to development, production for use, and the greening of urban environments as well as preservation of the wild."[43]

The environmental justice movement is the leading edge of a national and worldwide upsurge of people concerned about their own health as well as that of their families and communities. People are reaching beyond the isolation and fragmentation that plague our society, and realizing the underlying political nature of cancer, AIDS, birth defects, and reproductive disorders. Support groups for women with breast cancer, people with AIDS confronting the medical establishment, and food safety activists exposing the toxic practices of corporate agribusiness are refusing to remain silent and accept with resignation the recurring personal tragedies that so thoroughly shape contemporary life.[44] Sandra Steingraber, a poet, scholar, and cancer activist, criticized mainstream coverage of the cancer epidemic in a recent interview with the food safety journal *Safe Food News*. Most media accounts, she explained,

> shift the focus from carcinogens in the food chain to our behavior and the food choices we make. It's an effective way of blaming the victim... I'm interested in changing the whole structural system so we get the contaminants out of the food in the first place.[45]

The struggles of environmental justice activists offer important lessons, and inspiration, to the millions of people facing a myriad of contemporary assaults on their lives and well-being.

Chapter 7

The New Forest Activism

As the environmental justice movement has raised an important challenge to traditional environmentalism from without, a new generation of forest activists has brought a more confrontational and visionary outlook to issues that lie at the very core of the mainstream environmental agenda. For nearly a century, traditional conservation groups, from the National Wildlife Federation to the Sierra Club, largely defined the terms of public discussion around issues such as forest conservation, wildlife protection, natural resources, and land development. The spectrum broadened somewhat in the 1970s, with the emergence of legal- and policy-centered groups such as EDF, NRDC, and the independent Sierra Club Legal Defense Fund. But, as we have seen, these groups quickly staked out positions well within the boundaries of official environmentalism.

In the 1980s and 1990s, a very different kind of conservation movement has emerged, spurred by the development of a new science, conservation biology, and a new quasi-organization, Earth First! Conservation biology is the product of a new activist generation of ecological scientists who are no longer willing to limit their role to merely cataloguing the destruction of species and their habitats. Conservation biologists focus instead on the recovery of ecosystems, seeking a proactive role in designing resilient wilderness reserves and restoring threatened ecosystems. They have lobbied to establish buffer zones and corridors connecting protected wilderness areas, in an effort to facilitate migration and thus diversify the genetic pool of protected species.[1]

Earth First! has been sensationalized in the media for its advocacy of tree spiking and other forms of "monkeywrenching," or eco-sabotage. But in the development of a new approach to forest activism, it has represented much more than that. In its early years, Earth First! was part publishing house, part media stunt, and a producer of inspirational traveling "roadshows" on wilderness issues. Its slogan, "No Compromise in Defense of Mother Earth," was emblazoned on protest banners throughout the country. Its original founders, angered by U.S. government moves to limit the protection of large roadless areas within the National Forest system, hoped to expand the scope of acceptable debate within environmental circles.[2] Dave Foreman, the movement's best-known and most controversial spokesperson, described the goal of Earth First! as "sparking a fundamentalist revival within the environmental movement," hoping to influence the mainstream groups to adopt a less compromising stance, and shift their focus from aesthetics and recreation toward the preservation of biological diversity.[3] Foreman and his allies cultivated an image as "reluctant activists," forced into action by circumstances, who would much rather be exploring the wilderness on their own or partying around a campfire than organizing a radical movement.

Yet the style of activism that emerged from the scores of groups around the country that rallied under the Earth First! banner in the late 1980s was far from reluctant. It was exuberant, seriously playful, and well steeped in both conservation biology and the anarchic spirit of direct action that emerged from the anti-nuclear and peace movements of the previous decade. Some Earth First!ers participated in various forms of monkeywrenching, but for most, the late-night escapades extolled and mythologized in the movement's publications were largely a supplement to the careful study of locally endangered ecosystems and the diverse forms of public activism in their defense. Many were adherents of the official Earth First! philosophy of deep ecology, while others ascribed to a far more eclectic synthesis of ecological and New Left perspectives.[4]

Soon it became clear that the back-to-the-landers, anarchists, and feminists that were increasingly drawn to the movement not only contradicted Foreman's carefully crafted "Rednecks for Wilderness" image, but were also doing most of the ongoing organizing work in numerous local Earth First! affiliates. In northern California's redwood country, Earth First!ers formed a local branch of the old anarcho-syndicalist labor union, the Industrial Workers of the World (IWW), to forge alliances with dissident loggers and mill workers against the exploitative working conditions in the timber industry and the export of lumber mills to Mexico. Foreman responded to this and other unexpected developments with tracts in defense of private property and condemnations of what he termed an incipient takeover of Earth First! by "class struggle social justice leftists."[5] In 1990, California Earth First!ers renounced monkeywrenching in favor of high-profile public activism and created Redwood Summer, a successful and colorful campaign of nonviolent civil disobedience in the redwoods.[6]

In the fall of 1990, facing federal conspiracy charges resulting from an FBI sting operation in Arizona, Foreman resigned from Earth First! along with the entire *Earth First!* journal staff. Foreman described various recent changes in Earth First! in rather harsh terms, and renounced what he described as "a transformation to a more overtly counterculture/antiestablishment style and the abandonment of biocentrism in favor of humanism."[7] Redwood Summer organizer Judi Bari, who brought a strong feminist and pro-labor perspective to Earth First! in northern California—and paid dearly for her high visibility in the movement when her pelvis was shattered by a bomb planted under the front seat of her car during a Redwood Summer organizing tour—responded:

> The only way to preserve wilderness and the only way to save our planet's life support system from collapse is to find a way to live on the earth that doesn't destroy the earth. In other words, Earth First! is not just a conservation movement, it is also a social change movement.[8]

Defending the Last Redwoods

The fate of northern California's last remaining ancient redwood forests appeared sealed in 1985 when the Houston-based Maxxam conglomerate staged a hostile takeover of a local Scotia, California timber company called Pacific Lumber. Pacific Lumber held title to most of Humboldt County's remaining uunprotected redwood forest, including several thousand acres of the most intact primeval redwood habitat left on earth. Maxxam soon more than doubled the pace of logging in the redwoods to pay off its junk bonds, leveling tens of thousands of acres of second growth forests and isolated old growth patches. Local activists responded by carefully mapping the forests, petitioning state agencies, and challenging the company in court. While the redwoods themselves have no legal standing, activist lawyers successfully linked the fate of the forest to the survival of an endangered seabird, the marbled murrelet, which is only able to nest in intact old growth forests.

Still, the redwoods continued to fall. Activists began blockading logging equipment, scaling redwoods that were about to be cut down, and on a few occasions, driving metal spikes into endangered trees to discourage logging. In 1989, in an effort to forge alliances with dissident loggers and mill workers in the region, activists associated with Earth First! and the IWW renounced clandestine actions such as tree spiking and launched a long-term campaign of public civil disobedience to save the ancient redwoods.

The 1990 Redwood Summer campaign brought up to 3,000 demonstrators to the logging sites, corporate offices, and town centers of northern California. Threats and physical intimidation by timber company officials and their supporters continued long after the May 1990 car bomb attack on organizers Judi Bari and Darryl Cherney; however, demonstrations, lawsuits, and region-wide educational campaigns continued as well. Every Timber Harvest Plan filed with the California Department of Forestry was challenged on legal and scientific grounds. Hundreds of people were arrested for trespassing onto Maxxam's logging sites; some camped out for days at a time on platforms hoisted amid the limbs of ancient redwoods. Activists in the region revealed Maxxam's involvement in a failed savings and loan institution in Texas and proposed that the millions of dollars in junk bonds that were seized by federal regulators be traded for the redwoods.

In 1995, Maxxam tried to reclassify its logging operations as emergency salvage efforts, following the industry-wide trend, and sought exemptions from federal and state environmental laws. The 1,700-year-old core redwood stands were becoming more isolated, and could soon become highly vulnerable biological islands in a sea of clearcut devastation. A closely timed court injunction in 1995—immediately following a rally of 2,500 people and the largest mass arrest to date—prevented Maxxam from stepping up its logging at the very close of that summer's marbled murrelet nesting season.

In the fall of 1996, activists in redwood country again faced an imminent threat of "salvage" logging and responded in even greater numbers. More than 6,000 people descended on the small logging town of Carlotta, California, and nearly 900 were arrested for trespassing on company land in the largest act of civil disobedience in the history of the forest protection movement. Demonstrations and human blockades at Pacific Lumber's timber gates continued for months and, on several occasions, virtual activist villages were created on high platforms amid the treetops. Protests continued in San Francisco as well; on one occasion, activists climbed 200 feet up the vertical cables of the Golden Gate Bridge and unfurled a banner highlighting the urgency of saving the redwoods.

Two weeks after the largest of these demonstrations, a deal was struck between U.S. government negotiators and Maxxam owner Charles Hurwitz. Maxxam would receive more than $380 million in federal and state lands in exchange for some 7,500 acres of its 190,000-acre holdings. The Clinton administration and California Senator Dianne Feinstein claimed credit for saving the redwoods, but activists in California remained unsatisfied. The 7,500 acres, they argued, were only a fraction of at least 60,000 acres needed to sustain an intact old growth ecosystem. Maxxam would have nearly a year to submit a Habitat Conservation Plan for their holdings, a plan that would likely permit continued destruction of marbled murrelet habitat. The deal would handsomely reward Hurwitz for his backhanded financial dealings, even while he remained the object of three federal lawsuits stemming from his role in the $1.6 billion Texas savings and loan debacle.

The demonstrations continued almost daily, as Maxxam's Pacific Lumber company resumed hauling redwood logs out of the region, sometimes in direct violation of state forestry regulations. Nonviolent demonstrators faced unusually rough treatment from state and local police forces, people suspended amid the treetops had their lives threat-

ened repeatedly, and arrestees were sometimes locked in maximum security cells while they awaited processing. Still, the campaign persisted.
"Whether to continue or not is not a question," said Cecelia Lanman,
program director of EPIC, the Arcata-based organization that has long-
sustained legal interventions in defense of the redwoods, "We've got ten
years behind us and possibly another ten in front."[9]

Regional and International Organizing

In the 1990s, activists across the country have created diverse new organizational forms to further the no-compromise defense of wilderness
that Earth First! had so successfully introduced. The *Earth First!* journal
moved to Eugene, Oregon after a difficult transitional period, and today
offers the most dynamic, varied, and politically engaged chronicle of
new campaigns and movements. In 1996, Earth First! activists throughout the West launched a "Campaign to End Corporate Dominance,"
seeking alliances with social justice, labor, and community groups. The
Campaign's first public event was in San Francisco, where several local
groups joined to protest Shell Oil's ongoing destruction of land and people around the world. Nine Ogoni activists in Nigeria, including the poet
Ken Saro-Wiwa, had recently been hanged for their opposition to Shell's
destruction of their homeland, making the corporation an important focus for ecology and social justice activists worldwide.[10] While many
groups, including the "Ecotopians" of northern California, continue to
work primarily under the banner of Earth First!, others have formed a
variety of new regional, national, and international activist networks.

Much of the persistent, long-range work in defense of local ecosystems has been taken up by regional groups with names like the Alliance
for the Wild Rockies, Heartwood, the Southwest Center for Biological
Diversity, and Restore: The North Woods. These groups combine legal
interventions, local organizing, and media campaigns, and some offer
assistance to smaller, local groups living near the most unique and endangered forests. While spokespeople for the Sierra Club and the Wilderness Society are still far more frequently quoted in the national press,
these other groups sustained much of the opposition to the new wave of
"salvage" logging that swept the country in 1995-96, and have brought

well-coordinated campaigns against timber exports, wood chipping, and other emerging issues into previously unorganized parts of the Northeast and South.

One of the most impressive of these new regional formations is Heartwood, which began as an Indiana-based network of activists committed to preserving the remaining hardwood forests of the central Midwest. It has grown to include some eighty affiliated groups throughout the Midwest and South. Heartwood offers timely legal assistance and small grants to local, backwoods activists, and publishes a regional journal that offers an astute, holistic perspective on larger issues of regional interest, from the dangers of corporate dominance to the search for alternative fibers for making paper.[11] "We've gone from a forest protection organization to a community of people working to protect the forest," explains Heartwood founder and executive coordinator Andy Mahler. "We recognize that to protect the forest we must first find, organize and provide a supportive community for the people who are working for forest protection."[12]

Their network, like most others, invariably faces tensions over structure, personalities, and chronic funding shortages. These difficulties may be an unfortunate but necessary consequence of maintaining both an uncompromised agenda, and the organizational openness and integrity that helps to protect small groups such as Heartwood from the pressures of co-optation. Heartwood remains an important model of how a diverse network of leading-edge activists can be united by a commitment to participatory organization and an intense devotion to the forests that its members know best.

In other regions, key issues, rather than specific organizations, have been the catalyst to bring people together. For example, in the Northeast, eco-activists of varying political outlooks united for several years in an effort to halt utility purchases of electric power from Hydro-Quebec. The Canadian company's planned hydroelectric dams would have flooded some 1,800 square miles of previously undisturbed wilderness in the James Bay region of northern Quebec. Hydro-Quebec came to represent the combined threat of massive-scale hydroelectricity, stepped-up commercial logging, and other forms of industrial development in a vast, ecologically unique sub-Arctic region.

Many U.S. opponents of the Hydro-Quebec dams were primarily motivated by the James Bay region's unique boreal forests and wetlands, with their teeming populations of caribou and freshwater seals, as well as abundant feeding grounds for migratory birds. Others focused on the struggle of the indigenous Cree and Inuit peoples to sustain their traditional lifeways amid the sometimes overwhelming pressure of forced modernization; and still others concentrated on the economics of large-scale power purchases, which represent a powerful disincentive for local and regional alternative energy development. Together, in close cooperation with Cree activists, but with only a minimum of ongoing coordination, groups representing these diverse outlooks won the curtailment or cancellation of many of the planned purchase agreements between Hydro-Quebec and electric utilities in the northeastern United States.

The diverse activities of grassroots activists, students, union members, and everyday citizens all contributed to the steady erosion of political support for the Hydro-Quebec contracts. Maine was the first state to turn down Hydro-Quebec power, requiring utilities to strengthen their conservation plans instead. Contracts with Vermont utilities were reduced by about a third, due to declining electric demand along with successful referendum drives in Burlington and other communities; these contracts might have been defeated altogether were it not for the active intervention of a Democratic governor with close political ties to the utilities and Wall Street. Probably the most decisive blow was the cancellation in the spring of 1992 of a $13 billion contract with the New York State Power Authority. Activists in Quebec and the United States continued to pressure state and utility officials, while native solidarity activists spread the word about James Bay throughout the United States and even Europe. While steps to deregulate the utility industry still raise the prospect of further power purchases from Quebec, the 1994 suspension of the largest and most devastating of Hydro-Quebec's megaprojects remains one of the outstanding political victories of grassroots environmentalists in the region.

Another important struggle that has linked eco-activists in the United States and Canada has been the campaign for Clayoquot Sound, a portion of Canada's Vancouver Island that is home to one of the world's largest remaining lowland temperate rain forests. The region's ancient red cedars live to more than 1,000 years old and its Sitka spruce reach up to 300 feet. For fifteen years, local environmentalists and First Nations people worked to stop logging in the area. They attended public hearings, negotiated with government officials, and on occasion, blockaded logging roads. In 1993, two timber companies, Interfor and MacMillan Bloedel, were granted permission to log nearly three-quarters of the remaining ancient forest, virtually everything that was not already set aside as parkland.

That summer, activists in British Columbia launched what soon became the largest campaign of civil disobedience in Canadian history. More than 12,000 people from across Canada and around the world participated in a peace camp near the shores of Clayoquot Sound. Over 850 people were arrested for peacefully blocking logging roads, and supporters included people from all walks of life, among them several forestry workers who realized that there would soon be no forest left if logging continued at current rates. The effort grew into an international campaign supported by some 150 organizations.

In the summer of 1995, a scientific panel commissioned by the provincial government recommended an end to clearcut logging in Clayoquot Sound. Future logging would be limited by the imperative to preserve both the ancient forest ecosystem and the cultures of the region's First Nations people. Under continuing international pressure, the government agreed to abide by all of the panel's 120 recommendations. Continuing violations of this mandate, however, have sparked repeated calls for direct action in defense of the region's pristine ecosystems. Greenpeace, in close cooperation with local grassroots activists, has helped to bring people to Clayoquot Sound on a number of occasions—including a 1996 blockade by both land and sea—and direct action campaigns in defense of old growth forests have appeared in other, more remote parts of the province as well.[13]

Meanwhile, international grassroots campaigns have focused on the companies throughout North America and Europe that buy paper manufactured by MacMillan Bloedel from the pulp of British Columbia's ancient trees. Companies use this paper mostly to print newspapers and telephone books. Protests have been carried out at the Toronto Stock Exchange, at the Canadian Consulate in London, and at the annual shareholders' meetings of MacMillan's most visible corporate customers, including GTE, Pacific Bell, Nippon Telephone and Telegraph of Japan, and the *New York Times*. In 1995, the *Times* canceled its contract with MacMillan Bloedel, following a persistent campaign by local grassroots activists in New York City in cooperation with the Rainforest Action Network and negotiators from NRDC.[14]

Big Timber Moves East

With the rapid disappearance of the old growth forests of the northwestern United States, timber companies are looking to places once considered unsuitable for modern, large-scale extractive logging to sustain the growing international trade in lumber, whole logs, wood chips, and pulp. As "salvage" logging has expanded rapidly throughout the West, the pulp and paper industry has targeted the southeastern United States for an expansion of logging and the construction of a new generation of highly polluting pulp and paper mills. Areas of northern New England are also facing new threats to their survival; activists in Maine, for example, defeated proposals for a major port facility designed to encourage the export of the region's forest products.

Throughout the eastern states, the arrival of industrial-scale logging is interrupting the long-term recovery of mature forest ecosystems at an historic halfway point, just when the forests' annual biomass production has begun to level off and the potential economic return is the greatest. This is a crucial stage in the potential recovery of the region's original forest ecosystems. "The timber corporations of the United States are beginning their next round of what has come to be viewed as a 100 year east-to-west rotation," explained Mathew Jacobson of the Vermont-based Green Mountain Forest Watch.[15] Clearcut lands are often sold to real estate developers and speculators for subdivisions and vacation homes, assuring that intact forests will not soon return. State and federal agencies have responded to the threat of overdevelopment by promising incentives to sustain the logging industry, rather than setting ecologically necessary land aside for the preservation of biological diversity.[16]

Eco-activists have begun to forge a more coherent response to these renewed threats to temperate forests in the United States and around the world. At a gathering in Tasmania, Australia in 1992, Earth First! activists and others from Vermont, Montana, and California joined with Australian forest activists to form the Native Forest Network (NFN). Inspired, in part, by the overwhelming success of the California-based Rainforest Action Network in developing a highly visible international movement for the protection of tropical rainforests, this new network has helped temperate forest activists in different parts of the world to share ideas and strategies, as well as support each other's campaigns with coordinated direct actions. Internationally, the vast taiga of eastern Siberia, the unique eucalyptus forests of southeastern Australia, and the temperate rainforests of southern Chile, among others, are all facing the ravages of intensified commercial logging.[17] In the United States, the Native Forest Network has also come to fill some of the organizational vacuum that arose from ongoing disputes over the future of Earth First! With a more defined and accountable organizational structure, NFN has eschewed the personality-driven politics of Earth First! and sought ways to support local activists in a more sustained fashion. NFN actions have a distinctly anti-corporate character, and on several occasions, simultaneous sit-ins, rallies, banner hangings, and other actions in several different countries have highlighted the transnational character of the continuing threat to the world's forests.

The Native Forest Network also embodies a different outlook on the movement as a whole. "Our goal is to politicize the forest movement," explained Orin Langelle, who attended the Tasmania gathering and helps to coordinate an NFN regional office in Vermont. "Some groups focus on setting up nature reserves and think they can protect biodiversity without changing the system. To be realistic, we have to stop all corporate assaults on the planet." Anne Petermann, eastern North American contact person for the Network, continued, "We don't accept wilderness as a single issue separate from urban concerns, waste, consumption patterns and all the rest. As forest activists, we are broadening our focus from just stopping cutting to who the land really belongs to, where the wood goes, and the nature of the global capitalist market."[18]

The Network's first North American conference in 1993 emphasized the struggles of Native activists from across the United States and Canada, from James Bay to the Navajo reservation in Arizona, and featured representatives from several indigenous nations, along with organizers from Australia, England, and Scotland. Indigenous activists have helped to reinforce the understanding that preserving forests and other native ecosystems is a matter of survival, not just an abstract theoretical or aesthetic concern. In 1996, the NFN sent a group to southern Mexico to explore the response of the indigenous Zapatista rebels to government and corporate attacks on the region's endangered Lacandon rainforest.

In the southern United States, NFN activists have launched high-profile campaigns to highlight the accelerating pace of wood chip exports to overseas pulp mills; their actions included the dramatic hanging of a banner reading "Stop Exporting Forests and Jobs" from a 120-foot crane at Kimberly-Clark and Scott Paper's export dock in Mobile, Alabama.[19] In the West, NFN organizers have helped to develop a grassroots response to the threat of "salvage" logging, and have sustained a long-term Earth First! campaign in central Idaho to save one of the largest intact forest ecosystems in the continental United States.[20] In the Northeast, NFN joined with Earth First!ers and more traditional environmentalists to defeat the proposed port facility on Sears Island, on the central Maine coast, which would have destroyed important breeding grounds for fish in the Gulf of Maine while permitting the export of some 600,000 tons a year of wood chips from the forests of northern New England.[21]

Native Forest Network activists in New England have also proposed a synthesis of ecological, social, and labor activism under the banner of "revolutionary ecology." They emphasize links between environmental and social issues, and have begun to articulate a new vision for the social and ecological renewal of the besieged northern forest region. A recent pamphlet on the subject states:

> Revolutionary Ecology calls for the fundamental transformation of all human activities which threaten evolutionary potential. This belief stems from a consciousness about the interconnectedness of all life, and the realization that human beings are not separate from nature.... Revolutionary Ecologists... work for an end to all forms of domination—sexism, racism and corporate control of land for profit, to name a key few.[22]

NFN activists have also developed a distinct approach to ecological and social restoration, based on their concept of a Traditional Ecological

Autonomous Zone (TEA-Zone). This has emerged in contrast to the higher-profile efforts of the government-sponsored Northern Forest Lands Council as well as the Wildlands Project, a strikingly nonpolitical attempt to implement the methods of conservation biology developed by many of the people who departed from Earth First! along with Dave Foreman in 1990. The Wildlands Project, for all its valuable educational and scientific work, focuses largely on the identification and mapping of endangered ecosystems.[23] In contrast, the goal of establishing TEA-Zones

> is a vision of ecological sanity, of autonomy from the suffocating constraints imposed by transnational corporations and their global economy, and of support for traditional ways of life that are in resonance with the land and in solidarity with the indigenous people of the region.[24]

This approach rejects the misanthropic notions of many "biocentric" activists who often unwittingly reinforce the traditional dualism of "humanity vs. nature," instead seeking to "reintegrate human societies into dynamic and complete holistic ecosystems." Ecological restoration is thus seen as inherently inseparable from the cultural and economic renewal of the region's communities.

Questioning the Mainstream

While people in the Native Forest Network and other newer activist networks do not always agree on the particulars of strategy and political outlook, they are often united in their opposition to the continuing compromises of official environmentalism. Steve Holmer of the Western Ancient Forest Campaign explained, "We have to view the national groups as a third branch of Congress and lobby them as constituents." Mike Roselle, a long-time activist who helped to found Earth First! and was associated with its more activist wing, as well as with Greenpeace and the Rainforest Action Network, continued, "We have to out-lobby them to prevent their compromised agendas from defining the issues.... We don't need their money, we work harder, and we're better at what we do."[25] A group of dissenting Sierra Club activists voiced a similar analysis in their response to the Club's endorsement of the troublesome 1995 Montana Wilderness Bill:

> When a portion of the environmental community stops engaging in honest advocacy for ecosystems, and begins to engage in political calculus, that portion of the environmental community effectively becomes just another level of the legislature.... Now, those who seek to be honest with the elected legislature about the necessary prescriptions for the environment must first lobby this quasi-legislative portion of the environmental community before their lobbying efforts with the elected legislature will have any meaningful effect.[26]

The role of the mainstream environmental groups in the campaign against Hydro-Quebec's plans to dam the rivers of the James Bay region is somewhat unique in this regard. National environmental groups like the Audubon Society, the Sierra Club, and NRDC often took a back seat to local community activists, and were sometimes able to play a constructive, clearly defined role around the James Bay issue. The Audubon Society was the first organization to publicize the issue nationwide, and NRDC used its influence to arrange a well-publicized hearing for the Cree nation's Grand Chief, Matthew Coon-Come, before the New York State legislature. On several occasions, though, the national groups sought to capture the initiative around James Bay, with promises of more funds and exposure for local campaigns. Grassroots campaigns made James Bay a highly visible issue in communities throughout the Northeast, and local activists ultimately criticized the mainstream groups for their incessant turf battles, broken promises, and continued exploitation of the issue in their direct-mail fundraising appeals. NRDC, in particular, continued featuring the threat posed by the Great Whale hydroelectric project in their fundraising mailings long after work on it was suspended.

On local and regional forest issues, the national groups—and mainstream regional organizations, such as the Conservation Law Foundation in New England, and various states' Natural Resources Councils—contribute legal, scientific, and lobbying resources to issues of key importance to local activists. But their lobbyists also engage in behind-the-scenes efforts that anger local activists, as we have seen. Grassroots activists who are primarily focused on the integrity of locally endangered ecosystems often take a dim view of the relatively intangible and elusive benefits of backroom political horse trading.

Repeated political concessions by the national Sierra Club and Audubon Society on issues of regional importance have fueled an insurgency within the ranks of those two organizations, which are unique among the mainstream groups in maintaining networks of local chapters throughout the country. For example, the Kalmiopsis Audubon Society chapter in southern Oregon defied the national organization and joined with others to challenge the Clinton administration's Northwest forest plan. Grassroots opposition from within the ranks helped to keep the Sierra Club from joining with Washington-based environmentalists in support of NAFTA and from supporting anti-immigration legislation in California in the name of population control.[27] Still, when a Florida-based Audubon chapter attempted to secede from the national organization in protest against the Society's allegedly cozy relationship with Waste Management, Inc. and other corporate donors, Audubon officials reportedly fired the chapter's director and changed the locks on the office door.[28]

In the Sierra Club, the debate between local chapters and the national organization came to a head during a five-year campaign by Club members in support of a proposal to end commercial logging in all National Forests. Organizers of this drive called themselves the John Muir Sierrans, and described it as a crusade to return the organization to the values of its honored founder. Opponents of the logging ban proposal—including Dave Foreman, who was elected to the Sierra Club board in 1995—argued that the inflexibility of such a stance would limit the Club's ability to influence federal policies or maintain strategic positions in defense of the most ecologically important forests. "I get quite frustrated with true believers who hold onto some idealistic notion of no compromise," Foreman told a reporter from the Associated Press, apparently with little intended irony.[29] David Brower, also a recently elected board member of the Club, initially expressed skepticism toward the proposal, but later announced his support for a policy against National Forest logging. On Earth Day 1996, it was announced that the logging ban had passed by a two-to-one margin, winning the votes of more than 30,000 Sierra Club members. While a relatively small percentage of the Sierra Club's half-million contributors, this was considered a high turnout for a Club election, spurred in part by members' outrage at the all-too-visible effects of "salvage" logging throughout the western and southern states.[30]

The late 1990s are a critical time for forest activists. While numerous local campaigns continue to be won through the persistence and dedication of small, underfunded groups of activists, the bigger picture remains uncertain. The escalation of "salvage" logging aroused people in defense of the forests to an unprecedented degree. Yet corporate efforts to accelerate the pace of logging and promote the wholesale export of raw forest products are only a part of an equally unprecedented capitalist feeding frenzy that is today threatening ecosystems and communities of people throughout the world. To adequately confront this reality will require a far greater level of determination, as well as international coordination of forest campaigns. While official environmentalism remains on the defensive, despite demonstrated public support for more protective measures, local groups are not always able to reap the political fruits of their victories.

Michael Donnelly of Friends of the Breitenbush (Oregon) Cascades, another intervenor against the resumption of ancient forest logging in the Northwest that accompanied the Clinton forest plan, has urged that the movement as a whole renounce the self-destructive "insider" mentality of the mainstream groups, with their reliance on promised favors from politicians tied to the Democratic Party. "[T]he reason we are losing ground," he suggests, "is that for years the forest movement has been dominated by an inside-the-Beltway mindset and a too-cozy relationship with the Democratic Party and… big foundations."[31]

Donnelly urges that activists abandon the false "realism" of the Washington-based groups and more fully express the widespread public support for meaningful environmental protection. "Every deal that has been cut in the name of our movement has failed us," he writes, and "has cost us deeply spiritually, as well as on the ground." His proposed solutions are rather straightforward: continue identifying and then raising support for endangered places; use the political and legal process whenever possible to protect native ecosystems; end the mainstream groups' self-defeating defensiveness; and stop making deals. "All native ecosystems are worthy, all are critical, none are superfluous," he writes.

Regaining the moral high ground for environmental initiatives is a central priority for activists, along with summoning political will to reach beyond the limits of past compromises. While appeals to the powers-that-be on their terms offer an illusion of respectability and access to power, assertive actions that give voice to a plainly pro-environment majority promise far more lasting results. As forest activists increase their awareness of the social, political, and international realities that shape the future of the forests and of all life, they better articulate the socially transformative potential of principled ecological activism.

Chapter 8

Ecological Movements in the Third World

International campaigns by organizations such as Greenpeace, the Rainforest Action Network, and the Native Forest Network are unfolding in a climate of growing ecological awareness by people throughout the world. Nowhere is this more apparent than in southern Asia, Latin America, and other so-called less-developed regions. The emergence of articulate and sometimes militant Third World voices in the ecology movement during the past decade offers a necessary counterpoint to the persistent myth that such awareness is largely a product of First World affluence.[1] In societies where people still live close to the land, the ecological integrity of that land is far from a luxury. Indeed, for people struggling to sustain traditional ways of life amid sometimes overwhelming development pressures, maintaining their home region's forests, soils, water, and wildlife is a matter of day-to-day survival. The ideas and actions of ecological movements in the Third World thus complement the efforts of grassroots eco-activists in the United States, and also offer an important challenge to the highly publicized international campaigns of mainstream environmental groups.

In Third World countries today, growing numbers of people have been forced from the land into crowded, pollution- and disease-ridden cities, where they are utterly dependent on the exigencies and uncertainties of the global marketplace to satisfy their basic needs. Scholars and activists with a critical internationalist perspective have come to see these social and economic dislocations as the underlying cause of poverty, malnutrition, and social decay. These frequent dislocations, in turn, are largely the product of a vicious cycle of highly destructive commercial and industrial development.[2]

Vandana Shiva, widely acknowledged as the most articulate international voice of the new Third World ecological outlook, sees such development—which she defines as "capital accumulation and the commercialization of the economy for the generation of 'surplus' and profits"—as the main cause of poverty and dispossession throughout the world today. For Shiva and other Third World ecologists, this is merely the latest stage in a centuries-old process of colonization that degrades the natural world, exploits and excludes women, and causes the erosion of cultures that have thrived for thousands of years in a mutually sustaining relationship with the land upon which they depend. Shiva writes:

> "Development" could not but entail destruction for women, nature and subjugated cultures, which is why, throughout the Third World, women, peasants and tribals are struggling for liberation from "development" just as they earlier struggled for liberation from colonialism.[3]

Since the late 1980s, activists in the North have become increasingly aware of movements of people struggling to protect their traditional lands from the ravages of the global market economy. Rainforest activists have drawn attention to the plight of the Penan on the island of Borneo, the Yanomami of the Brazilian Amazon, and numerous other peoples who have put their lives on the line to resist incursions by multinational timber companies onto their traditional territories. The assassination of prominent labor organizer Francisco (Chico) Mendes in 1988 raised public awareness in the North of the Brazilian rubber tappers, who have intervened against the colonization of the Amazon rainforest by mining and cattle ranching interests, hydroelectric developers, and other destructive enterprises. In Kenya, women organized through the world-renowned Green Belt Movement have planted more than twenty million trees as a measure against deforestation and the destruction of traditional lifeways.[4]

One of the most dramatic of the Third World's blossoming ecological movements has been the Chipko, or tree-hugging movement, which was initiated by indigenous women in the Himalayan highlands of northern India in the 1970s and spread rapidly across the country. Merging a traditional Hindu devotion to the integrity of the forests with the more recent tradition of Gandhian nonviolence, the women and men of Chipko have struggled against the exploitation of native forests and the displacement of indigenous ecosystems by plantations of commercially valued trees. Fasting, embracing ancient trees, lying down in front of logging trucks, and removing planted eucalyptus seedlings that strain precious groundwater supplies, the people of Chipko have asserted that the forests' role in replenishing the soil, water, and air must take precedence over their exploitation as a source of exotic timber for export.[5]

Larry Lohmann of *The Ecologist* magazine, who spent many years living and working in Thailand, highlights the importance of understanding the uniqueness and diversity of these movements. Movements such as Chipko are rarely simply "environmental" in the terms used by most Westerners. They emerge from a complex interplay of social, political, cultural, historical, and ecological factors, and more often than not, they defy Western dualisms of public vs. private ownership, morality vs. self-interest, biocentrism vs. anthropocentrism, militancy vs. pragmatism. They emerge from people's determination to protect traditional communal systems of livelihood, production, and allocation, rooted in distinct cultural and social patterns, from the intolerably destabilizing pressures of Western development. Lohmann writes, "Environmental knowledge and action, in Thailand as elsewhere, is locally specific, dependent on a constant, fluid interplay between theory and practice, and embedded in the democratically evolving practices of ordinary people."[6]

"The so-called environmental crisis in Africa," writes development critic Ben Wisner, "far from being a simple matter of population pressure creating vicious cycles of poverty, land degradation, famine, and further spirals of compensatory female fertility, is a crisis caused by the loss of local control over land and labor."[7] This reality, along with the effort to maintain cultural integrity in the face of a homogenizing global culture that denies and devalues traditional systems of knowledge, lies at the root of the struggle of the Ogoni people of Nigeria against the exploitation of their region's oil resources, of the opposition of people in Ghana to the flooding of their land to generate electricity for aluminum smelting, and of the resistance of the Maasai of Tanzania against threats to their pastoral ways by international "ecotourism." South African activist and scholar Yash Tandon writes:

> [P]rivate ownership of land and of nature's resources is, for the African, an unnatural phenomenon. It is profoundly antisocial and anti-humanist. Land and its resources should only be held as a trust to the community and to all nature's living creatures. Its entrustment to individuals is an act against humanity and life itself.[8]

Genetic Imperialism

As multinational corporations have stepped up the extraction of commodities such as timber and minerals—and have made Asia and Africa a dumping ground for the North's toxic wastes—they have also set out to colonize the genetic resources and indigenous knowledge of Third World peoples.[9] The pleas of activists in the 1980s that tropical rainforests should be protected for the wealth of useful, largely unknown biological products they contain have been transformed into a new agenda of biological colonialism. Corporations are surveying remote areas of the world for medicinal plants, indigenous relatives of common food crops, exotic sweeteners, sources of naturally occurring pesticides, and even the genetic material of once-isolated indigenous peoples. The biotechnology industry has proved particularly solicitous of plants, animals, and people that display unique genetic traits, which can be transferred—using recombinant DNA technology—to common crop varieties, bacteria, and other life-forms for future study and commercial exploitation.[10]

The traditional peoples who are largely responsible for the centuries-long cultivation and protection of beneficial plants and animals receive little if any benefit from these activities. Samples are collected, often by university-based researchers, with the aid of the local people who are most knowledgeable about local foods and medicines. The samples are sent to laboratories in urban centers where genetic traits are studied, products are developed, and patents are obtained that grant the company that supported the research a proprietary right to its findings.

Biotechnology companies often seek broadly sweeping patents that offer a monopoly on all possible products from a given natural source; traditional knowledge is thus transformed into a source of commercial products to be sold worldwide at a substantial profit.

For example, India's neem tree, which has been tapped as a source of insecticidal oil, medicines, and other products since ancient times, is now becoming the proprietary property of Western corporations, such as the U.S. chemical giant W. R. Grace. Anti-cancer drugs extracted from the rosy periwinkle of Madagascar have produced well over $100 million in profits for the Eli Lilly company, but are unlikely to be made available in their country of origin. The prospecting of living material reached a new height in 1995 when the U.S. National Institutes of Health received a patent on living cells cultured from the tissues of an indigenous Hagahai person from the remote highlands of Papua New Guinea. Activists saw this as an alarming step toward the establishment of a worldwide trade in human genetic material.[11]

For activists around the world, these developments represent a qualitatively new stage in the exploitation of the South's resources by northern economic interests. The protocol on Trade-Related Intellectual Property contained in the 1994 GATT empowers the World Trade Organization to compel countries to enforce patent rules developed by northern governments, including the widespread patenting of living organisms and their genetic material. So far, only India has resisted this pressure; in March of 1995, the upper house of the Indian parliament indefinitely tabled a proposal that would have brought the country's patent laws into compliance.[12]

India's resistance to patenting life is the culmination of many years of activism by Indian farmers against the corporate control of agriculture. Organized farmers in India and other Third World countries are aware that, under the guise of fighting hunger, corporate agribusiness has heightened social inequality in agricultural regions and made people increasingly dependent on the corporate-dominated global economy. At the same time, industrial farming methods have lowered groundwater levels, poisoned the land with chemicals, and undermined the species diversity that has long sustained indigenous agriculture.[13] Farmers in the southwestern Indian state of Karnataka have focused on the increasing dominance of Cargill and other transnational corporations, and the threat they pose to land, water, and regional food security. In 1992, activists entered Cargill's regional office in Bangalore, removed records and supplies of seeds, and tossed them into a bonfire, reminiscent of the bonfires stoked by British textiles during India's independence movement. The following summer, 200 members of the state's peasant organization dismantled Cargill's regional seed storage unit and razed it to the ground.[14]

In October 1993, half a million farmers joined a day-long procession and rally in Bangalore to protest corporate control of agriculture, the patenting of seeds and other life-forms, and the new trade and patent rules required by the then-proposed GATT agreement. Their demands included a strong affirmation of the tradition of free cultivation and exchange of seeds by India's farmers.[15] S. M. Mohamed Idris of the Penang, Malaysia-based Third World Network described the farmers' predicament in these terms:

> Unlike the colonialism of the past, this new colonialism is more subtle, more invisible and therefore more dangerous. The rich countries and their corporations have already taken most of our natural resources, our minerals, our trees, our soils, as raw materials for their industries. Now that these resources are almost gone, they want to take away our rich and diverse biological materials, our seeds and our genetic resources.[16]

In 1996, 100 farmer-activists attacked Bangalore's first Kentucky Fried Chicken outlet, breaking windows and electrical outlets to protest the fast food industry's environmental unsustainability, cruelty to animals through factory farming, human health hazards, and the resulting erosion of traditional agricultural and social values. During a protracted legal and political battle, activists in Karnataka had discovered that Kentuckey Fried Chicken products contain nearly three times the level of monosodium glutamate allowed by state law, and that the company had plans to invest $40 million in building restaurants all across the country. Charges of attempted murder against the protesters and one of the movement's most prominent spokespeople were dropped in the face of international protest.[17]

Debts for Nature?

People in the so-called developing countries have also challenged the commodification and enclosure of land, often encouraged by U.S.-based environmental organizations in their effort to export northern models of environmental protection. In response to the growing Third World resistance to international debt payments during the 1980s, mainstream environmentalists and international bankers developed the concept of "debt-for-nature swaps." Commitments to preserve and "sustainably manage" parcels of tropical forest and other ecologically important lands have been traded for write-offs of small portions of several African and Latin American countries' debt, a total of $200 million worth by 1996.[18] Organizations such as the World Wildlife Fund, Conservation International, and the Nature Conservancy have sponsored and actively promoted debt-for-nature swaps as vehicles for "the greening of international finance."

The first and perhaps best publicized of these swaps was launched in 1987, when the Frank Weeden Foundation of Connecticut—the same foundation that funded the Sierra Club's controversial programs on population and immigration issues—granted $100,000 to Conservation International for the purchase of $650,000 in unpaid debt from a Citibank affiliate in Bolivia. In exchange, the Bolivian government agreed to support the expansion of the Beni Biological Reserve, an ecologically unique area containing some of the world's largest remaining reserves of mahogany and tropical cedar. The Reserve would be protected "to the maximum extent possible under Bolivian law," according to Conservation International, and would be surrounded by a much larger "multiple use and conservation" buffer zone, for a total of almost four million acres. The Bolivian government agreed to allocate $250,000—mostly from funds generated through U.S.-sponsored food aid—toward the management of the project. Conservation International offered training, technical support, and other forms of international assistance for the project, along with advice on the "sustainable use" of the precious mahogany forests.[19]

Supporters of the project asserted that the entire area might have been stripped of trees in a few years had Conservation International not intervened, while critics argued that the entire project was merely a vehicle for its more rational exploitation. Some observers report that logging in the buffer zone has increased steadily since the project began: for example, twice as much mahogany was removed in 1988 as in 1987. Contracts for seven new sawmills in the area were approved immediately before the debt swap went into effect, but residents of the area were not consulted before the agreement was signed, even though much of the land was already in dispute between logging companies and the area's native inhabitants.[20]

So-called "sustainable development" experts divided the land into experimental parcels slated for varying levels of tree harvesting, from the most limited to the most intensive.[21] For the native people, these trees would have been used to build homes and canoes, and to shelter local wildlife for generations to come. The Moxeno and Chimane people have seen northern environmentalists thwart their efforts to manage the land as a community, instead supporting the practice of the Bolivian government—and many others in Latin America—to subdivide native lands into individual private plots.

As they question the legitimacy of all debt payments to international banks, activists in Latin America and elsewhere have pointed out the particularly insidious nature of this nonsolution to the alleged "debt crisis." First, the amount of land set aside for a small amount of debt relief is so large that countries would have to surrender vast amounts of territory to achieve a significant reduction in their indebtedness. Second, the land rights of indigenous peoples, as well as the wishes of the most local environmentalists, are generally ignored. Many Third World critics speculate that areas to be preserved are selected primarily for the benefit of the biotechnology industry's germ plasm prospectors. Debt swaps, according to Ecuadoran environmentalist Esperanza Martínez, allow northern countries to impose "new forms of dependence and extraction of riches."[22] Further, debt swaps can be seen as a way to neutralize environmental opposition to neo-colonialism throughout the South. Paralleling the compromises of mainstream environmentalists in the U.S., such efforts encourage "the consolidation of a sector in [our] movement disposed to support the strategy of the United States and international banks," according to Manuel Baquedano, president of Chile's Institute for Political Ecology.[23]

Corporate interests clearly have much to gain by enlisting environmentalists to do their bidding. In 1991, for example, the Natural Resources Defense Council was found to be engaged in secret negotiations among the oil giant Conoco, the government of Ecuador, and a confederation of the Ecuadoran Amazon's indigenous nations. Seeing oil development in the region as inevitable, NRDC's negotiators, including Robert Kennedy, Jr., believed they would be able to get a better deal for the Amazonian peoples. When a group of Huaorani people opposed to any oil development in their homeland contacted the Rainforest Action Network (RAN) and other groups exposed the impending deal, ultimately leading to the departure of Conoco from Ecuador, an international campaign against other oil companies operating in the region, and initial steps toward government recognition of traditional land rights.[24]

The World Wildlife Fund and other mainstream groups have also helped to create national parks in several African countries. The parks, conceived on the North American model, are advertised as pristine places where wild animals and their habitat can be preserved without human disturbance. But this often happens at the expense of indigenous peoples, who have been living alongside wild animals since time immemorial, and in many cases, fought for centuries to keep slave traders, poachers, and colonists out of these areas. Without native protection, wildlife habitat may be designated for preservation today, but is more vulnerable in the long run. In Kenya and Tanzania, for instance, the pastoral Maasai people have protected elephants and other animals from hunters since the beginning of European colonialism but are now excluded from national parks created with the support of U.S. environmentalists. The Maasai and other groups displaced in the name of environmental protection have been moved to more marginal lands and are sometimes reduced to begging from wealthy foreign tourists who are able to purchase permits to engage in sport hunting. Moringe Parkipuny, a Maasai elder who represents his people in the national parliament of Tanzania, explained:

> To us in Africa, the disappearance of the elephant is just one aspect of the major problem of colonialism.... The conflict, as we see it, is between indigenous peoples and the policies imposed on them by for-

eign governments. These policies discriminate against us by making wild animals more important than indigenous peoples. They have also turned our people against wild animals, because they feel that wildlife is now being used as a weapon to destroy us.[25]

Blaming the Poor

While concerns about population growth and immigration in the United States have been exploited by those who would sever the fundamental link between ecology and social justice, Third World activists face a far more extreme agenda. A systematic exploration of the politics of population is beyond the scope of this book; suffice it to say, the population issue has largely become a smoke screen to obscure the patterns of colonialism and exploitation that are primarily responsible for the destruction of the South's ecological integrity.[26] Discussions of overpopulation invariably focus on countries in Africa and southern Asia, rather than Holland, for example, which probably has the world's highest population density, or Japan, which has long imported much of its food, timber, and other necessities.[27] Population growth in the Third World is certainly a matter of ecological concern, but it is a symptom, rather than a cause, of environmental and social degradation.

Western pundits, such as Robert Kaplan of the *Atlantic Monthly* in his widely quoted polemic "The Coming Anarchy," see a grim future for Africa and other "underdeveloped" regions of the world. In their apocalyptic visions, this is an inevitable consequence of nature "beginning to take its revenge."[28] This view is supported by many environmental groups working in the international sphere, such as the World Wildlife Fund which in the late 1980s, described the world's poor as the "most direct threat to wildlife and wildlands."[29] Ecological thinkers and activists in Third World countries raise a very different set of questions. Is "nature" responsible for the horrifying statistics offered by Kaplan and others—African countries losing 80 percent of their rainforests, people forced to migrate to dangerous and overcrowded cities, etc.—or are such problems the consequence of an intensified neo-colonialism that has stripped their land bare and turned much of the world into what author Tom Athanasiou terms "an international debtor's prison"?[30]

Even those institutions most responsible for the present state of affairs are being pressed to acknowledge who is really overconsuming the earth's resources. The World Bank, for example, has helped drive countless countries into debilitating cycles of poverty and dependency, in the name of "structural adjustment," a systematic effort to reorient the world's economies toward debt repayment, privatization of public services, and the promotion of foreign investment. Yet even the Bank is compelled to admit that industrialized countries, with barely 20 percent of the world's population, consume well over 80 percent of the world's goods.[31] Between 1900 and 1990, although the world's human population tripled, fossil fuel use increased thirtyfold and industrial output increased fiftyfold.[32] A more graphic example is cited by the Malaysian activist Martin Khor, who decries the "gross inequalities in the use of natural resources epitomized by the fact that New Yorkers use more energy commuting in a week than the energy used by all Africans for all uses in a year..."[33] There is clearly nothing inevitable about the relationship between population and consumption, especially when considered in regionally specific terms.

For most mainstream commentators, in the South as well as the North, and for many mainstream environmentalists, the answer to inequality is more development, often carried out with a veneer of environmental sustainability. We have seen that development, for many Third World activists, is merely the latest incarnation of the 500-year legacy of European colonialism. As Muto Ichiyo of the Tokyo-based Pacific-Asia Resource Center describes it, "Economic development, which was supposed to raise the world out of poverty, has so far only transformed undeveloped poverty into developed poverty, traditional poverty into modernized poverty designed to function smoothly in the world economic system."[34] It brings toxic hazards, such as Bhopal (where families of the victims of the 1984 chemical explosion are continuing to pursue legal charges against the executives of Union Carbide), and sweatshop industries that assault people's health and well-being.[35] For British political ecologists Oliver Tickell and Nicholas Hildyard, "[c]asting environmental problems in the language of development diverts attention from the policies, values and knowledge systems that have led to the crisis—and the interest groups that have promoted them."[36]

One expression of the current development paradigm has been the active participation of some U.S.-based environmental groups in government-funded international development efforts. International development assistance ostensibly designed to encourage the use of environmental technologies is often used as a wedge to satisfy the needs of transnational capital. A recent report by the U.S. Agency for International Development (AID), for example, advocated "the forging of environmental policies to favor private sector, market-based solutions... and supporting market-based approaches to biodiversity preservation and enhancement."[37] Technical assistance to address environmental problems is, for the most part, tied to the enactment of measures to limit foreign investors' liability for environmental damages. In 1993, $132 million in such assistance was funded by AID and channeled through the international activities of environmental organizations such as the World Wildlife Fund, Nature Conservancy, Conservation International, and World Resources Institute.[38]

As Vandana Shiva often points out, development does much more than perpetuate poverty and sustain the institutions of northern domination. It systematically degrades the knowledge, skills and cultural practices that have made it possible for people to thrive completely outside of a commercial context for thousands of years. In India, development turns once self-reliant farmers into "credit addicts and chemical addicts";[39] in Africa, it turns indigenous pastoralists into beggars. Even in the West, in the boreal forests of northern Quebec, for instance, it has meant the relocation of many recently intact Cree villages into prefabricated neighborhoods entirely dependent on imported consumer goods. Once relocated into the global market—physically, economically, and culturally—people invariably confront the same debilitating social ills that affect urbanized and suburban people throughout the world.

In the late 1980s and early 1990s, the concept of "sustainable development" became the accepted agenda for reconciling environmental protection with economic development. The term emerged from a series of UN studies and commissions, culminating in the oft-quoted 1988 Brundtland Commission report, *Our Common Future*, and the 1992 UN Earth Summit in Rio de Janeiro.[40] While the Rio conference made "sustainable development" a household term among mainstream environmentalists, and helped to enshrine it as the official policy of government agencies throughout the world, many activists in both the North and South see it as a fundamental contradiction in terms.

The principle of sustainability, a cornerstone of ecological thought embodying the regeneration of natural cycles and the promise of a successful weaving of human lifeways into them, has been severely distorted by the capitalist imperative of unencumbered growth. In contrast to the perpetual dynamic balance between human communities and the natural world envisioned by social ecologists, sustainable development advocates have joined forces with the global status quo within the framework of a crude, population-centered determinism. Jim McNeill, principal author of *Our Common Future*, explained it this way in a volume prepared for the Trilateral Commission on the eve of the Rio Earth Summit:

> If human numbers do double again, a five- to ten-fold increase in economic activity would be required to enable them to meet their basic needs and minimal aspirations.... Is there, in fact, any way to multiply economic activity a further five to ten times, without it undermining itself and compromising the future completely? *Can growth on these orders of magnitude be managed on a basis that is sustainable?* [emphasis added][41]

With a subtle and increasingly common turn of phrase—and questionable use of statistics—the project of making development environmentally sustainable has been transformed into one of sustaining development and economic growth. The earth's ecosystems cannot possibly survive a five- to tenfold increase in economic activity—certainly not the kind of economic activity that we in the industrialized North have come to take for granted, and only recently begun to question. With Third World cities already choking on pollution, and global climate change threatening to thoroughly disrupt the ecological balances that sustain life, it is difficult to imagine the consequences, for example, of providing private automobiles to each of China's 300 million city dwellers or enough factory-raised animals to feed Kentucky Fried Chicken to the non-vegetarian portion of India's population. Two hundred years of industrial development in the North occurred largely at the expense of the lands, resources, and people of the South. Where will the emerging

middle classes of the developing world's cities find the equivalent resources to appropriate in the name of development? The world may see
a great deal more of the "jobless growth" that sustains an economy
based increasingly on unproductive financial speculation, but what
promise does this offer to the tens of millions of people who have been
forced off the land and into the maelstrom of the global cash economy?

Realizing the long-range impossibility—and the immediate social and
ecological consequences—of the Western model of development, ecologists and traditional peoples throughout the Third World are seeking a
different kind of vision for the future, a vision that embraces indigenous
traditions while rejecting the mythical benefits of replacing subsistence-
based economies with ones that rely on buying and selling commodified
goods.[42] Campaigns to resist intrusions of the market economy against
traditional lands and economic practices are rarely reported in the official international press, but such efforts have spread throughout the
world, becoming more organized and more politically conscious.

Farmers from Ecuador to West Africa and the Philippines are return-
ing to indigenous farming methods, banning the use of chemicals and
modern machinery in their traditional territories. Fishing communities in
India and the Philippines have established coastal zones from which
mechanized commercial fishing boats are banned.[43] Activists in Malaysia
forced the cancellation of a $5 billion mega-dam project, the second larg-
est of its type in the world, which would have displaced 9,000 people.
Adherents to a landless people's movement in Brazil have occupied traditional lands, rejecting the control of absentee landowners committed to
raising cash crops. People throughout southern Mexico, inspired by the
example of the Zapatista rebels of the state of Chiapas, are defying the
corrupt political oligarchy that has dominated the country for nearly
seventy years. The Zapatista rebellion of January 1994, coinciding with
the enactment of NAFTA, pledged to reverse the Mexican government's
recent abolition of constitutionally guaranteed communal land rights.
One town in central Mexico expelled officials who supported the construction of luxury hotels, condominiums, and a golf course on indigenous lands, declaring a "free municipality" independent of the state
government.[44] As the editors of the British journal *The Ecologist* have explained:

Indeed, as the structures of enclosure begin to falter and break down under the stress of economic recession, international debt, popular protest and everyday resistance to the anonymity of industrialization, new life is breathed into even the most seemingly dismal communities as people rediscover the value of coming together to resolve their problems.[45]

What role can ecological activists in the North play in furthering the movements of people in the South? As Third World representatives at the 1992 Earth Summit emphasized, changes in the North's patterns of consumption are a prerequisite to meaningfully addressing the needs of the poor. As the Third World Network's Martin Khor described the situation:

> Since their basic needs are already fulfilled, the minority spend their incomes on superfluous and luxury consumption, and indeed the system requires them to do so to avoid... recession. The poor have basic needs but too little resources to fulfill them. Thus much of the world's finite resources are being depleted or degraded to become inputs to the production of luxuries.... At the international level, it should be realized that the present crisis is generated by the unsustainable economic model in the North, inappropriate development patterns in the South, and an inequitable global economic system that links the northern and southern models.[46]

As inequalities in wealth and power within the industrialized societies begin to parallel the huge disparities between the North and South, it is obvious that the ecological crisis cannot be addressed without seriously confronting the underlying causes of poverty and inequality.

By unquestioningly adopting the "globalist" perspective of transnational corporations, northern environmentalists have unwittingly accepted the oppressive and anti-ecological mind-set of global corporate management. The false globalism put forward by international institutions, from the United Nations to the World Bank and International Monetary Fund, has set the stage for increasing control by those institutions over land and resources, sometimes under the guise of protecting the environment. "The global," explained Vandana Shiva, "does not represent the universal human interest; it represents a particular local and parochial interest which has been globalized through its reach and control," specifically, the interests of the corporate global managers.[47] Their outlook denies the rights and sovereignty of peoples throughout the world, expropriating and patenting their knowledge while placing conditions on access to the North's environmental technologies. It mandates structural adjustment and the creation of managed rainforest preserves to forestall climate change, while refusing to limit the North's fossil fuel emissions, which are chiefly responsible for disrupting the earth's climate. The tacit acceptance, and even the celebration, of a managerial globalism by many northern environmentalists has become yet another obstacle to addressing the root causes of environmental and social destruction. As Shiva has written:

> The image of planet Earth used as a visual in the discourse on global ecology hides the fact that, at the ethical level the global as construct does not symbolize planetary consciousness. The global reach by narrow and selfish interests does not use planetary or Gaian ethics. In fact, it excludes the planet and peoples from the mind, and puts global institutions in their place. The concept of the planet is invoked by the most rapacious and greedy institutions to destroy and kill the cultures which use a planetary consciousness to guide their daily actions.[48]

Perhaps more than ever, an ecological outlook requires that we understand how the world looks when one steps outside the boundaries of a northern, industrial, consumerist worldview. The traditional knowledge of indigenous peoples as well as the social and economic analyses of Third World activists are helping not only to unmask the green facade of neo-colonialism, but to challenge the political complacency of many northern environmentalists. This challenge has become especially urgent as mainstream environmental groups legitimate the disingenuous adoption of environmental rhetoric by the U.S. government, the World Bank, and other institutions. "Given the key role they are fated to play in the politics of an ever-shrinking world," Tom Athanasiou writes, "it is past time for environmentalists to face their own history." Environmentalists have become advocates, sometimes inadvertently, "merely for the comforts and aesthetics of affluent nature lovers," he continues. Today, this is no longer tolerable. "They have no choice. History will judge greens by whether they stand with the world's poor."[49] Adopting such a stance, and heeding the messages of Third World ecologists, may ultimately help us to discover what is most sustainable in our own diverse cultures as well.

Chapter 9

Unifying Movements: Theory and Practice

Each of the movements we have explored in the preceding chapters has substantially broadened the scope of ecological activism. Campaigners for environmental justice, the new regional and international networks of forest activists, and the emerging ecological movements of the South are all reaching beyond the limited objectives and compromised agendas of mainstream environmentalism, confronting the power of corporations and giving voice to a more holistic vision of an ecological future. They offer a more thorough understanding of the roots of the ecological crisis, a focus on the institutions most responsible for the current state of affairs, and hope for a popular response commensurate with the magnitude of the problem. These movements are helping activists across the United States and around the world to reach beyond the politically expedient to what is ecologically and ethically necessary.

But how might such disparate voices come together to develop a holistic ecological movement that is more than the sum of its diverse parts? How do we begin to fully realize the socially transformative potential of ecological thought and action? Can we begin to develop a new political culture that transcends entrenched patterns of political disempowerment and cultural passivity, and reasserts the power of politically aware people to change the world?

People across a wide spectrum of social movements agree that this is an exceptionally difficult time to raise such questions. The realities of life in a world dominated by unprecedented concentrations of private power seem almost overwhelming. No place on earth remains unaffected by the ruthless practices of an ecocidal global order. An expansive worldwide monoculture of accumulation and greed threatens the planet's very ability to sustain life, making it increasingly difficult to imagine a peaceful transition to a cooperative, ecological society.

As we have seen throughout this book, the self-limiting pragmatism of mainstream environmentalism offers little hope in the face of such powerful social and economic forces. While those committed to politics as usual will continue to seek compromise and settle for what momentarily appears most expedient, the future of the ecology movement depends far more upon those who see past the limits of short-term realities and raise the possibility of an ecological, democratic, and egalitarian society. Ecological movements played a central and often unrecognized role in overturning the invincible totalitarian societies that once dominated eastern Europe. Opposition to industrial practices that severely threatened people's health—and the health of their rivers, lakes, and forests—helped to fuel the revolutions that brought those societies to a sudden and unanticipated end. We can no longer delay the creation of an ecological democracy movement in the Western industrialized world that will begin the vitally necessary transition to a peaceful ecological future.

In the 1980s and 1990s, various movements in the United States and around the world have explicitly tried to integrate the lessons of issue-oriented ecological struggles with a broader vision of social and political transformation. While none of these movements has realized its full transformative potential, each offers lessons that might help to enlighten the next wave of ecological revolutionaries. In particular, the movement for a Green politics as well as the emergence of bioregional and ecofeminist sensibilities offer a more comprehensive, future-focused perspective, along with a conscious blending of ecological and social activism. Each has inspired activists engaged in immediate, near-term struggles and spawned a unique, visionary outlook toward how we might live sustainably on the earth. Each, in its own way, has helped to realize the reconstructive potential of an ecological worldview.

Green Politics

The movement to develop a Green politics in the United States was launched in 1984 at a small gathering in St. Paul, Minnesota, and within a few years grew into a nationwide confederation of more than 300 affiliated local and regional groups. Most of the original members drew their inspiration from the emergence of Green political movements and parties in Europe, but it soon became clear that U.S. Greens were looking to Europe for a variety of reasons. Some looked to the Greens as an international multi-issue movement that was beginning to articulate a fundamental critique of industrial capitalist society, and as a necessary step toward the development of Green political parties. European Greens joined the most visionary elements of the ecology, peace, and social justice movements, and framed detailed proposals for the ecological transformation of society.

Others drew more specifically from the early electoral successes of the European Greens, as they began to win seats in national and state parliaments all across the continent. This offered a challenge to promote Green ideas within a far more constrained electoral system than exists in Europe. Most U.S. Greens have participated in both grassroots organizing and local electoral efforts, seeing the two as basically complementary and mutually supportive. A growing tension, however, between social movement-oriented activists and those who aspired to success within the existing electoral system soon came to dominate discussion and debate among the Greens in this country.[1]

Along the way, the Greens created an impressive national network, committed to grassroots participatory democracy at all levels of its operations. Many groups began to realize the possibilities for a holistic, multi-issue approach to Green activism: Greens helped to defeat municipal waste incinerators in communities from Maine to Seattle; they rallied in support of Native-American treaty rights and against multinational mining interests in the upper Midwest; they planted gardens and helped to rebuild inner-city communities in Detroit and elsewhere; they spoke out against corporate environmentalism and launched alternative, community-based Earth Day events; they merged environmental and anti-war activism during the Persian Gulf War; and they developed alternative approaches to town, city, and county planning all across the country. In northern Indiana, Greens formed an alliance with unionized workers to stop the construction of an extremely toxic painting plant; in Portland, Oregon, they established a long-lasting inner-city land trust; and in Maine, they launched the statewide referendum against clearcutting the forests, along with a successful initiative for publicly funded election campaigns. Greens also elected scores of people to local offices all across the United States, while remaining largely independent of the two major political parties.

Between 1988 and 1990, hundreds of Greens in local chapters around the country participated in the development of a visionary national Green Program. The program affirmed the Greens' commitment to economic and social justice, along with an ecological and spiritual outlook that sees the integrity of life on earth as its central organizing principle. It addressed everything from agriculture, energy, land use, and waste management to economics, social justice, education, and health. A detailed program plank on economics began:

> To Greens, the earth and its natural systems cannot be owned; they are to be respected and cared for in accordance with ecological principles. Concepts of ownership are provisional and temporary, to be employed in the context of stewardship and social and ecological responsibility. The Greens call for an ecological economic system that is based on democratic and decentralized cooperative and public forms of ownership, not excluding small businesses—a new way that goes beyond the economic systems prevailing in the world today.[2]

But a national political movement capable of promoting meaningful structural changes in society requires more than a well-crafted program. Despite the Greens' impressive record in various local campaigns, countless local groups proved unable to sustain their sense of commitment and vision for the long run. In many urban areas, the dominant political culture of single-issue activism made it difficult for the Greens to maintain a clear identity and sense of focus amid an ever shifting picture of local activism. For many chapters, membership proved transient as local issues ebbed and flowed. Hundreds, perhaps thousands of people joined the Greens for a few weeks or months, reveled for a short while in the opportunity to work closely with people who shared common values, but never become fully engaged in the long-term development of the organization.

For many long-time Greens, struggles within the national organization proved a continual distraction from local work: seemingly endless debates over organizational structures, decision-making styles, administrative difficulties, membership rules, and the like drew attention from their engagement in matters of immediate local and national concern. A 1992 attempt at a coordinated national action plan aroused only limited participation, despite surprisingly sympathetic media coverage. This effort sought to integrate the Greens' continuing involvement in anti-nuclear activism with Green Justice campaigns in the inner cities, as well as support for Native-American activists seeking to counter that year's commemoration of the quincentennial of Christopher Columbus' arrival on these shores. Ironically, those seeking to steer the Greens toward a more traditional political party structure condemned these campaigns as an unreasonable national imposition on the priorities of local groups. Soon, with dwindling organizational resources at the national level, the formation of Green political parties in various states became the de facto national strategy of the Greens.[3]

Finally, it was the lure of electoral success that may have irrevocably diluted the transformative potential of the Green politics movement. In California, where a state Green Party had been on the ballot since 1991, Greens sent inquiries to several prominent national figures, in search of a presidential candidate for their 1996 primary election. When the renowned consumer advocate Ralph Nader responded in the affirmative, a chain of events ensued that further steered the Greens from the development of a diverse national network of grassroots activists toward an inspired, but fundamentally compromised, effort to create a new national political party.

The 1996 Nader for President campaign certainly brought more national media attention to the Greens than any previous undertaking. Nader's uncompromisingly anti-corporate agenda began to open areas of debate that had long been excluded from the national political scene.

In some states, the campaign helped to draw scores of new activists into the ranks of Green organizations. Greens soon discovered, however, that presidential politics has an insidious logic all its own. Petition gathering, fundraising, and restructuring Green organizations to conform with various electoral rules often displaced imaginative grassroots activism, and the hope of national recognition superseded many Greens' professed commitment to a locally centered grassroots democracy. Campaign organizers encouraged ambitious individuals to override the concerns of grassroots Greens who hesitated to become immersed in presidential politics, giving rise to competing organizations developed in several states.

Despite Nader's personal commitment to encouraging local electoral efforts, fewer Green candidates participated in local races in 1996 than any year since the decade began. Years of efforts to broaden the social base of the Green movement were compromised by Nader's reluctance to embrace issues important to many activists. Ecofeminists, gay activists, and people of color who had long been reassured that their concerns were central to the Green political agenda once again found themselves marginalized. Greens committed in principle to a politics of local initiative and a decentralized confederalism felt their efforts were being compromised by the growing association of the Greens with presidential politics. While the national clearinghouse of the Greens continues to encourage diverse grassroots approaches to organizing, and local and regional groups continue doing leading-edge political work under the Green banner, the dream of a unified national Green organization joining local community organizing with independent electoral activity today seems as remote as ever.[4]

Bioregional Visions

A movement of people committed to a bioregional vision of social transformation emerged about the same time as the Greens, but immediately set out in a somewhat different direction. While Greens mainly concerned themselves with ecological and social policy and political activism, the bioregional movement was far more concerned with ecological living and culture. Still, bioregional groups have initiated numerous visionary campaigns in defense of local ecosystems and communities, along with some of the most creative expressions of contemporary ecological consciousness.

The bioregional movement is rooted in the simple but radical notion that the definition of where one lives should be shaped by fluid, natural ecological boundaries rather than arbitrary political ones. Bioregions are natural regions defined by mountain ranges, river watersheds, vegetation, and soil patterns, as well as by traditional patterns of human settlement. The watershed, or drainage basin, of a particular river system is often the central feature that symbolizes bioregional interdependence and the unifying idea that "we all live downstream."[5] For many rural activists, including those who have gone back to the land in recent decades, a close examination of the natural landscape offers a great deal of insight into how people first came to inhabit a particular place. For urban dwellers, bioregionalism promises a fuller appreciation of everyone's rootedness in natural cycles. On the scale of a bioregion, one can better understand how to live in an ecologically sustainable fashion, how the activities of more self-reliant communities of people can complement the patterns of nature that most typify their home place. Principles of community self-reliance and local self-governance, inherited from both Native-American and contemporary eco-anarchist roots, have long played a central role in defining the political sensibility of those drawn to a bioregional outlook.[6]

In the early 1980s, bioregional organizers in California and in the Ozarks of southern Missouri proposed convening a Community Congress as a forum for further developing and implementing a bioregional vision. Congress participants would represent diverse sectors of their community, creating a cooperative and non-statist model of bioregional governance. The Ozark Area Community Congress began in 1980 and has convened annually ever since. Ozark activist and homesteader David Haenke wrote that the Congress was designed

> to set itself as an unofficial "legislative" and coordinating body for the ecologically sustainable human systems in the Ozarks... Its purpose was to advocate, strengthen, and finally hook these systems together to form an infrastructure which could sustain human life directed by ecological [principles].[7]

The first North American Bioregional Congress occurred in 1984; it developed detailed resolutions, adopted by consensus, on subjects such as forests, water resources, health, culture, and the greening of cities. The Bioregional Congress also initiated the process that led to the founding meeting of the Greens later that year.

Biannual continental congresses and gatherings became a regular feature of the bioregional movement throughout the 1980s and 1990s. While continually refining and strengthening the bioregional vision, the congresses also struggled with questions of inclusiveness. Aiding the formation of bioregional groups in Canada and Mexico became a central priority, along with affirming a leadership role for native peoples and other activists of color from all over the continent. Though bioregionalists maintained a significant local presence in several areas of the country—northern California, the Ozarks, the Pacific Northwest, the hill country of north-central Texas, and the Great Lakes region, to name a few—a strong anti-organizational bias made it difficult to develop the means to spread the bioregional vision more widely throughout the continent. Gatherings were organized by relatively informal councils of activists who agreed to meet during the two years between events, and a more formal organization of bioregionalists only came into being in 1996. This was also the year of the first continental bioregional gathering to take place in Mexico, near a community called Tepoztlán, which only a year earlier had halted a major resort development, expelled a corrupt political leadership, and declared itself a free municipality independent of the state government.[8] Bioregionalists from Mexico and the United States aided the organizing activities of local people in this effort.

The politics of radical disengagement from the dominant system have long played an important role in the bioregional movement. In British Columbia, in 1988, the Bioregional Congress declared its commitment to

> a strategy of disengaging from the dominant political and economic system to more adequately confront its excesses and injustices... Strategies of non-cooperation (boycotts, war tax resistance, supporting co-ops and collectives, creating sustainable local economies, etc.) can put people in a better position to take back what is ours and break the shackles of consumerism.[9]

In 1990, with war looming in the Persian Gulf, the Congress' Rainbow Peoples' (people of color) Committee proposed a "Declaration of Eco-Independence from centralized government; from profit, oil, and drug addiction; from the patterns of domination that perpetuate this war economy."[10]

Despite the inherent radicalism of the bioregional idea, however, cultural rather than political aspects of bioregionalism have come to the fore in recent years. Gatherings have de-emphasized the drafting of and reaching consensus on new proposals, and concentrated more on information sharing, personal renewal, and celebrations of bioregional cultures. Though countless visionary projects, including a growing international "green cities" movement, have evolved out of the Bioregional Congresses, bioregionalism as a new politics of place has taken somewhat of a backseat to bioregionalism as an enriched cultural and ethical sensibility.[11] Bioregional sensibilities are clearly having an effect on the mainstream of society: all across the continent, awareness of the watershed as an organizing principle of ecological living has influenced regional planners, architects, and environmental educators, as well as countless artists, poets, and musicians. Yet it remains to be seen whether increased ties with Mexican activists and the emergence of a new bioregional organization will help to renew the more overtly political and revolutionary elements of bioregionalism.

Ecofeminist Voices

In the spring of 1980, some 800 women active in the peace, anti-nuclear, and various countercultural movements gathered in Amherst, Massachusetts for a landmark conference entitled Women and Life on Earth. It was at this event that the idea of ecofeminism, which had emerged from a variety of social and philosophical currents during the 1970s, first became identified as the philosophy of a social movement. Inspired by a series of women's peace actions—and, eventually, long-term encampments—at military bases in Europe, the women who gathered in Amherst initiated a series of women-only demonstrations at the Pentagon and other U.S. military installations. Their manifesto, drafted largely by the well-known feminist author Grace Paley, stated in part:

We understand all is connectedness. We know the life and work of animals and plants in seeding, reseeding and in fact simply inhabiting this planet. Their exploitation and the organized destruction of never to be seen again species threatens and sorrows us. The earth nourishes us as we with our bodies will eventually feed it... We know there is a healthy sensible loving way to live and we intend to live that way in our neighborhoods and our farms in these United States, and among our sisters and brothers in all the countries of the world.[12]

Ecofeminism has roots in feminist psychology, French critical theory, social ecology, and numerous other schools of thought, but it largely grew out of discussions central to the development of women's movements in the United States. Early ecofeminists sought to address what had become a key question for radical feminists in the 1970s: Do women have a special personal connection with the natural world or is this a cultural myth that ultimately reaffirms patriarchal gender roles? Refusing to either embrace or entirely reject an historical woman/nature connection, ecofeminist pioneers such as Ynestra King called for a more dialectical approach to this important question.

Patriarchal societies have traditionally justified the denigration of women and nature in very similar ways, King and others reasoned, and therefore women who have lived the consequences of this history of oppression do have a distinct role to play in the development of ecological thought and action. To reverse the patriarchal domination of women and nature, however, requires a fuller understanding of the historic roots of patriarchy and, ultimately, a radical reharmonization of all people with the natural world. Exploring the historic parallel between the subjugation of women and the desire of people, particularly men, to control nature has led many ecofeminists to the conclusion that an ecological future requires an end to all forms of relationship that are based upon domination rather than cooperation.

According to King, both feminism and ecology "demand that we rethink the relationship between humanity and the rest of nature, including our natural, embodied selves." This rethinking offers a hope for weaving together various existing strands of feminist thought, making possible "a new ecological relationship between nature and culture, in which mind and nature, heart and reason, join forces to transform the systems of domination, internal and external, that threaten the existence of life on Earth."[13] Starhawk, internationally known for her role in the development of an earth-centered feminist spirituality, has helped to create a unique synthesis of neo-pagan ritual and determined political action, as part of a San Francisco-based affinity group. She writes:

> The primary insight of ecofeminism is that all issues of oppression are interconnected, that to understand how to heal and liberate the world, we must look at the relationships between the various systems by which power is constructed. In an ecofeminist vision, there is no such thing as a struggle for women's rights separate from a struggle to repair the living systems of the earth that sustain life, or a struggle for gender equality that can be divided from a struggle for equality along lines of race, culture, economics, ancestry, religion, sexual orientation, or physical ability.[14]

In recent years, ecofeminism has evolved in many directions. Though some critics view this as evidence that ecofeminism is simply too eclectic and incoherent to meaningfully inform social movements, the underlying sensibility of ecofeminism has clearly had a profound influence on a wide array of movements and theoretical projects.[15] Ecofeminists are a crucial part of all the diverse ecological movements of our time, as well as continuing struggles against militarism and for an earth- and people-centered approach to international development. There are uniquely ecofeminist approaches to psychology and cultural criticism, the rediscovery of earth-centered spiritualities, and activism on behalf of animals.[16] Ecofeminists have contributed to the bioregional movement, to Earth First!, and in numerous important ways to the development of the Greens.[17]

Ecofeminist scholars offer a unique perspective on a wide range of issues concerning the relationship between nature and culture. Australian philosopher Val Plumwood, for example, has developed a comprehensive ecofeminist critique of Western dualism and the distortions of reason that stem from its historical identification with "the cultural identity of the master." Her ecofeminist philosophy challenges the ways our concept of humanity has "been constructed in the framework of exclusion, denial and denigration of the feminine sphere, the natural sphere and the sphere associated with subsistence."[18] Other ecofeminists have pioneered critiques of postmodernism, romanticism, science, and technology, and were central in articulating a new feminist politics of the body.[19] While ecofeminism has matured largely as a personal sensibility and a philosophical perspective, rather than a distinct social movement, its contributions to an array of movements remain diverse and powerful.

For example, ecofeminists have brought a commitment to feminist group process into various ecological movements. Feminist approaches to consensus decision-making, active listening, and various ways that groups can nurture everyone's individuality and personal empowerment have strengthened countless local campaigns, from the peace and anti-nuclear movements to today's anti-toxics and forest campaigns, bioregional congresses, and the Greens. The old feminist adage that the personal is political continues to serve as an important guidepost for the development of a movement committed to an ecologically, socially, and personally sustainable future.

Ecofeminists have also been highly visible participants at UN conferences and other international forums on issues of immediate concern to women. By weaving active ties among women's ecological movements around the world, they are evolving a genuinely multicultural approach to ecological thought and are beginning to realize the hope for "an inclusive and global analysis of oppression," as described by ecofeminist Greta Gaard. The dominant worldview "militates against an appreciation of the enriching potential of the diversity of life and cultures, which instead are experienced as divisive and threatening," explain Maria Mies and Vandana Shiva (ecofeminists from Germany and India, respectively) in a recent book.[20] A movement for an ecological future thus needs to more consciously embrace diversity and difference, both in the natural world and within human societies.

Activists and Ecophilosophers

Ecofeminism is only one of several philosophical currents that have influenced the development of ecological activism in the 1990s. Two of these currents, social ecology and deep ecology, have been widely debated and discussed among activists, scholars, and poets alike.[21] Each has raised fundamental questions regarding humanity's place within the natural world and inspired philosophical debate throughout the ecology movement. These perspectives have heightened many people's understanding of the limitations of traditional environmentalism, and the need for a more coherent and holistic ecological worldview.

While a full exploration of the philosophies of deep ecology and social ecology are well beyond the scope of the present discussion, it is important to consider how these divergent approaches are influencing the development of ecological activism today. Public perceptions of these particular ecophilosophies have been largely shaped by a continuing debate among their leading advocates that was initiated by social ecologist Murray Bookchin at the first national conference of the Greens in 1987.[22] Both of these philosophical outlooks, however, have played an important role in various wings of the movement, and raised countless activists' appreciation for the complex and sometimes contentious relationship between ideas and action in social movements.

Among ecological activists, deep ecology is generally associated with Earth First! and other projects dedicated to the preservation of wilderness, that shrinking portion of the natural world that remains relatively free of persistent human influences. Deep ecologists perceive wilderness as the "real world," the setting where natural evolution may continue, free of the manipulations and disruptions that they chiefly associate with human presence. Deep ecology activists, such as Nova Scotia forest activist David Orton, view it as the basis for "an alternative, non-human-centered vision" capable of "undermining the Earth-destroying human-centered status quo which is everywhere around us."[23] While some deep ecologists celebrate the ability of human beings to embody a planetary consciousness—in the words of theologian Thomas Berry, to "enter into the larger community of living species"—others have gravitated toward a rather vulgar misanthropy, viewing humanity as an ecological aberration, an obstacle to evolution, and even a cancer on the biosphere.[24]

Social ecologists, on the other hand, emphasize the emergence of humanity as a unique and admirable product of natural evolution. Human presence is seen as a realization of nature's potential for self-consciousness, and of the principles of freedom and cooperation, which both have origins in the very *telos*—the underlying logic—of natural evolution.[25] In the social sphere, according to Murray Bookchin, the founding philosopher of social ecology, "to become human is to become rational and imaginative, thoughtful and visionary, in rectifying the ills of the present society."[26] Social ecology is most associated with movements that stress the creative side of human nature, particularly such activities as organic agriculture, ecological design, small-scale eco-technology and Green politics.

Deep ecology advances the development of an "ecological self," capable of transcending human destructiveness and achieving a fuller appreciation of life as a whole. Social ecology seeks the roots of ecological destruction in particular social institutions—capitalism and the nation-state—and argues that an ecological society can emerge from forms of local political engagement that directly challenge these institutions. Social ecologists view environmental destruction as the outcome of the historical project of dominating nature, a powerful myth that emerged dialectically from aberrant relationships of domination within early human societies. Opposition to all forms of domination in society thus becomes a prerequisite for effective ecological activism.

Deep ecology's praxis is chiefly contemplative and spiritual, with activism seen as an expression of an individual's personal transcendence of an anthropocentric, or human-centered, worldview.[27] It is a heroic and often individualistic approach to activism, one that tends to dismiss efforts to link environmental and social concerns as expressions of innate human arrogance. Social ecology, in contrast, is founded on a radical critique of existing social and political institutions; it sees the active public sphere, the reassertion of community and citizenship, and the development of new political institutions, such as face-to-face popular assemblies and confederations of free cities and towns, as steps toward the development of an ecological society.[28]

The tenor of the ongoing debate between deep ecology and social ecology reflects the two schools' vastly different philosophical and historical assumptions. It also reflects the distinct social standing of the two often conflicting perspectives. Deep ecology, as a rather widespread cultural phenomenon, means many different things to different people. It has been embraced by nature writers, theologians, and philosophers from a variety of schools. Social ecology, a more unified approach to philosophy and social criticism, has largely emerged from with the work of one author, Murray Bookchin.[29] While numerous other activists and social critics embrace aspects of Bookchin's approach, his fierce insistence on the coherence of social ecological theory has, at times, restrained its full development as a diverse and evolving school of thought.[30] By comparison, deep ecology is described by its founder, the Norwegian philosopher Arne Naess, as inherently open-ended. It has thus been far easier for its adherents to develop and interpret it as they wish, leading to an array of expressions, as well as criticisms.

People in Earth First! began questioning their own movement's association with deep ecology shortly after Bookchin first launched his polemic in 1987. Bookchin's critique was sparked by a string of virulently misanthropic statements by Dave Foreman, Edward Abbey, and other prominent deep ecologists, statements that were seen as having a dangerously racist and anti-humanist tone. They characterized African starvation and the AIDS crisis as natural remedies for overpopulation, and called for the closing of U.S. borders to protect "our" biodiversity from those lacking a northern European cultural heritage, among other rhetorical barbs.[31] People working to raise awareness of wilderness issues in San Francisco and other urban areas saw these comments as an affront to their own commitment to cultural as well as biological diversity. As the Earth First! movement evolved into the 1990s, questions about the adequacy of deep ecology became more prevalent.[32]

Though these activists were rarely swayed by philosophical critiques of deep ecology, many began to appreciate its inherent limitations as an outlook for inspiring activism. While bold actions in defense of wild places throughout North America continue to be rooted in the spiritual ties to place that deep ecology often arouses, a philosophy that largely fails to recognize a positive role for human communities within a natural context can hardly be expected to inspire an inclusive political movement capable of challenging a fiercely anti-ecological status quo. Many activists perceived a fundamentally elitist strand in deep ecology, which systematically excludes many of the people who could best help to create a more holistic movement.

Carl Anthony, director of the Earth Island Institute's Urban Habitat Program and a leading voice for environmental justice, has observed, for example:

> Deep ecology is in touch with something, but the desire of a tiny fraction of middle- and upper-middle-class European Americans to hear the voice of the earth could be, in part, a strategy by people in these social classes to amplify their *own* inner voice at a time when they feel threatened, not only by the destruction of the planet, but also by the legitimate claims of multicultural communities clamoring to be heard.[33]

Peggy Sue McRae, a frequent contributor to the *Earth First!* journal, expresses cynicism toward deep ecology's embrace of an expanded identification with the nonhuman world, seeing this as merely a product of an imperialistic white male ego:

> Like the drug addict, the male ego needs more and more identity just to maintain itself. To grant women, birds and trees our own separate ego identities would be a disaster. It would leave a huge, gaping rip in the fragile fabric of the male ego.[34]

The leading proponents of deep ecology themselves demonstrate a profound ambiguity toward activism. Social philosopher Bill Devall, for example, questions whether "an active political stance is any longer appropriate with a broad ecological self," and posits the alternative of a "zenlike acceptance" of both human creativity and human destructiveness.[35] Others, however, continue to promote deep ecology as a foundation for activism. Judi Bari, for example, vehemently dissociates herself from the misanthropic wing of deep ecology, but defends the philosophy as an adequate, even revolutionary response to capitalism, authoritarian socialism, and patriarchy.[36] David Orton has advanced a distinct variety of "socialist biocentrism," and continues to promote Devall and George Sessions' rather ambiguous "deep ecology platform," in an effort to separate himself from "human-centered" leftists who merely append ecological concerns to an interminable laundry list of issues. Still, Orton has recently joined those who question the adequacy of deep ecology as a guide for human activity in nature.[37]

Social ecology has also been critiqued as a philosophical basis for ecological activism. Many who are appalled by the misanthropic views of some deep ecologists are equally skeptical of social ecology's more utopian outlook on human potential. An unmediated embrace of human creativity often rings false in view of today's deadening cultural passivity, acquisitiveness, and rampant consumerism. Critics of ecosystem management, biotechnology, and other contemporary technological excesses have raised objections to Bookchin's embrace of human "intervention" into the natural world. While Bookchin himself has consistently opposed abusive attempts to manage or simplify the natural world, his views are readily misinterpreted in an intellectual climate thoroughly shaped by the most blatantly anti-ecological industrial and cultural practices.

Bookchin's recent emphasis on human "intervention," in contrast to his earlier advocacy of a softer-edged "participation" in evolution, is largely in response to deep ecology's persistent anti-humanism.[38] Yet this has encouraged critics to paint his work with a broad brush of acquiescence to manipulation and control of the natural world.[39] Bookchin's philosophical defense of reason and the project of the European Enlightenment raises considerable doubt among generations of activists who have experienced only the worst excesses of a highly instrumental, technocratic, and profoundly destructive rationality. Furthermore, his famous intolerance toward perspectives that differ from his own has discouraged many critics from reflecting upon the important nuances of his historical and philosophical perspective.[40]

Many radical ecologists express hopes for a reconciliation of these two philosophies, hoping to unite the evocative and poetic qualities of the best deep ecology-inspired writing with social ecology's philosophical coherence and uncompromising political and social critique. Ecofeminists and bioregionalists, in particular, have each offered their own philosophical contributions as possible steps toward bridging the gap. While the idea of a more unified ecological philosophy remains an attractive one for many activists, it is important that such efforts not overlook the important critical issues that this continuing debate has raised.

Toward a Green Economy

As ecologists have sought to clarify philosophical aspects of their worldview, they have also redoubled their efforts to advance an ecological approach to economics. Faced with an increasing conflict between ecological values and the demands of an economic system that thrives on unlimited greed and acquisition, economists, public policy analysts, and activists alike have struggled for a solution. For some, the goal is to modify the workings of the current system to bring environmental factors into traditional economic calculations. But for many ecologically minded people, this is merely an attempt to force the square peg of capitalist market thinking into the round hole of ecological processes. A fuller reconciliation of social and ecological values requires that we challenge the hegemony of economically centered thinking, and begin to realign social and political institutions with ecological patterns.

Economists seeking to bring environmental factors into their calculations rely on two key analytical innovations: they have inserted the effects of pollution and other environmental effects directly into microeconomic calculations, and they have supplemented macroeconomic indicators such as the GNP to account for the long-range depletion of natural resources. Classical economics largely excludes environmental factors from consideration, viewing them as external to economic activity. In several states, regulators have required utilities to include environmental "externalities" in their comparisons of the costs of various sources of energy. Environmental economists also describe pollution taxes as a way of adjusting prices to reflect environmental "externalities." Such measures, however, are rarely if ever initiated by corporations acting, as they must, in their own economic self-interest; they are generally the result of political interventions into the marketplace, designed to placate demands for stricter environmental regulations.

Measures such as these can accurately reflect the environmental consequences of economic activities only where environmental factors are readily quantified in economic terms. We have already seen how such projections are rarely satisfactory, from either an environmental or an ethical perspective. Thus, "internalizing externalities," as economists call this process, offers a valuable but insufficient tool to highlight the environmental costs of economic activities.

Numerous economists have further argued that if the macroeconomic calculations that shape policy decisions were to incorporate ecological considerations, then the market itself could evolve toward a more ecological paradigm. Economist Herman Daly, for example, has long proposed that the depreciation of natural resources and other environmental costs be subtracted from the net national product to develop a more meaningful measurement of national income.[41] For Al Gore, whose book *Earth in the Balance* helped to convince many activists that the Clinton administration would make environmental issues a high priority, replacing the GNP with an index that accounts for resource depletion is a compelling national obligation.

Even the World Bank has taken some steps toward acknowledging environmental values in this way. A recent Bank-sponsored study attempted to rank the world's nations on the basis of their total wealth, including natural, manufactured, and human "resources." The study ranked Australia and Canada as having the greatest national wealth, per capita, with the United States ranking a distant twelfth.[42] Despite some debatable assumptions about the stability of raw material prices and the relative value of different land uses, such studies begin to offer a more realistic gauge of the consequences of development. They may serve as a warning to countries, from Nigeria to Norway, that have undertaken programs of rapid economic expansion at the expense of long-term reserves of natural resources. Whether the World Bank study will in any way alter the Bank's own aggressively pro-development lending policies is, of course, another question entirely.

Changes in other economic measures, such as discount rates (a correction for anticipated changes in future value), depreciation formulas, and other factors, have been suggested as ways to help bring the economy more in line with ecological realities. Other countries' financial and regulatory systems have also been put forward as models of a more "sustainable" capitalism. For example, many environmentalists cite the longer time frame that Japanese corporations bring into their economic calculations. But Japanese manufacturing companies and the banks they borrow from are often parts of a single huge corporate entity with holdings in scores of different economic sectors.[43] This enshrines vast concentrations of wealth and economic control, and many Japanese conglomerates are ranked among the world's leading environmental villains. Mitsubishi, for instance, is one of the world's largest importers of wood products, and is considered responsible for massive forest destruction in seven tropical countries, as well as Canada and Siberia. Mitsubishi has been targeted for a worldwide boycott by the Rainforest Action Network since 1990.[44]

Europe, too, is often seen as a harbinger of a "green capitalism," even though it is home to some of the world's biggest transnational polluters—the German chemical giant BASF and the French Rhone Poulenc corporation are two examples. Europe's recent successes in reducing pollution and promoting environmental technologies are less a product of "greener" corporations than of decades of social and environmental legislation, advanced and defended by a popular and militant labor movement. European social movements have placed significant economic, social, and cultural constraints on how corporations treat the environment, as well as their employees—constraints that are seriously threatened in this age of global corporate concentration.

The collapse of the totalitarian system of state ownership of the economy that once held sway in the Soviet Union and other avowedly "socialist" states helped to invigorate arguments that capitalism would lead the world toward ecological sustainability. The former Soviet bloc left a legacy of radioactive contamination of land, air, and water; the destruction of untold lakes and rivers by massive dams, irrigation networks, and industrial pollution; and the ecocidal effects of unregulated pesticide use, among other horrors. These are often described as the consequences of a socialist dream gone awry. For former Soviet dissident Zhores Medvedev, these environmental atrocities are rather the result of an unrelenting "pursuit of the short-term benefits and artificial comforts of a consumer society."[45]

The Soviets recklessly pursued economic parity with their capitalist rivals, linking access to political power with exaggerated and unrealistic production quotas. As in many less-industrialized countries seeking to establish themselves as economic powers—a status shared by Russia well into the 20th century—economic policies were carried out at the expense of both ecological and social values. Today, an increasingly desperate Russia is rapidly selling off its natural resources, most notably the oil reserves and the vast boreal forests of Siberia, to Western corporations in exchange for necessary infusions of capital. In China, as well, unprecedented economic growth and increased foreign investment are creating a legacy of air pollution, acid rain, and nearly insurmountable water pollution and waste disposal problems.[46]

Recent experiences affirm what many activists and thinkers have long believed: that the mechanisms of the capitalist market are fundamentally incapable of reversing these legacies of ecological destruction. What lessons does this offer our own born-again advocates of an unbridled "free market"? Can the capitalist imperative of economic growth be reconciled with the protection of ecosystems and the maintenance of natural balances? Will "free market" environmentalists eventually devise policies that encourage environmental sanity, or is a fundamentally different approach called for?

In Europe, far more than the United States, the collapse of the Soviet bloc has sparked a reassessment of the underlying nature of capitalism from a variety of perspectives. The acquiescence of even many radical economists to the presumed inevitability of a market system has made the search for a more critical understanding of capitalism an urgent one. Perhaps the most systematic treatment of the role of the market in promoting environmental degradation is that of German economist Elmar Altvater. In his 1991 book, *The Future of the Market*, which was translated into English in 1993, Altvater explored the implications of the collapse of the former Soviet bloc for the further evolution of market relationships and world trade, as well as the ecological consequences of an unchallenged acceptance of market values.

"Market efficiency has been achieved by drawing upon nature's reserves as if they were limitless," Altvater argues, explaining that:

> A "positive feedback mechanism" may thus be set up between the economic system and nature. Interest-rate signals force the production of a surplus through the overexploitation of natural resources. The degraded natural basis of production and consumption then makes it more difficult to achieve profits commensurate with the rate of interest. The debt crisis has negative ecological effects, while the degradation of nature intensifies the debt crisis.[47]

Thus, the progressive deterioration of the natural world under capitalist accumulation becomes a self-perpetuating and ever accelerating process. Altvater's analysis of the incompatibilities between nature and the market revolves around several key points:

- The market views natural resources as infinite and, therefore, economically valueless. This is the problem of "externalities" as highlighted by many schools of mainstream resource economists. Ecological considerations are largely beyond the scope of the economic system and enter into financial calculations only as a result of persistent political intervention.

- The payment of interest and the extraction of profits require enhanced rates of exploitation. As capital has become more mobile and profits in the global market have become increasingly tied to financial speculation, the pace of exploitation has increased in step. Today's global economy has been described as a huge fire sale, in which all prudent considerations are cast aside in the pursuit of more commodities at ever more impressive bargains.

- Price signals in the marketplace are especially unreliable indicators of value. This is especially true for goods and "intangibles" that are not specifically produced for sale. Neither can interest rates offer meaningful information about future conditions. Qualitative differences are obliterated, even in the most well-meaning efforts to quantify ecological values.

- The practice of discounting (i.e., adjusting financial calculations to correct for anticipated future changes) inherently devalues the future. This is true whether one is concerned with future investments or the sustenance of ecosystems and human lives, as we have seen. The higher the interest rate, the more short sighted economic decisions become. Economic models and projections of future possibilities inherently disguise and obscure ethical choices.

- Treating natural qualities as market commodities violates the integrity of whole ecosystems. Private ownership divides ecosystems into salable parcels that are divided over time into successively smaller units. The focus on economic "property rights" cannot help but violate the integrity and the interdependence of living systems.

- Ecological damage is not adequately corrected by simple financial compensation. While technologies of ecological restoration on a small scale have advanced considerably in recent years, it is nearly impossible to imagine replacing a thousand-year-old native forest, an offshore reef depleted of its native fish populations, or a vast underground aquifer contaminated with pesticides and industrial chemicals.

A society that extols greed, acquisitiveness, and the unlimited accumulation of personal wealth simply cannot be expected to honor the integrity of life on earth. The profound disjuncture between human societies and the rest of nature, historically a product of the co-evolution of capitalism, industrialism, and the nation- state, lies at the heart of our present social and cultural malaise.[48] Capitalism thrives on the myth of "the alleged self-healing virtues of unconscious growth," as economic historian Karl Polanyi described it more than half a century ago.[49] This myth, entirely unprecedented in human history before the rise of capitalism, has degraded societies and debased cultures wherever it has been unleashed, from 18th-century England to today's "free trade" zones. Its consequences for the integrity of the earth's living ecosystems are becoming more apparent with each passing year.

A wide array of intermediate steps, piecemeal reforms, and temporary holding actions are clearly necessary to restrain the system's worst excesses. But not all reforms are alike. Some help plant the seeds for a more ecological way of life, while others may make it more difficult for far-reaching alternatives to emerge. Today's debates about the direction of ecological activism may determine whether alternatives will be in place before cataclysmic events force them upon us in a much more socially disruptive manner.

Perhaps the most unrealistic approach is to continue blithely trusting in the current global status quo. The global capitalist marketplace has given us a world in which hyper-ambitious traders at computer terminals in Singapore, Zurich, or New York can trigger the collapse of a nation's currency, its food supply, or an entire ecosystem before anyone can even begin to discuss the consequences. Less than 10 percent of the $3-4 trillion that flows through the international economy every day is tied to any purpose beyond pure speculation.[50] This system has turned the world into a gambling casino, compelling whole nations of people to compete for corporate favors in what can only become a perpetual race to the bottom.

In the face of overwhelmingly powerful and destructive economic forces, it seems increasingly difficult to imagine a fundamentally different form of economic and social organization. There is no clear blueprint for an ecological economy, and no generally agreed upon strategy for creating one. Yet, there are a number of key features that logically follow from ecological principles, and a variety of models, both historical and contemporary, that offer ideas and inspiration.

People working to envision a green economy have drawn upon a wide diversity of sources from the gift-based economies of many aboriginal cultures and pre-capitalist village economies throughout the world, to contemporary experiments such as the consumer cooperative movement, community land trusts, municipal utilities, worker-managed manufacturing firms, barter and community currency networks, and numerous others.[51] Larger alternative networks, such as the worker-owned Mondragon cooperatives of the Spanish Basque country and the Seikatsu consumer cooperatives of Japan, have each made substantial compromises with the dominant economic systems in their particular corner of the world, but still offer important models of cooperation. Each involves hundreds of thousands of people working toward a more harmonious relationship with their neighbors and the land they depend upon for their survival.[52]

With these and other models in mind, activists have begun to flesh out the essential features of an ecological economy. Such an economy would be decentralized along bioregional lines, limiting concentrations of economic power, while encouraging activities that are consistent with the health of both natural and human communities. It would be materially diverse, respecting a multiplicity of lifeways and cultural expressions that mirror the earth's ecological and cultural diversity. Technological know-how would be devoted to minimizing energy use, rigorously recycling nonrenewable materials, and substituting human ingenuity for the profligate consumption of the earth's resources. An ecological economy would cast decisions in terms of their long-range consequences, perhaps reintroducing the Iroquois tradition of evaluating decisions by their likely effects seven generations hence. It would operate within what physicists call a steady-state, eschewing the imperatives of growth and accumulation that continually reinforce the anti-ecological character of contemporary society.

To formulate policies that embody principles of economic justice, while taking the long-range sustenance of communities and ecosystems fully into account, an ecological economy would be democratic and community-controlled. Economic decisions need to be made in the open by everyone who is affected by them, not by distant unaccountable corporate or state bureaucracies. Decisions that affect people across many different communities and regions would be coordinated from the bottom up, based on a confederal model of cooperative organization. This would apply to everything from trade policies and the protection of the environment and human rights, to perhaps the coordinated production of those few goods that might still require large capital investments and economies of scale.[53]

Of course, changes in the structure of economic institutions will not, by themselves, teach us how to best reconcile the imperative of social justice with the needs of the biosphere as a whole, the desire for regional autonomy with the imperative of justice and equity across regions, and other persistent social dilemmas. Still, an economy that ceases to support the appropriation of vast resources by a minuscule portion of the human population would offer society considerably more breathing room to address such apparent conflicts. The emergence of an ecological economy and an ecological society will require profound changes on the social and cultural, as well as the political and economic levels, and a radical shift in the underlying relationship between the economy and society.

In a green economy, ecological and ethical values need to become the centerpiece of economic and social decisions. In traditional societies, the economy is "submerged in social relationships," according to Polanyi— that is, in social, cultural, and religious values as well as time-honored patterns of reciprocity and redistribution.[54] The idea of a hegemonic economic sphere that thoroughly dominates social and political choices is a very recent invention in human history. A market economy "demands nothing less than the institutional separation of society into an economic and political sphere," Polanyi wrote. "Nineteenth century society, in which economic activity was isolated and imputed to a distinctive economic motive, was, indeed, a singular departure."[55] The market economy dictates the creation of a "market society," one in which every aspect of our lives is divided, measured, packaged, and given a price tag.

In contrast, an ecological economy is, above all, a moral economy, a phrase Murray Bookchin has borrowed from the historian E. P. Thompson's pioneering studies of preindustrial British society.[56] In a moral economy, economic relationships are expressions of interdependence and care, not of aggression and exploitation. This requires a fundamental recasting of social institutions and a profound shift in human relationships that can only take hold in a social environment that fully nurtures cooperation and mutuality rather than competition and greed.

It is this goal of transforming human relationships that ultimately underlies many of today's economic experiments, from food cooperatives and working collectives to community gardens and land trusts. It also lies at the center of Green, bioregional, and ecofeminist approaches to social and ecological activism. Greens and bioregionalists have consciously engaged in alternative economic activities as a part of their organizing efforts, but this is only the beginning. A far more engaged synthesis, bringing together movements that challenge the present status quo with movements to create living alternatives, is necessary if we are to confront present inequities in wealth and power, while planting the seeds of an ecological society.

Food cooperatives and worker-owned businesses within a capitalist market society quickly lose their utopian impulse as they become absorbed into the day-to-day routines of economic survival; often, they merely become a part of the system they were envisioned to replace.[57] Political movements lacking a reconstructive vision of a better society breed frustration, burnout, and a self-limiting politics of expediency and short-term gain. Only within the context of a more fully developed ecological movement and only with a comprehensive ecological critique can these oppositional and reconstructive currents truly converge, nurturing a holistic process of social transformation. In such a setting, economic alternatives and forward-looking social movements can begin to reach their full potential to become, as described by Martin Buber nearly a half century ago, the "cell-tissue" of a new society.[58]

Chapter 10

Ecology, Community, and Democracy

In the summer of 1996, the influential and increasingly controversial Pew Foundation released the results of an opinion poll suggesting that public confidence in the mainstream environmental movement may be at an historic low. This confirmed what people involved in grassroots environmental action have been saying for a long time: that the strategies of compromise and accommodation, of patiently working within the constraints of today's stifling political debate, do not inspire people's trust, most probably because these strategies are incapable of turning the tide of ecological destruction.[1] The poll was especially remarkable for its source: for many years, the Pew Foundation has played a central role in defining the mainstream agenda that the poll criticizes. Perhaps more than any other environmental funding source, Pew has steered its grant recipients toward an agenda focused narrowly on legal reform and national legislation, often to the exclusion of more challenging grassroots approaches to environmental problems.

Michael Colby, director of the food safety advocacy group Food & Water, has termed this legislation-centered approach "activist malpractice," citing the all too common tendency of mainstream organizations to "initiate a grass-roots campaign with the expectation to lose."[2] Food & Water has distinguished itself for more than a decade with its dynamic efforts against food irradiation, toxic pesticides, and genetically engineered foods. Its largely successful crusade to prevent the radiation treatment of fresh foods to increase their shelf life has taken the form of a national consumer campaign aimed at corporations: supermarket chains, food processors, wholesale distributors, and the irradiation facilities themselves. While anti-irradiation laws were passed in a handful of states, Food & Water's campaigns of direct pressure on the food industry played a far more central role in restraining this dangerous and aggressively promoted technology.

In contrast to the endless variety of grassroots campaigns for food safety, environmental justice, biodiversity protection, controls on urban development, and other ecological concerns, mainstream strategies in the 1990s have been dominated by a narrowly legislative approach. Distressingly shortsighted campaigns for temporary moratoriums and phaseouts of toxic practices, partial protections for limited patches of wilderness, and other such measures have long dominated the efforts of mainstream environmentalists. Activist constituencies are repeatedly rallied behind proposals that are both compromised in scope and unlikely to be enacted. Colby describes it this way:

> Activist leaders, particularly those with a legislative focus, tend to treat the struggles more as some kind of game than an essential struggle for the health and well-being of the public and the environment. Why else would groups so readily trade real reform for hollow, watered-down compromises that do little except bolster reputations and give the false impression of victory?[3]

When the Republican Party gained control of Congress in 1994, the mainstream groups rushed to defend existing environmental laws within an even more constrained framework of compromise. The resulting efforts helped to forestall the immediate threat to particular laws, but could not by themselves shift the environmental debate beyond a discouragingly defensive and reactive kind of politics. Citizen lobbying efforts can be an important part of a well-coordinated environmental campaign, but there is only defeat in the offing for strategies that would turn grassroots activists into passive supporters and letter writers for environmental lobbyists.

The mid-1990s saw the beginnings of a shake-up at the top of some of the largest Washington-based environmental groups. Some have made concerted attempts to cast their efforts in more grassroots terms. When environmental lawyer Mark Van Putten assumed the position of CEO of the National Wildlife Federation in 1996, he described his mission as one to "reinvigorate the real roots of the conservation movement."[4] The Wilderness Society also chose a new top officer in 1996, and the Sierra Club elected a twenty-three-year-old activist and founder of the Sierra Student Coalition as its new president.[5] The Sierra Club's national legislative office now issues weekly electronic alerts to activists and has gradually, though reluctantly, strengthened its positions on issues of primary concern to grassroots Club members.

Other changes are of a more cosmetic nature. The Natural Resources Defense Council, for example, sent out countless direct-mail appeals highlighting issues that were initiated and developed by grassroots activists—issues such as the preservation of the Arctic wilderness surrounding James Bay, struggles against ancient forest logging in British Columbia's Clayoquot Sound, and the expansion of wilderness protection in Utah. While NRDC supported various aspects of all these campaigns, its persistent direct-mail solicitations barely disguise the Council's rather limited, backroom approach to activism—a 1996 mailing even pledged that the organization would be "mobilizing grassroots opposition in all 50 states."[6] Mainstream environmental media blur the distinction between grassroots and elite-driven activism even further. A new Canadian environmental publication calling itself *Grassroots Magazine* was heavily promoted on the Internet in 1996 and featured such improbable grassroots figures as actors Robert Redford and Jack Nicholson, Hillary Rodham Clinton, and ecoentrepreneurs Ben Cohen (of Ben & Jerry's ice cream) and Anita Roddick (of the scandal-ridden cosmetics outfit The Body Shop).[7]

Large national organizations can sometimes play a positive supporting role in grassroots campaigns, offering much-needed legal assistance, scientific expertise, and media access. This has been demonstrated in the James Bay and Clayoquot Sound campaigns, among others. But these are still exceptions to the rule. The largest, best-funded organizations are far more likely to undercut the grassroots, claim credit for their accomplishments, and try to maneuver activists toward demoralizing and ineffectual compromises. This has occurred repeatedly around National

Forest issues, food safety, NAFTA, and many other key ecological struggles. It happens not only at the national level but at the local and state levels, as well—for example, during the campaign initiated by the Greens to ban clearcutting in the forests of Maine. Similarly, a grassroots campaign to prevent the aerial spraying of toxic herbicides over corporate-owned forest land in northern Vermont was repeatedly discouraged and undermined by regional foundations and the state's leading conservation groups, which then proceeded to use the issue in their own fundraising mailings. Organizations committed to the environmental status quo continue to appropriate the image of grassroots politics, exacerbating activists' distrust of these organizations. Meanwhile, politicians like Bill Clinton persist in manipulating the images of environmentalism even as they promote compromises that seriously weaken a comprehensive ecological agenda.

The heart and soul of the ecological movement does not lie with multimillion-dollar organizations based in Washington, D.C. nor with politicians who glibly speak environmental rhetoric to disguise their subservience to the agendas of corporate America. It lies with millions of people all across the country and around the world, most of whom do not strongly identify with any organization. They include numerous hikers and gardeners, educators and naturalists, poets and dreamers, swimmers and ballplayers, fishing and hunting enthusiasts, as well as uncompromising defenders of animals. Whether they live in rural areas or in the city, people are concerned about the quality of the air they breathe, the water they drink, and their living and working environments. These are people who politicians believe they can take for granted, people whose environmental commitments are so often caricatured as wide but not deep. Yet when environmental quality is threatened, when there is a challenge to the natural elements that affect everyone's health and quality of life, even those who express their aspirations in the most conventional terms can reach a quite different understanding of the social and political system that constantly gives rise to such threats.

Gordon Durnill, a conservative lawyer and Republican political operative, became an ardent defender of the environment and public health during a five-year term as U.S. chair of the International Joint Commission, which is dedicated to overseeing the health of the Great Lakes on behalf of the U.S. and Canadian governments. "[M]ost of the people worried about an environmental problem are not motivated by political philosophy," he stated in his 1995 book, *The Making of a Conservative Environmentalist*. "They are motivated by a specific environmental problem in their community and by the desire to correct it." His concluding chapters are dedicated to the notion that liberals have failed the environmental movement and that conservatives should jump in to fill the void. "Liberals have said all the words environmentalist[s] love to hear but failed to provide the people with environmental protection," he explains. "Should not conserving our natural resources, our way of life, our quality of life, . . . the prevention of adverse human health effects be a conservative goal, as opposed to the current regulatory efforts at the tail end of the industrial chain?"[8]

Durnill is absolutely right about the motivations that arouse environmental activism and the failure of conventional liberal solutions. But his conclusion suggests a perhaps willful oversight of some important political realities. The fact is that conservatives in this political era are rarely interested in conservation. They are most fundamentally committed to preserving and extending the vast inequalities in wealth and political power that form the very basis of "our way of life." Sustained efforts to protect the environment and human health more often lead to a different conclusion: that environmental destruction is an outgrowth of the very same imbalances in wealth and power that have made it so difficult for most people to take part in the political and economic decisions that shape their everyday lives.

Mainstream liberals have largely failed the environmental movement, just as they have failed the causes of social justice, world peace, and the advancement of genuine democracy. They promote economic growth as the main goal of social policy, and support measures that ultimately advance the centralization of political and economic power. In this age of corporate downsizing and global competition, liberals and conservatives alike are far too willing to bow to corporate agendas, scapegoat the poor, and promote slightly different variants of the same anti-social and anti-environmental policies. Liberals will embrace social justice and environmentalism when it is politically expedient, and adopt the language of populism when it helps them win an election. They have joined the ideological Right in denouncing big government, while simultaneously aiding the expansion of corporate power, maintaining military forces and "defense" spending at Cold War levels, and underwriting an unprecedented growth in prisons and police forces in the United States. The experiences of activists all across the country demonstrate that a third way—a much more expansive ecological outlook—is needed to transcend the ideological boundaries of a political spectrum too often defined by the fundamentalist Right and the neoliberal center. Such an outlook would fully embrace the radically democratic promise that underpins the revolutionary legacy of ecological thought and action.

Toward a Democratic Culture

Wherever people perceive an immediate threat to the environment, to their health, or to the integrity of their community, a tremendous wealth of energy and creativity can be brought to bear to resist that threat. Persistent political engagement teaches invaluable lessons about the institutions that, by their very nature, concentrate wealth and power and promote short-term gain over long-term sustainability. But sadly, even the most inspiring issue-oriented campaigns often have a distressingly transient and elusive character. A profound paradox underlies the American myth of democracy; to unravel this paradox might offer some clues as to how a more sustained variety of activism may be realized.

In the 1970s, with the social movements of the late 1960s still very much a part of the political landscape in the United States, the elite Trilateral Commission published a study of what it termed the "crisis of democracy" in the industrialized world. In contrast to most people's experience, their crisis was not about overcoming obstacles to democratic practice. Rather, they perceived an "excess of democracy" that, in the words of the study's introduction, "appear[s] to have generated a breakdown of traditional means of social control, a delegitimation of political and other forms of authority, and an overload of demands on government, exceeding its capacity to respond."[9] A "democratic distemper" had swept the United States, according to Samuel Huntington of Harvard's Center for International Affairs; society had become overly polarized because too many people had come to expect a voice in public affairs. Lamenting the apparent demise of the pervasive public apathy of the 1950s, Huntington explained:

> In the past, every democratic society has had a marginal population . . . which has not actively participated in politics. In itself, this marginality on the part of some groups is inherently undemocratic, but it has also been one of the factors which has enabled democracy to function effectively.[10]

Two decades later, the "democratic distemper" of the 1960s and 1970s would appear to have largely been cured. Millions of once politically active citizens have withdrawn into their private lives, unable to sustain the hope that their views and their desires carry much weight in the public sphere. A vast portion of the public, perhaps even a large majority, has now fallen into the role that Huntington would have consigned to the "marginal population." The absorption of mainstream environmentalism into the routines of business-as-usual is only one symptom of the widespread decline in democratic participation and democratic expectations that the Trilateralists of the 1970s so ardently hoped for.

In the late 1980s, social historian Richard Flacks set out to examine the causes of this decline in democratic participation. "A major paradox of American social and cultural development," Flacks explained, "is this: more than any society we have the idea of democracy in our origin and legitimation; yet to a very large degree this society has failed to sustain institutional or cultural means to foster ready individual interest in democratic participation."[11] Rather than nurturing habits of active democratic engagement in the United States, Flacks pointed out, we have inherited an increasingly selfish understanding of liberty— a counterpoint to, rather than an aspect of, freedom—that idealizes self-sufficiency in the private sphere far more than public engagement and active interdependence. In times such as ours, this creates a radical disjuncture between everyday life and the democratic ideal of a people able to make their own history. In the absence of a civic culture of active democratic engagement, we are in danger of losing touch with the most basic inheritance of the democratic revolutions of the 17th and 18th centuries, what French political analyst Daniel Singer has described as "the conviction that society, and therefore life, can be radically altered by political action."[12]

This strikes at the core of our ideas of what freedom is all about. Throughout the 1996 presidential campaign, Bill Clinton asked "whether we want a country of people all working together or one where you're on your own."[13] While Clinton's rhetorical commitment to community and cooperation is largely reserved for campaign seasons, this phrase summarizes, albeit simplistically, one of the most fundamental dilemmas of our time: does freedom arise from the pursuit of narrow self-interest or from the shared activity of working in a community for the sake of the common good?

Everywhere we see signs that people are disheartened by the increasing individualism and atomization of American life and crave a greater sense of community. In today's thoroughly commodified and increasingly authoritarian society, all kinds of packaged solutions to this craving have emerged, from evangelical religious revivals and expensive, walled-in housing developments to "chat rooms" on the Internet. For those willing and able to pay the price, these artificial and highly controlled synthetic communities may offer some meager relief from the denatured social and ecological reality that plagues today's suburban-dominated society.[14] But they rarely satisfy the fundamental human impulse for cooperation and community that they may be designed to redirect or alleviate.

The rapid growth of electronic communication over the Internet is a particularly striking example of this. Innovations in communications technology are enthusiastically celebrated by many, if not most, political activists; however, these innovations have for the most part exacerbated the decline of activism and the loss of real community. While it is now easier than ever before to create intentional "communities" of common interest through the various electronic networks, it is often at the expense of the face-to-face, person-to-person communities that make real social and political engagement possible. The quantity and immediacy of information that is now quickly disseminated among networks of activists is truly unprecedented. In the context of an engaged political movement, this information can dramatically enhance activists' awareness of underlying issues and of kindred struggles around the world. But today it often has a hollow ring, a rarefied absence of engaged reality, that is hardly ever compensated for either by its volume or its speed. Information, and even community, in its soulless electronic form, is being reduced to yet another commodity that we consume in the privacy of our own homes, increasingly removed from a public sphere capable of bestowing real meaning and creating real change.

An ecological sensibility offers the hope of a more creative solution: the promise of working cooperatively in towns and neighborhoods to rebuild genuine human ties among neighbors, while renewing our sense of active interdependence with the natural world of which we are a part. Whether efforts at ecological reconstruction take the form of a community garden, a farmers' market, abandoned land turned into a park, or a campaign against corporate interference with the integrity of one's community, activism at the local level helps to reclaim public space and nurture a sensibility that can begin to save our culture from the ravages of corporate dominance.

Yet today's political debates, in the United States and much of the industrialized world, are dominated by efforts to privatize public services, weaken environmental protections, and advance economic policies that merely heighten the unprecedented concentrations of wealth and privilege. The ideal of engaged citizenship in an active public sphere has been replaced by a cult of individual gain that Adam Smith and other early progenitors of capitalism could scarcely have imagined. We are taught to view ourselves as consumers and taxpayers rather than as citizens and community members. "All that makes sense is private life," lamented Susan Sontag in a recent essay on the unwillingness of Westerners to address the urgency of the tragic civil war in Bosnia. The trends toward "[i]ndividualism, and the cultivation of the self and private well-being" have seemingly obliterated the impulse toward community and cooperation, and blunted our ability to assert the power of human dignity in the face of profound injustice.[15] Progressive voices remain muted, even as the voices of the Christian Right continually affirm their mission to intervene in public affairs and claim a right to "dominion" over public life and morals.[16]

Cycles of Activism

Historians have uncovered some consistent patterns in the development of popular social movements. But although these patterns sometimes appear to mirror biological cycles of emergence, maturation, and decline, they are in reality the product of particular social factors, and are shaped by the actions of powerful institutions and well-organized groups of people.[17] In some ways, historical trends do shape the culture and expectations of activists. Social movements often experience distinct phases of popular mobilization, during which their goals may become accepted by a wider public and subsequently institutionalized into more traditional organizational forms. The acceptance of a movement's goals can be immediately preceded by a period of heightened uncertainty and feelings of inadequacy among activists. When activism wanes, people rarely take full stock of what they have accomplished. Depending on just how fully realized the aims of a movement have become, there may be a longer or shorter period of time before public controversies are newly aroused and large numbers of people become activated once again. There may be more or less of a political backlash against the institutionalization of a social change movement's goals.

The mainstream media generally depicted the early 1990s as a period of rising backlash against the environmental movement. Highly manipulated campaigns by property rights and "wise use" activists were granted a far higher public profile than the more widespread efforts of local environmental activists. Public support for environmental protection helped to keep legal measures in place, even as opposition to environmental regulation became ever more vocal and strident. But as we have seen repeatedly in the second half of this book, the striking inadequacies of the mainstream environmental agenda continue to spark new movements and new mobilizations. Often, these are formed in response to a corporation trying to expand the reach of its operations at a particular community's expense. The movement against the James Bay dams, as well as the alliance between indigenous communities and other rural dwellers against copper and zinc mining in the upper Midwest are clear illustrations of this. So are many countless organizing efforts against the excesses of urban development that have appeared over the years in large and small cities alike.

Other new movements emerge in response to renewed threats to communities that already share a long history of resistance. The reemergence of nonviolent direct action movements in the forests of the Pacific Northwest in response to the excesses of the 1995 "salvage" logging law is a particularly dramatic recent example. Finally, new scientific understandings of long-known environmental hazards, as well as previously unrecognized environmental threats, have contributed to the resurgence of efforts against pesticide-laden foods and toxic chemical manufacture, styrofoam, and other increasingly well-understood issues. In each of these areas, the established national environmental groups have lagged far behind the efforts of grassroots eco-activists. If mainstream environmentalism appears to be in decline, its grassroots counterpart maintains its health and integrity by being continually reborn.

The landmark environmental laws of the 1970s were unique among government regulations in their detailed requirements for public hearings and open public processes for their implementation. This reflected, albeit in a rather limited way, the legacy of the popular social movements of the 1960s. Since the mid-1980s, opportunities for public involvement have become more constrained. Government officials collaborate with industry representatives to restrict public participation, relax requirements for public notice, and shorten the available time for people to comment on controversial administrative decisions. In the 1990s, many states have further circumvented requirements for public notification, for example, by allowing companies to withhold environmental data from the public in exchange for more comprehensive internal environmental audits.[18]

These changes, carried out in the name of "flexibility" and the "streamlining" of regulations, not only encourage secrecy and evasion by corporate managers but seriously curtail everyone's fundamental right to understand and challenge threats to their health and safety. When environmental professionals collaborate with government and industry to limit the role of affected communities in decision-making, they reinforce the popular skepticism that the official voices of environmentalism are capable of acting in the broader public interest. Mainstream environmentalists far too often demonstrate a stronger commitment to the legislative process than to the outcome of a contentious environmental debate.

The problematic role of professional mainstream activists is endemic to a diverse spectrum of popular movements. We have seen in Chapter One how large foundations encourage the professionalization and institutionalization of movements, partly to co-opt emerging leaders and blunt new movements' potentially radicalizing edge. Political scientist Sidney Tarrow has reviewed several accounts from the women's and gay rights movements expressing the dismay of grassroots activists at the conspicuous shift toward legalistic remedies that followed the professionalization of these movements.[19] Communities have seen their best organizers become absorbed into various official bureaucracies; education and social service agencies have "in the name of *compassion* . . . effectively transformed many citizens into clients," in the words of social critic Stanley Aronowitz.[20] This transformation breeds paternalism and privilege in place of empathy and mutual aid, an understanding generally recognized by social activists in the 1960s and only recently co-opted by those who would simply abolish public-sector social services. For dedicated, thoughtful people in a highly individualistic and competitive society, there are few alternate ways to earn a living while carrying on the work of the movement. But why should the imperatives of personal survival and advancement deprive communities of their best fighters for social and environmental justice? How can communities sustain the long-term, system-challenging activism that is central to the realization of a just and ecological society?

Richard Flacks, in a recent essay, described the demobilizing consequences of national movement organizations neglecting grassroots community-building for hollow campaigns of direct mail and pre-programmed letter writing:

> Thus every movement has a kind of dual organizational structure—a set of national organizations with large centralized staffs, which function largely as lobbies for particular interests . . . , and, distinct from those, a vast decentralized array of local groups, some of which may be locals or chapters of national organizations but many of which are

not. Local activism is the key resource for democratization. This resource continues to be available—but it is in danger.[21]

"Democratization depends on the revitalization of direct action and the revival of utopian dissent," Flacks argues, echoing those who seek a renewed ecological radicalism.[22]

In the environmental movement, bridging the gap between professional and grassroots activism is central to the emergence of a more holistic ecological perspective. Activism against a variety of environmental assaults—such as nuclear power, ecosystem destruction, and toxic waste—has taught thousands of people the pitfalls of trusting their lives and their future to unaccountable experts. People from all walks of life, and with widely differing educational backgrounds, have mastered the scientific and technical underpinnings of a vast array of issues, and have acquired the skills to challenge government and industry's hired experts.

For the historian and pioneering social critic Ivan Illich, challenging the cult of the expert is the centerpiece of resistance to a disabling culture of consumerism and commodification, and the starting point for a program of social reconstruction:

> The credibility of the professional expert, be he scientist, therapist or executive, is the Achilles heel of the industrial system. Therefore, only those citizen initiatives and radical technologies that directly challenge the insinuating dominance of disabling professions open the way to freedom for nonhierarchical, community based competence. . . The first step . . . is a skeptical and nondeferential posture of the citizen toward the professional expert. Social reconstruction begins with a doubt raised among citizens.[23]

Thus, efforts by mainstream environmentalists to "represent" affected communities in their conflicts with corporations and government agencies are not only an affront to those communities but a hindrance to the effectiveness of the movement and the liberatory potential of ecological activism. The illusion of access to power conceals a stifling inability to shift the terms of debate. Neither democracy nor ecological sanity is well served by a political culture in which most people have withdrawn from the public sphere and look to professional organizers and lobbyists to do their activism for them. Democratizing information and cultivating an informed skepticism toward official experts both remain key elements of sustained and effective ecological activism.

It has become more difficult in recent years for small grassroots groups to acquire and maintain the resources for prolonged interventions in the political arena. Nearly every organization that hopes to engage in a meaningful campaign for ecological sanity today faces troubling choices regarding its long-term survival. With foundations imposing more constraints on the strategies and methods of organizations they will support, activists are often forced to choose between the integrity of their campaigns and the maintenance of their organization.

Large organizations with suites of offices and well-paid professional staffs are certainly the most susceptible to funding pressures, but they increasingly limit the activities of small grassroots organizations as well. There is intense pressure on nearly every organization to limit its activities and make peace with the dominant system in order to procure the funds and other resources necessary to sustain itself for the long haul. Competition for scarce funds can heighten internal tensions, making it difficult for organizations to plan beyond their most immediate short-term needs. The insidious cycle of competition and co-optation needs to be broken. Activists need to develop alternate means for supporting grassroots organizations and strengthening personal relationships within the communities they seek to serve. Perhaps a more sustained commitment to community building can help to relieve the movement from the disproportionate influence of large foundations and wealthy donors. This is yet another reason for ecological activists to be more fully engaged in local struggles for social justice and democratic renewal.

What Kind of Movement?

While the Pew Foundation's 1996 poll signaled a widening acknowledgment of the limits of mainstream environmentalism, most commentators seeking to address the movement's failings have called for little more than a reinvigorated form of business-as-usual. They accept the view that the major national environmental groups should set the agenda for the movement as a whole, and urge that they do their job better. Perhaps Washington environmentalists need to pay closer attention to radical stirrings at the grassroots, become more attuned to larger cultural and spiritual currents, spend more time in the woods. Many would-be critics remain committed to a politics of behind-the-scenes compromise and access to power, hoping that a renewed environmental movement might emerge from the boardrooms of environmental businesses or rise from the ashes of Washington's short-lived "Republican revolution."

Some Washington-based groups have responded in their own way to the call for a more aggressive political stance. For example, the mainstream environmental movement played a more visible role in the 1996 congressional elections than ever before. The League of Conservation Voters targeted a dozen members of Congress for defeat, highlighting their role in promoting a virulently anti-environmental agenda.[24] The Sierra Club spent ten times as much as ever before in support of pro-environment candidates, a total of $7.5 million.[25] Such efforts are a necessary step but are far from sufficient to alter the terms of environmental debate. Indeed, the most noticeable result may have been to encourage candidates on both sides of the issues to drape their campaigns in green cloth, advancing the corporate greenwash by once again promoting environmental image over substance.

The second Clinton administration will almost certainly be more bedecked in environmental imagery than the first. Reauthorization of numerous environmental laws, from the Endangered Species Act to the Superfund, is long overdue, and all but the most adamant anti-environmentalists are anxious to move forward on these issues. Clinton will most likely seek modest improvements in environmental policy to draw attention away from worsening poverty and rising corporate power. He will also probably continue to try to mollify environmental skeptics with more land swaps and corporate giveaways, "flexible" regulations based on statistical assessments of risk, and various "free market" policy innovations. The debate in Washington will almost certainly continue to obscure the daily environmental threats facing communities across the United States and around the world.

Meanwhile, growing numbers of grassroots activists see the machinations of policymakers and lobbyists in Washington as largely irrelevant to the development of a renewed ecological movement. Clearly, a hostile

Congress or administration can abolish public health protections, unleash "salvage" logging, or condemn endangered species to extinction in the course of an afternoon's debate. On the other hand, federal legislation at best offers small, incremental improvements in environmental policy, improvements that contribute little toward long-range ecological sanity. It rarely helps to further the development of a political movement able to challenge entrenched power and advance a more thoroughgoing ecological vision.

What kind of movement can begin to set the stage for a more fully realized ecological vision for the 21st century and beyond? While activists rightly have little confidence in formulaic answers to such questions, a few common features emerge from the more successful ecological campaigns of the past decade. Hopefully, these can serve as guideposts for those who seek a more promising path forward. Some specific features of a renewed ecological movement include:

Diverse networks of grassroots activists, organized and coordinated from the ground up. Activists working on similar issues and facing an increasingly unified corporate agenda need to find ways to work together across the boundaries of geography, ethnicity, social class, and specific issues. Broader networks of activists help to sustain the momentum of a movement beyond the life-span of any single campaign. Local groups may have ties to several regional and national networks, sometimes sharing legal and technical resources with larger, better-funded organizations. It is essential, however, that they retain the prerogative to set their own agendas and speak to their own communities' priorities.

Greater cooperation between ecological activists and those engaged in other social movements. Ecological activism cannot exist in a vacuum. People's concern for the natural environment—or lack thereof—is shaped by all of the other circumstances of their lives. A healthy environment is necessary for the development of healthy human communities, and relationships of justice and equity in the social sphere are necessary for people to live in harmony with nature. On a more pragmatic level, social and ecological activists confront the same concentrations of corporate power. Corporate policies of eliminating workers, forcing communities to compete for jobs, and degrading the natural world for the sake of higher profits are all cut from the same cloth. In the difficult times ahead, social and ecological activists need to be more wary of efforts to set them against one another, and far more ready to support and enhance each other's struggles.

A more holistic approach to issue-oriented politics. Most day-to-day activism is centered in specific, relatively short-term campaigns around issues that directly affect people's lives and the immediate imperatives of ecosystem survival. These are the pressing everyday concerns that engage and inspire people to take time out of their busy lives to address ecological problems, and try to effect change in the world at large. But rather than settling for the false pragmatism of a one-dimensional approach to issues, activists can highlight the ways in which immediate issues reveal overarching structural problems. U.S. activists opposed to the damming of the James Bay region of Quebec integrated concerns about wildlife and pollution, the region's indigenous peoples, and the effects of imported electricity on their own state and regional economies. Such a holistic approach can strengthen political alliances around an issue, while emphasizing wider, more systemic concerns: How is political and economic power wielded in a particular city or region? How can communities develop institutions of direct democracy to regain control over the decisions that affect their lives? Campaigns for immediate reforms need to stress the potential for fundamental structural changes.

A more conscious synthesis of oppositional movements with those seeking to develop and demonstrate ecological alternatives. Many people are reluctant to become involved in environmental campaigns because they see no alternative to the present order of things. A reconstructive ecological vision, illustrated with practical living examples of a more ecological way of being, can enhance the life of a community and offer activists greater sustenance to get through the hard times. A stronger link to social and ecological activism can also forestall the co-optation of alternative institutions by the corporate status quo. If we want to create a world in which everybody, not just the affluent few, can live ecologically, we need to raise awareness of the inherently *political* nature of personal lifestyle choices, and resist efforts to reduce ecological living to the consumption of fashionable "green" consumer goods. The reconstructive dimension of ecology is also its utopian dimension, an awareness best illustrated through a lively array of cultural and spiritual expressions, as well as a sustained commitment to political activism, direct action, and the practice of direct democracy.

Enhanced international links with like-minded people and movements in other parts of the world. The global corporate economy has transformed all issues into international ones. People in other countries, particularly in the less-developed South, are exploited for cheap labor and simultaneously treated as scapegoats for our social and economic ills. Their lands have become the dumping grounds for the North's industrial wastes, and their indigenous knowledge is coveted by the North's agrochemical and pharmaceutical industries as "intellectual property" to be appropriated for profit. Successful alliances between environmental justice activists in the Southwest and their neighbors across the Mexican border have demonstrated the potential of international campaigns to expose the myths of "free trade" and oppose corporate schemes that so often set communities with common problems against each other. Real-life ties of solidarity and cultural understanding are the best antidote to the myth that the solution to the South's social and economic ills lies in the attainment of a high-consumption Western lifestyle.[26]

A defiance of political and economic orthodoxies, and a refusal to be limited by the false realism of status quo politics. What kinds of economic structures are most consistent with an ecological worldview? How can we organize our communities so as to regain a living harmony with the natural world of which we are a part? Questions such as these need to move to the forefront of ecological activism. If the institutions of global capitalism are antithetical to the survival of life, we can no longer live our lives or structure our activist campaigns as if these institutions were inevitable. There is little hope for ecological renewal in a world where corporations are sovereign and are granted more rights than people or ecosystems. Forward-thinking activists are challenging corporate charters, declaring that companies that refuse to respect the land and the people should not have the right to operate in their state or region. They are building local economies and asserting their independence from the whims of transnational capital. They are engaging in persistent direct action in defense of the integrity of living ecosystems. But these are just first steps. A much wider range of creative actions is necessary if we are to realize the vision of a self-managed society that embodies and enhances the mutualism and integrity of the natural world.

A renewed ecological movement would also embody a much fuller understanding of the meaning of democracy. An ecological democracy would reach far beyond the limits of the formal, procedural democracy that people in the United States have come to accept and take for granted. Today most people are resigned to going to the ballot box once every four years to choose among barely distinguishable alternatives. Long before the formal election cycle begins, candidates embark on aggressive fundraising drives, in which they must prove their obedience to what is ultimately, despite rhetoric to the contrary, an aggressively anti-ecological status quo. Legal scholar Jamin Raskin has termed this phenomenon the "wealth primary."[27] Alternatively, an ecological democracy empowers everyone to participate fully, openly, and directly in the decisions that affect their lives, in both the political and economic spheres. It facilitates projecting community needs far into the future, considering the impact of our decisions on all of the living beings with which we share our place on the earth. Communities can join together by building confederations of towns and neighborhoods that foster grassroots ties of interdependence and mutual aid among people who share a bioregion, a continent, and a planet.

Ecological democracy is about creating new political and economic institutions of decentralized power and community control, along with the solidarity and civic integrity that makes it possible to resist the intrusions of those who would assert political or economic power from without. Ecology's holistic and reconstructive outlook offers hope for transcending the parochialism and selfishness that is now continually reinforced by the pressure to compete for scarce capital and resources. Confederations of communities rooted in principles of mutuality and self-reliance, and skilled in resisting outside economic pressures, may ultimately discover how to dissolve the power of today's global institutions.

Political commentators of all ideological stripes now recognize that public confidence in the institutions that control and dominate our lives has reached an unprecedented low. The widespread, but often highly manipulated, popular distrust of government may now be evolving toward an informed rejection of the secretive rule of corporations as well.[28] Those who wield political power, along with their opportunistic strategists and media consultants, hope that this disdain for powerful institutions will serve to reinforce a crippling cynicism toward all aspects of public life. This is a frequent outcome of much of the "negative" political advertising that now dominates electoral campaigns. But growing resentment toward state and corporate power could also be the foundation of a revived popular movement for a more fully realized democracy. Mainstream environmentalists—with their unbroken faith in the political process, their illusions of access to power, and their commitment to a discredited and ill-defined political "center"—have rendered themselves largely irrelevant to this emerging discussion. The challenge for grassroots eco-activists is to join with their neighbors to offer a renewed public voice for ecology, community, and genuine democracy.

The 1990s began amid predictions that this would be the decisive decade for transforming society's relationship to the earth's environment. Countless activists and environmental scientists proclaimed that the 1990s would be the last chance to reverse ecological collapse before damage to the earth's ability to sustain complex life reaches the point of no return.

As the decade has rushed past the halfway mark, there has clearly been no such reversal. Indeed, environmental scientists and activists have alerted us to a seemingly endless litany of new assaults on the integrity of the earth's living ecosystems. Since 1990, we have seen the ecological collapse of North America's Atlantic fisheries and continuing declines in the population of songbirds and amphibians, two of the most accepted indicators of overall ecosystem health. Cancer rates continue to rise, and the quality of the world's soils and water supplies continues to decline. In the United States, nearly two years of intensified "salvage" logging threatened the survival of many of our last remaining intact forest ecosystems. Exports of urban and industrial wastes to the Third World have escalated as disposal costs in the United States continue to rise, and recycling and waste reduction efforts stagnate. Hundreds of new chemicals continue to be developed and produced each year, despite growing evidence of the mutagenic and hormone-disruptive effects of whole classes of industrial and agricultural chemicals. The genetic engineering of plants and animals has emerged from science fiction novels and cloistered laboratories into the worlds of food production and medicine, as the biotechnology industry begins to infiltrate everyday industrial and agricultural practices.[29]

Efforts to curb pollution, sustain living ecosystems, and forestall the effects of global climate change have all been restrained by a powerful combination of environmental complacency and anti-environmental backlash. Despite a steady rise in environmental awareness in the United States and around the world, movements for ecological transformation are still only rarely able to challenge the power of entrenched economic and political interests. The shortsighted practices of politics-as-usual have proved thoroughly inadequate to confront the urgency of this situation. In a period of increasing worldwide poverty, coupled with unprecedented concentrations of wealth and power, we can no longer take even limited environmental progress for granted. More than ever, it is necessary to toss complacency aside, and create a more politically sophisticated and defiant worldwide ecological movement.

It is impossible to know with any certainty whether the cycles of ecological decline that have become so utterly apparent in just the past few decades can be reversed. It is impossible to reliably predict whether our grandchildren will inherit a world in which the diversity of life will flourish, or a world that is so thoroughly degraded that humanity only survives through a spiraling and ultimately futile dependence on ever more intrusive technological interventions. It is our human nature to survive and adapt, but also to hope, to dream, and to celebrate our biological and spiritual ties to all life on earth. It is this dimension of human consciousness that refuses to accept a future of declining expectations, and compels us to put ourselves on the line for the integrity of our communities and our bioregions.

Ecological activists in the 1990s have been all too willing to merely adapt to worsening environmental and social conditions. The pursuit of private life and everyday survival has driven far too many good-hearted people to abandon the world of politics to the power-obsessed, the ego-driven, and those who follow the dictates of authoritarian social and religious movements. But the challenges of our time have also sparked a new search for the deepest political, social, and spiritual roots of our ecological and social problems. They have invigorated a new grassroots movement, willing to defy the norms of an anti-political and anti-ecological culture and to challenge institutions that only understand the language of power and greed.

The renewed grassroots ecology movement gets its strength and inspiration from the persistent struggles of those who have long resisted pollution, toxic waste, and environmental racism; from the militant defenders of the forests and the oceans; and from those who are working to realize a new ecological vision for the future of our cities and towns. Activists in the North are learning the stories of the tree huggers of India, the rubber tappers of the Brazilian Amazon, and the Mayan rebels of the southern Mexican rainforest. Their stories offer hope to all of us who share a vision of a greener future. It is a hope for a new ecological revolution that is gentle but uncompromising, realistic but utopian—a revolution that embraces our interdependence and celebrates our creativity. It is a revolution that cries out to earth-loving people worldwide, calling us to speak in a united voice for healing, cooperation, and a peaceful, more compassionate future.

Notes

Notes to the Introduction

1. For a comprehensive history of the struggles around James Bay, see Al Geddicks, *The New Resource Wars* (Boston: South End Press, 1993), pp. 15-27; also Alicia Fierer and Cris Moore, "James Bay: Anatomy of a Campaign," *Z Magazine*, October 1992, pp. 50-52, and Brian Tokar, "Grassroots Victories, Lobbyist Gridlock," *Z Magazine*, February 1995, pp. 47-53. Book-length accounts from Canadian authors include Sean McCutcheon, *Electric Rivers: The Story of the James Bay Project* (Montreal, Quebec: Black Rose Books, 1991), and Michael Posluns, *Voices from the Odeyak* (Toronto, Ontario: NC Press, Ltd., 1993).
2. Bradley Angel, "Sovereignty and Environmental Justice,"*GroundWork* (San Francisco: Tides Foundation), no. 5, February 1995, pp. 18-19; Peter Montague, "Violence in Indian Country Over Waste," *RACHEL's Environment and Health Weekly*, no. 404, August 25, 1994; conversation with Bradley Angel, January 1996.
3. While such struggles clearly have policy and legislative dimensions, local activists retained the initiative, and traditional forms of environmental lobbying generally took a backseat, as we will see in the chapters that follow.
4. Quoted in Tom Athanasiou, *Divided Planet: The Ecology of Rich and Poor* (Boston: Little, Brown, 1996), p. 233.
5. Tom Athanasiou, *Divided Planet*, p. 241.
6. Athanasiou, *Divided Planet*, pp. 239-41, Prattap Chatterjee and Matthias Finger, *The Earth Brokers: Power, Politics, and World Development* (New York: Routledge, 1994), especially Chapter Seven.
7. According to the *Wall Street Journal* (May 4, 1995), corporate profits rose 13 percent in 1993 and 11 percent in 1994. For the 500 largest U.S. corporations, as surveyed by *Fortune* magazine (May 15, 1995), profits rose an astounding 54 percent in 1994, despite modest gains in corporate revenues and a sluggish 3

percent gain in employment. International figures tell a similar story (*Fortune*, August 7, 1995). On the stratification of wealth in the U.S., see Keith Bradsher, "Inequality of Wealth Gap Widens in U.S.," *New York Times*, April 17, 1995.

8. For instance, Monsanto has received environmental business awards for its efforts to cut toxic waste emissions, even as it supports the activities of anti-environmental writers and lobbyists, and sues small dairy companies for identifying products that are free of Monsanto's genetically engineered Bovine Growth Hormone. See, for example, Peter Montague, "How They Lie," *RACHEL's Environment and Health Weekly*, nos. 503-4, July 18 and 25, 1996.

9. Chitrita Banerji, "Interview with Bruce Babbitt," *Conservation Matters* (Boston: Conservation Law Foundation), winter 1994-95, p. 17.

Notes to the Prologue

1. Susan Sontag, "AIDS and its Metaphors," *New York Review of Books*, October 27, 1988, quoted in Tom Athanasiou, *Divided Planet: The Ecology of Rich and Poor* (Boston, MA: Little, Brown, 1996), p. 56.

2. Quoted in Edwin W. Teale, *The Wilderness World of John Muir* (Boston, MA: Houghton Mifflin Co., 1954), pp. 315, 320.

3. Donald Worster, *Nature's Economy* (San Francisco, CA: Sierra Club Books, 1977), p. 266.

4. Described in Philip Shabecoff, *A Fierce Green Fire: The American Environmental Movement* (New York: Hill and Wang, 1993), pp. 35-36; also, Duane A. Smith, *Mining America: The Industry and the Environment, 1800-1980* (Lawrence, KS: University Press of Kansas, 1987), pp. 67-74. The Marysville farmers' thirty-year struggle ended in an 1884 federal court decision protecting the entire Yuba River watershed from mine discharges.

5. Quoted in Worster, *Nature's Economy*, p. 267.

6. Robert Gottlieb, *Forcing the Spring: The Transformation of the American Environmental Movement* (Washington, D.C.: Island Press, 1993), p. 26.

7. See, for example, Brian Tokar, "The 'Wise Use' Backlash: Responding to Militant Anti-Environmentalism," *The Ecologist*, vol. 25, no. 4, July/August 1995, pp. 150-56.

8. Gottlieb, *Forcing the Spring*, pp. 47-80.

9. Shabecoff, *A Fierce Green Fire*, pp. 71-74, 100-101; Gottlieb, *Forcing the Spring*, pp. 27-29.

10. "From Outrage to Action: The Story of the National Audubon Society," (New York: National Audubon Society, 1986).

11. Shabecoff, *A Fierce Green Fire*, p. 76.

12. Gottlieb, *Forcing the Spring*, pp. 157-58.

13. Gottlieb, *Forcing the Spring*, pp. 15-16, 43-44.

14. Gottlieb, *Forcing the Spring*, pp. 38-41; Katherine Barkley and Steve Weissman, "The Eco-Establishment," *Ramparts*, vol. 8, no. 7, May 1970, pp. 50, 54.

15. Gottlieb, *Forcing the Spring*, pp. 136-43, 149.

16. Peter Montague, "How They Lie," *RACHEL's Environment and Health Weekly*, no. 503, July 18, 1996.

17. Gottlieb, *Forcing the Spring*, p. 139; Shabecoff, *A Fierce Green Fire*, pp. 103-4. Henry Kendall, a nuclear physicist based at MIT, also gained national prominence as the founder of the Union of Concerned Scientists.

18. After the departure of David Brower in 1984, Friends of the Earth, long torn between its activist and lobbyist orientations, moved its main offices from San Francisco to Washington, D.C. and in 1989 merged once again with the Environmental Policy Institute (formerly Environmental Policy Center).

19. The Group of Ten would soon be filled out with the addition of the National Parks and Conservation Association. The equally established Defenders of Wildlife was excluded from the Group of Ten when National Wildlife Federation president Jay Hair dismissed it as "anti-hunting." Other groups were left out because they were not considered "active" in Washington (i.e., they were not engaged in the regular lobbying of Congress). See Mark Dowie, *Losing Ground: American Environmentalism at the Close of the Twentieth Century* (Cambridge, MA: MIT Press, 1995), p. 69, Gottlieb, *Forcing the Spring*, pp. 123-24.

Notes to Chapter One

1. Katherine Barkley and Steve Weissman, "The Eco-Establishment," *Ramparts*, vol. 8, no. 7, May 1970, pp. 50, 54.

2. Richard Berke, "Oratory of Environmentalism Becomes the Sound of Politics," *New York Times*, April 17, 1990.

3. Andrew H. Malcolm, *et al.*, "How the Oil Spilled and Spread: Delay and Confusion Off Alaska," *New York Times*, April 16, 1989, p. 1; Sharon Begley, *et al.*, "Smothering the Waters," *Newsweek*, April 10, 1989, pp. 54-57; and John Greely, "The Spills and Spoils of Big Oil," *The Nation*, May 29, 1989, pp. 738-40.

4. "Earth Day 1990 Principles of Corporate Sponsorship," Stanford, California: February 1990; conversation with Owen Byrd, April 1990; James Ridgeway and Dan Bischoff, "The Leveraged Buyout of Earth Day," *Village Voice*, April 24, 1990, pp. 25-30; and Dale S. Turner, "The Corporate Buyout of Earth Day, *Earth First!*, March 1990, p. 3: Brian Tokar, "Environment for Sale," *Z Magazine*, April 1990, pp. 23-28.

5. Philip Shabecoff, *A Fierce Green Fire*, p. 111.

6. Conservation Foundation director Sydney Howe, who secured a substantial loan for Earth Day organizing, was ostensibly fired for his efforts to steer the Foundation toward urban environmental and social justice concerns. See Robert Gottlieb, *Forcing the Spring: The Transformation of the American Environmental Movement* (Washington: Hill and Wang, 1993), p. 108.

7. *Ramparts* editorial, vol. 8, no. 7, May 1970, p. 3.

8. Barkley and Weissman, "The Eco-Establishment."

9. I.F. Stone, "How Earth Day Was Polluted," in *Polemics and Prophesies 1967-1970* (New York: Random House, 1970), p. 237.

10. Juan Gonzalez, "Getting Serious about Ecology," *New York Daily News*, April 24, 1995, p. 12. See also Brian Tokar, "After Earth Day," *Green Letter*, summer 1990, p. 10; Joshua Nessen, "Take It to Wall Street," *Z Magazine*, June 1990, pp. 52-55.

11. Participants in a 1990 conference, sponsored by eight state attorneys general in response to concerns about environmental marketing abuses, included representatives of Procter and Gamble, Dow Chemical, Archer Daniels Midland, the James River (paper) Corporation, and Amway. See Betsey Sharkey, "Will Green Marketers Get Red Light?" *Adweek*, March 12, 1990.

12. Gottlieb, *Forcing the Spring*, pp. 147, 161.

13. Quoted in Steve Chase, ed., *Defending the Earth: A Dialogue Between Murray Bookchin and Dave Foreman* (Boston: South End Press, 1991), p. 38.

14. Dave Foreman, "Making the Most of Professionalism," *Whole Earth Review*, March 1985, pp. 34-5; Les Line, 1991 interview, quoted in Christopher Boerner and Jennifer Chilton Kallery, *Restructuring Environmental Big Business* (St. Louis, MO: Washington University Center for the Study of American Business, 1994), p. 15.

15. Charles Mohr, "Environmental Groups Gain in Wake of Spill," *New York Times*, June 11, 1989, p. 31; Mark Dowie, *Losing Ground: American Environmentalism at the Close of the Twentieth Century* (Cambridge, MA: MIT Press, 1995), p. 175. Dowie's book helped to awaken many environmentalists to the waning influence of the mainstream groups.

16. Mark Dowie, *Losing Ground*, pp. 41, 248. Dowie reports that the mainstream national groups received 65 to 70 percent of their revenues from direct mail and 7 percent from foundations. Corporations were contributing $20 million a year to environmental groups, amounting to 6 percent of total corporate philanthropy (pp. 44, 49, 54). Thus, corporate donations are directed toward environmental causes at nearly two and a half times the rate of charitable donations overall.

17. Charles Mohr, "Environmental Groups Gain in Wake of Spill."

18. Data from the 1988 annual reports of the Sierra Club, National Audubon Society, Wilderness Society, and National Wildlife Federation, as reported in Brian Tokar, "Marketing the Environment," *Z Magazine*, February 1990, pp. 15-20.

19. Jim Donahue, "Environmental Board Games," *Multinational Monitor*, March 1990, pp. 10-12, with supporting documentation from Essential Information, Inc.

20. Quoted in Dowie, *Losing Ground*, p. 107.

21. Conversation with Steven Lester, Citizens Clearinghouse for Hazardous Waste, March 3, 1993; "Corporate Friends," *Environmental Action*, March/April 1989, p. 15.

22. Brian Lipsett, in *Everybody's Backyard* vol. 7, no. 3, November 1989, pp. 2-3.

23. Joni Seager, *Earth Follies: Coming to Feminist Terms with the Global Environmental Crisis* (New York: Routledge, 1993), p. 186. Emphasis in original.

24. See, for example, Boerner and Kallery, *Restructuring Environmental Big Business*; Ron Arnold, ed., "Getting Rich: The Environmental Movement's Income, Salary, Contributor and Investment Patterns," Center for the Defense of Free Enterprise, Bellevue, Washington, 1994.

25. For instance, the Washington-based Environmental Working Group reported in July of 1996 on the annual lobbying week of the virulently anti-environmental Alliance for America. Amid presentations by oil industry lobbyists, property rights agitators, and House Speaker Newt Gingrich, was a talk by Jonathan Adler of the anti-environmental think tank the Competitive Enterprise Institute.

Adler described his own version of a split between "Big Green" and the "grass-roots," in which dependence on direct mail, foundation support, and government grants are signs of dwindling "grassroots" support for an environmental agenda. "A Summary of Alliance for America's Fly-in for Freedom," *A CLEAR View*, vol. 3, no. 11, Washington, D.C.: Environmental Working Group, July 15, 1996.

26. Boerner and Kallery, *Restructuring Environmental Big Business*, pp. 7-10, 30. Interestingly, while their analysis implies that only the Nature Conservancy—the largest, and most corporate dependent of the organizations they studied—was able to avoid a significant downturn in the 1990s, their data demonstrates membership and revenue increases on the part of several groups extending well into the mid-1990s.

27. Brian Lipsett, "Dirty Money for Green Groups?" *The Workbook*, Southwest Research and Information Center, vol. 18, no. 1, spring 1993, p. 3.

28. Mark Dowie, *Losing Ground*, see footnote 16.

29. A thoughtful defense of the activist approaches of Greenpeace through this period is offered by Paul Wapner, "In Defense of Banner Hangers: The Dark Green Politics of Greenpeace," in Bron Raymond Taylor, ed., *Ecological Resistance Movements*, (Albany: State University of New York Press, 1995), pp. 300-314.

30. Various organizational changes during the late 1980s and early 1990s make it difficult to unambiguously report on Greenpeace's finances. In 1987, Greenpeace U.S.A. reported a budget of $22 million, almost entirely from contributions and donations. By 1992, Greenpeace U.S.A. had gone through at least two reorganizations, first spinning off Greenpeace Action as a separate entity. In 1992, Greenpeace U.S.A., the nonprofit wing, became the Greenpeace Fund, with a budget of $8 million and a fund worth $24 million, and Greenpeace Action became Greenpeace, Inc., with a $41 million budget and a negative fund balance. Both entities receive approximately 90 percent of their income in the form of contributions and donations.

31. Ronnie Cummins and Ben Lilliston, "U.S. Consumers & Farmers Battle Genetically-Engineered Soybeans," Pure Food Campaign, Washington, D.C., October 1996; Greenpeace press statements, October 10 and November 7, 1996; and Youssef M. Ibrahim, "Genetic Soybeans From the U.S. Alarm Europeans," New York Times, November 7, 1996; "Greenpeace Stops Genetically Engineered Soybeans Destined for Europe on Mississippi River," Greenpeace, November 19, 1996.

32. Barkley and Weissman, "The Eco-Establishment."

33. Joan Roelofs, "Foundations and Social Change Organizations: The Mask of Pluralism," *The Insurgent Sociologist*, vol. 14, no. 3, Fall 1987, pp. 31-72; "The Third Sector as a Protective Layer for Capitalism," presentation to the International Political Science Association, 1994 (unpublished manuscript).

34. The grant was from the Frank Weeden Foundation, which is closely linked with anti-immigrant causes. See Dowie, *Losing Ground*, pp. 163-65, also Chapter Eight, page 165.

35. Conversation with Andy Mahler, September 1996.

36. Pew Charitable Trusts, *Annual Report*, 1994, p. 17.
37. Stephen Salisbury, "Pew Charitable Trusts Develops a Hands-On Role," *Philadelphia Inquirer*, October 13-14, 1996. Salisbury, writing in Pew's home city of Philadelphia, examined the Trusts' increasingly controversial activities in areas from journalism and school reform to tourism marketing and restructuring local arts organizations, as well as in the environmental movement. He described Pew's overall philosophy as "professionalized, self-promoting corporate liberalism."
38. Jeffrey St. Clair and Alexander Cockburn, "Tainted Money, Toxic Sources," *Wild Forest Review*, October/November 1995, pp. 9-13.
39. Richard L. Grossman and Frank T. Adams, *Taking Care of Business: Citizenship and the Charter of Incorporation* (Cambridge, MA: Charter, Ink/CSPP, 1993).
40. John Stauber, "From Earth Day to Earth Pay," *PR Watch*, vol. 1, no. 3, spring 1994, p. 4. According to Stauber, Dorf & Stanton's clients include Chase Manhattan Bank, Hydro-Quebec, Ford, Monsanto, and Ciba-Geigy. The $6.5 million figure is from Dowie, *Losing Ground*, p. 202.
41. "An Environmental Petition to Newt Gingrich," Earth Day, Washington, D.C., 1995.

Notes to Chapter Two

1. Italo Calvino, "Smog," in *The Watcher and Other Stories* (San Diego, CA: Harcourt, Brace Jovanovich, 1971), p. 117.
2. For a series of comprehensive case studies, see *The Greenpeace Book of Greenwash* (Washington, D.C., Greenpeace International, 1992). On the proliferation of false environmental claims in advertising, see John Holusha, "Some Smog in Pledges to Help Environment," *New York Times*, April 19, 1990; Barry Meier, "Environmental Doubts on 'Green' Ads," *New York Times*, August 11, 1990; and John Holusha, "Coming Clean on Products: Ecological Claims Faulted," *New York Times*, March 12, 1991.
3. John Stauber and Sheldon Rampton, *Toxic Sludge is Good for You: Lies, Damn Lies and the Public Relations Industry* (Monroe, Maine: Common Courage Press, 1995), pp. 125, 140; also see Chapter One, note 25.
4. Robert N. Stavins, "Harnessing Market Forces to Protect the Environment," *Environment*, vol. 31, no. 1, January/February 1989, p. 5.
5. Senators Timothy Wirth and John Heinz, "Foreword" to *Project 88: Harnessing Market Forces to Protect Our Environment* (Washington, D.C.: Senate Offices of Wirth and Heinz, 1988), p. vii.
6. Stephen Breyer, "Analyzing regulatory failure, mismatches, less restrictive alternatives and reform," *Harvard Law Review*, vol. 92, no. 3, January 1979, p. 597.
7. James Ridgeway, "Catching the Wave," *Village Voice*, June 27, 1989; Todd Gitlin, "Buying the Right to Pollute? What's Next?" reprinted in the *Earth Day Wall Street Action Handbook* (New York, 1990).
8. U.S. EPA, "Auctions, Direct Sales and Independent Power Producers' Written Guarantee Regulations," *Federal Register*, vol. 56, no. 242, December 17, 1991; "Acid Rain Allowance Allocations and Reserves," *Federal Register*, vol. 57, no. 130, July 7, 1992.

9. Ian Torrens, quoted in Leslie Lamarre, "Responding to the Clean Air Act Challenge," *EPRI Journal*, April/May 1991, p. 23.

10. "CBOT board endorses submission to EPA to administer clean air allowance auction," *News from the Chicago Board of Trade*, January 21, 1992.

11. James Dao, "Some Regions Fear the Price As Pollution Rights Are Sold," *New York Times*, February 6, 1993; Matthew Wald, "Acid Rain Pollution Credits are Not Enticing Utilities," *New York Times*, June 5, 1995. EPA auction data is from the Acid Rain Program Home Page on the World Wide Web (http://www.epa.gov/docs/acidrain/ardhome.html).

12. Paul Klebnikov, "Pollution rights, wronged," *Forbes*, November 22, 1993, p. 128.

13. U.S. EPA, "EPA Allowance Auction Results: List of Bidders for Spot Auction," "Transaction Summary of the Allowance Trading System," both from the U.S. EPA World Wide Web site (see note 11).

14. Jeffrey Taylor, "CBOT Plan for Pollution Rights Market Is Encountering Plenty of Competition," *Wall Street Journal*, August 24, 1993.

15. Matthew Wald, "He doesn't call them dirty deals," *New York Times* Business section, May 13, 1992.

16. "Beyond Bumper Sticker Slogans: ECO Interviews Fred Krupp of EDF," NY: *ECO*, January 1994, p. 30.

17. Robert Stavins and Bradley Whitehead, "The Greening of America's Taxes," *Progressive Policy Institute Policy Report*, no. 13, February 1992.

18. Daniel Dudek, "Creating Self-Financing Environmental Markets," *Environmental Finance*, winter 1991-92, p. 512.

19. Al Gore, *Earth in the Balance* (Boston: Houghton Mifflin Co., 1992), pp. 345-6.

20. Alice LeBlanc, "The Third Wave," *Environmental Action*, Winter 1994, pp. 24-6.

21. Jeffrey Taylor, "Global Market in Pollution Rights Proposed by U.N.," *Wall Street Journal*, January 31, 1992.

22. Robert Stavins and Thomas Grumbly, "The Greening of the Market: Making the Polluter Pay," in Will Marshall and Martin Schram, eds., *Mandate for Change* (New York: Berkley Books, 1993), p. 202.

23. Stavins and Grumbly, "The Greening of the Market," pp. 197-99.

24. Breyer, "Analyzing regulatory failure," p. 596.

25. Robert Hahn and Robert Stavins, "Incentive-Based Environmental Regulation: A New Era from an Old Idea?" *Ecology Law Quarterly*, vol. 18, no. 1, 1991.

26. Paul Hawken, *The Ecology of Commerce* (New York: HarperCollins, 1993), p. 169.

27. Conversation with energy economist Charles Komanoff, November 1990.

28. David Lapp, "The Demanding Side of Utility Conservation Programs," *Environmental Action*, summer 1994, p. 29.

29. Amory Lovins' *Soft Energy Paths: Toward a Durable Peace* (New York: Harper and Row, 1977) elaborates arguments he first developed in widely quoted articles in the journal *Foreign Affairs* and in Friends of the Earth's journal, *Not Man Apart*.

30. Arnold P. Fickett, *et al.*, "Efficient Use of Electricity," *Scientific American*, September 1990, pp. 65-74; "Supply Curves Illustrate Enormous Potential of Efficiency," *Rocky Mountain Institute Newsletter*, Fall 1989.

31. David Lapp, in "The Demanding Side of Utility Conservation Programs" (note 28), cites twenty-eight states where direct payoffs to stockholders were tried.

32. Hardin B. C. Tibbs, "Industrial Ecology: An Environmental Agenda for Industry," *Whole Earth Review*, winter 1992, pp. 4-19.
33. Novo Nordisk Bioindustrial Group, *Enzymes at Work*, Bagsvaerd, Denmark, 1992.
34. Robert Stavins, "Harnessing the Marketplace," *EPA Journal*, vol. 18, no. 2, May/June 1992, pp. 21-25.
35. Hawken, *The Ecology of Commerce*, p. 73.
36. Curtis Moore, "Snooze, We Lose," *Friends of the Earth Journal*, September/October 1995, p. 8.
37. Louis Richman, "Managing Through a Downturn," *Fortune*, August 7, 1995, p. 59.
38. John Holusha, "Dow Chemical's Clean-Up Czar Unlocks the Gates," *New York Times*, September 20, 1992.
39. Tom Barron, "'SEM': the latest EHS buzzword," *Environment Today*, vol. 5, no. 3, March 1994.
40. Randal O'Toole, "Lies, Damned Lies and Statistics," *Forest Watch*, vol. 13, no. 9, April/May 1993, supplement section.
41. Alan Durning, *Saving the Forests: What Will it Take?* (Washington, D.C.: WorldWatch Institute), 1993.
42. Randal O'Toole, "Building an Alliance Between Environmentalists and Libertarians," Thoreau Institute, 1995.
43. Karl Hess, Jr., "Bringing the Market Home," *Wild Forest Review*, vol. 1, no. 4, March 1994, p. 28.
44. See, for example, *The Ecologist, Whose Common Future* (Philadelphia, PA: New Society Publishers, 1993); Helena Norberg-Hodge, *Ancient Futures: Learning from Ladakh* (San Francisco, CA: Sierra Club Books, 1991); and Edward Goldsmith, *et al.*, *The Future of Progress: Reflections on Environment and Development* (Devon, England: Green Books, Ltd., 1995).
45. Hess, "Bringing the Market Home," p. 29.
46. Andrew Stirling, "Environmental Valuation: How Much is the Emperor Wearing?" *The Ecologist*, vol. 23, no. 3, May/June 1993, pp. 97-103.
47. Maureen L. Cropper and Paul R. Portney, "Discounting Human Lives," *Resources*, no. 108, summer 1992, pp. 1-4.
48. John Adams, "Cost-Benefit Analysis: The Problem, Not the Solution," *The Ecologist*, vol. 26, no. 1, January/February 1996, pp. 2-4.

Notes to Chapter Three

1. Karl Polanyi, *The Great Transformation*, (Boston, MA: Beacon Press, 1957 edition), p. 139.
2. Polanyi, *The Great Transformation*, especially Chapters Six and Twelve.
3. Thomas W. Merrill, "Two Social Movements," *Ecology Law Quarterly*, vol. 21, no. 2, 1994, pp. 331-33; Jeremy Main, "Conservationists at the Barricades," *Fortune*, February 1970, pp. 145-51.
4. Robert S. Diamond, "What Business Thinks: The Fortune 500 Yankelovich Survey," *Fortune*, February 1970, p. 119.

5. Stephen Breyer, "Analyzing regulatory failure: mismatches, less restrictive alternatives and reform," *Harvard Law Review*, vol. 92, no. 3, January 1979, especially pp. 552-65.

6. U.S. General Accounting Office, *Environmental Protection Issues in the 1980s*, December 30, 1980, p. 11.

7. Philip Shabecoff, *A Fierce Green Fire: The American Environmental Movement* (New York: Hill and Wang, 1993), pp. 207-8, 211-12.

8. Alan Carlin, *et al.*, "Environmental Investments—The Cost of Cleaning Up," *Environment*, vol. 34, no. 2, March 1992, especially pp. 16-19. All figures are in constant 1986 dollars.

9. Philip J. Hilts, "Questions on Role of Quayle Council," *New York Times*, November 19, 1991; "Quayle Council Debate: Issue of Control," *New York Times*, December 16, 1991; Dana Priest, "Competitiveness Council Suspected of Unduly Influencing Regulators," *Washington Post*, November 11, 1991; Jessica Matthews, "Bush's Double Game," *Washington Post*, November 22, 1991; Rose Gutfeld and Bob Davis, "EPA Considers Delaying Rules Sought by Bush," *Wall Street Journal*, February 4, 1992.

10. Rose Gutfeld, "Quayle's Aide's Stake in Firm Criticized," *Wall Street Journal*, December 6, 1991; Philip J. Hilts, "Senators Question Panelist's Ethics," *New York Times*, December 6, 1991; Michael Ross, "Proposed Clean Air Rules Changes Spark Battle," *Los Angeles Times*, November 21, 1991; and Christine Triano and Nancy Watzman, "Conflict of Interest on the Council on Competitiveness," OMB Watch, Washington, D.C., December 1991.

11. Christine Triano and Nancy Watzman, *All the Vice President's Men*, OMB Watch, Washington, D.C., September 1991.

12. Triano and Watzman, *All the Vice President's Men*.

13. Keith Schneider, "Environment Laws Face a Stiff Test from Landowners," *New York Times*, January 20, 1992.

14. Al Gore, *Earth in the Balance: Ecology and the Human Spirit*, (Boston, MA: Houghton Mifflin, 1992), p. 269.

15. Gore, *Earth in the Balance*, pp. 337, 297. For a more complete analysis of Gore's book, see Brian Tokar, "An Environmental Presidency," *Z Magazine*, April 1993, pp. 23-28; and "Environmental Doublespeak," *The Ecologist*, vol. 23, no. 4, July/August 1993, pp. 157-58.

16. Keith Schneider, "Clinton Will Not Fight Toxic-Waste Incinerator," *New York Times*, March 18, 1993; Gore, *Earth in the Balance*, pp. 297, 337. *Everyone's Backyard*, summer 1993; Keith Schneider, "For Crusader Against Waste Incinerator, a Bittersweet Victory," *New York Times*, May 19, 1993; Paul Connett, "Put Integrity Back in the Balance," *Waste Not*, Work on Waste, Canton, New York, October 1993; and "Have We Got Your Attention Now Mr. President?", *Everybody's Backyard*, vol. 11, no. 3, July/August 1993, p. 5 (Falls Church, VA: Citizens Clearinghouse for Hazardous Waste).

17. Peter Montague, "An Update On Two Key Incinerator Battles," *RACHEL'S Hazardous Waste News* (now *RACHEL's Environment and Health Weekly*), no. 328, March 11, 1993.

18. Marian Burros, "U.S. Will Focus on Reducing Pesticides in Food Production," *New York Times*, June 27, 1993; Keith Schneider, "A Trace of Pesticide, an Accepted Risk," *New York Times*, February 7, 1993.

19. National Academy of Sciences, *Pesticides in the Diets of Infants and Children*, Washington, D.C., June 1993.

20. John H. Cushman, Jr., "Pesticide Bill Advances in House Without Rancor and Opponents," *New York Times*, July 18, 1996; National Coalition Against the Misuse of Pesticides, "Anti-Cancer Law Threatened in Congress," Washington, D.C., July 17, 1996; Global Action and Information Network, "Grassroots Coalition Opposes New U.S. Pesticide Bill," Santa Cruz, CA: July 26, 1996; Jennifer Ferrara, "The Great Pesticide Compromise," *Food & Water Journal*, summer 1996, pp. 28-29.

21. Vandana Shiva, "Violating People's Rights, Protecting Corporate Profits—The U.S. Interpretation of the Biodiversity Convention," *Third World Resurgence*, no. 34, June 1993, pp. 2-3.

22. Conversation with Andrew Kimbrell, August 1993.

23. Peter Cooper and Lori Wallach, *NAFTA's Broken Promises*, Public Citizen/Global Trade Watch, Washington, D.C., September 1995; Daniel Brook, "Toxic Trade," *Z Magazine*, September 1992, pp. 55-58; and John Ross, "Green Activists Feel Free Trade Pinch," Gemini News Service, November 2, 1995.

24. Mark Ritchie, "Trading Away the Environment," in Richard Hofrichter, ed., *Toxic Struggles* (Philadelphia, PA: New Society Publishers, 1993), pp. 209-18; Greenpeace U.S.A., "NAFTA and the North American Agreement on Environmental Cooperation: Side-stepping the Environment," policy brief, Washington, D.C., November 1993; and Susan Meeker-Lowry, "Maquiladoras: A Preview of Free Trade," *Z Magazine*, October 1992, pp. 25-30.

25. David S. Cloud, "Environmental Groups Look for Ways to Ensure a 'Green' Trade Agreement," *Congressional Quarterly*, November 28, 1992, pp. 3712-13; Steven Greenhouse, "Judge in a Ruling That Could Delay Trade Pact," *New York Times*, July 1, 1993; Bill Snape, "Environmental Groups Outline Proposal for NAFTA Side Agreements," Defenders of Wildlife, Washington, D.C., May 6, 1993; and Dianne Solis, "Trade-Off on NAFTA Side Accord on Environment Apparently Set," *Wall Street Journal*, July 12, 1993.

26. Chakravarthi Raghavan, "South to face new 'Trade-related' threats," *Third World Resurgence*, no. 45, May 1994, pp. 18-19.

27. Andrea Durbin, "European Community Targets U.S. Environmental Laws for Elimination at GATT," Friends of the Earth, Washington, D.C., 1994.

28. David Brower, "Why I Won't Vote for Clinton," *Los Angeles Times*, July 21, 1996. Brower became a supporter of Ralph Nader's presidential bid, organized under the auspices of various state Green parties (see Chapter Nine).

29. Todd S. Purdum, "President Issues Executive Order to Buttress Toxic Emission Rules, *New York Times*, August 9, 1995.

30. While ranching interests base their opposition on populist appeals to the individualist values of the "Old West," recent figures suggest that ranchers and mining employees constitute a rapidly shrinking share of the western workforce, now less than 1 percent. See Timothy Egan, "Interior Secretary Endures

Storms from All Directions," *New York Times*, August 28, 1994. On Clinton's capitulation, see Timothy Egan, "Sweeping Reversal of U.S. Land Policy Sought by Clinton," *New York Times*, February 24, 1996; Keith Schneider, "Clinton the Conservationist Thinks Twice," *New York Times*, April 4, 1993.

31. David Helvarg, *The War Against the Greens*, San Francisco, CA: Sierra Club Books, 1994), pp. 75-76.

32. Helvarg, *The War Against the Greens*, p. 137.

33. Gary Ball, "Wise Use Nuts & Bolts," *Mendocino Environmental Center Newsletter*, Summer/Fall 1992, p. 5. See also Brian Tokar, "The 'Wise Use' Backlash: Responding to Militant Anti-Environmentalism," *The Ecologist*, vol. 25, no. 4, July/August 1995, pp. 150-56.

34. Citizens for Sensible Safeguards, "Shirking Responsibility," January 1996, available from OMB Watch.

35. Keith Schneider, "Bold Plan Seeks to Wrest Control of Federal Lands," *New York Times*, April 8, 1995; David Helvarg, "The Anti-Enviro Connection," *The Nation*, May 22, 1995, pp. 722-23.

36. Keith Schneider, "Fighting to Keep U.S. Rules from Devaluing Land," *New York Times*, January 9, 1995.

37. See, for example, Jeffrey St. Clair, "Fantastic and Frightening Tales of Endangered Species," *Wild Forest Review*, vol. 2, no. 7, October/November 1995, pp. 24-28.

38. *A CLEAR View*, vol .3, no. 7, April 1996.

39. Ford Runge, "Comments on the Changing Landscape of Property: Evolving Public and Private Interests," in Charles Geisler and Gail Daneker, eds., "Property and Values: A Summary of Presentations at a Conference Sponsored by the Equity Trust, Inc., and the ABA Commission on Homelessness and Poverty," Cornell University, Ithaca, New York, 1996.

40. Quoted in Dale Hattis and David Kennedy, "Assessing Risks from Health Hazards: An Imperfect Science, " *Technology Review*, May/June 1986, p. 66.

41. These effects include alterations in endocrine, immune, and nervous system functions, as well as the increasingly well-documented synergistic effects of multiple exposure to chemicals. See, for example, Peter Montague, "The Emperor's Scientific New Clothes," *RACHEL's Environment and Health Weekly*, no. 393, June 9, 1994; Steven F. Arnold, *et al.*, "Synergistic Activation of Estrogen Receptor with Combinations of Environmental Chemicals," *Science*, vol. 272 , June 7, 1996, pp. 1489-92.

42. Interview in *Safe Food News* (now *Food & Water Journal*), spring 1993, p. 15.

43. Peter Montague, "The Risks of an Environmental Presidency," *RACHEL's Hazardous Waste News*, no. 359, October 14, 1993.

44. John H. Cushman, Jr., "E.P.A. Critics Get Boost in Congress," *New York Times*, February 7, 1994; See also, Natural Resources Defense Council, "Breach of Faith: How the Contract's Fine Print Undermines America's Environmental Success," New York, 1995.

45. Public Citizen, "Assault on Safety: The Plan to Strangle Health and Safety Rules in Red Tape," Washington, D.C., 1995

46. Gary Bass, *et al.*, "Eye of the Newt: An Analysis of the Job Creation and Wage Enhancement Act," OMB Watch, Washington, D.C., 1994.

47. John H. Cushman, Jr., "Industry Helped Draft Clean Water Law," *New York Times*, March 22, 1995; "Rewritten Clean Water Act Gains in House," *New York Times*, May 12, 1995; and "House Votes Major Changes in Clean Water Act from 70's," *New York Times*, May 17, 1995.

48. NRDC press statement, November 13, 1995; Sierra Club Legal Defense Fund memo, April 13, 1995.

49. William Broad, "Budget Cuts Would Hit Hard at Civilian Science," *New York Times*, May 22, 1995; Malcolm W. Browne, "Budget Cuts Seen by Science Group as Very Harmful for U.S. Research," *New York Times*, August 29, 1995.

50. Editorial, "House of Environmental Horrors," *New York Times*, August 7, 1995.

51. John H. Cushman, Jr., "Environment Gets a Push from Clinton," *New York Times*, July 5, 1995; Editorial, "A Greener White House," *New York Times*, November 26, 1995; and Michael Kranish, "Clinton setting strategy for '96: Recently a subtle emphasis on education, the environment," *Boston Globe*, November 25, 1995.

52. John H. Cushman, Jr., "G.O.P. Backing Off from Tough Stand over Environment," *New York Times*, January 26, 1996; Alison Mitchell, "Clinton Asks Tax Breaks for Toxic Waste Cleanup," *New York Times*, March 12, 1996.

53. John Stauber and Sheldon Rampton, *Toxic Sludge is Good for You: Lies, Damn Lies and the Public Relations Industry* (Monroe, ME: Common Courage Press, 1995), p. 125.

54. Ron Faucheaux, "The Grassroots Explosion," *Campaigns and Elections*, December/January 1995, pp. 20-30 ff.

55. Cushman, "Environment Gets a Push from Clinton."

56. Wilderness Society, "New Public Opinion Survey Shows Westerners Want Public Lands Protected," November 24, 1995; Timothy Egan, "In Utah, a Pitched Battle Over Public Lands," *New York Times*, November 13, 1995. For an insightful analysis of the western cultural roots of the "wise use" movement, see Ralph Maughan and Douglas Nilson, "What's Old and What's New About the Wise Use Movement," Idaho State University, 1993.

57. Kieran Suckling, "Poll: Arizonans Support Logging Injunction by 2-1," *Southwest Biodiversity Alert*, no. 33, Southwest Center for Biological Diversity, September 17, 1996.

58. Matthew Wald, "Fuel Prices Rise with Clean Air Rules," *New York Times*, November 9, 1994; Agis Salpukas, "New Gas Arouses Grass-Roots Ire," *New York Times*, February 18, 1995; and Stephen Lester, "MTBE: Ozone Solution or a New Kind of Pollution?" *Everyone's Backyard*, Citizens Clearinghouse for Hazardous Waste, spring 1995, pp. 14-16.

59. Richard L. Grossman and Frank T. Adams, *Taking Care of Business: Citizenship and the Charter of Incorporation* (Cambridge, MA.: Charter, Ink/CSSP, 1993).

60. Times Beach Action Group, "PCB Deception Surrounding Bliss Sites," information packet, November 1995; conversation with Steve Taylor, March 1996. See also, Renate Kimbrough, *et al.*, "Epidemiology and Pathology of a Tetrachlo-

rodibenzodioxin Poisoning Episode," *Archives of Environmental Health*, March/April 1977, pp. 77 ff.

61. Victor Navasky, "Confederacy of Injustices," *The Nation*, February 26, 1996, p. 33.

62. International Joint Commission, "Eighth Annual Report on Great Lakes Water Quality," Ottawa and Washington, D.C., July 1996; Robert Costanza and Charles Perrings, "A Flexible Assurance Bonding System for Improved Environmental Management," *Ecological Economics*, vol. 2, 1990, pp. 57-75; Peter Montague, "The IJC's Eighth Report " and "Dealing with Uncertainty," *RACHEL's Environment and Health Weekly*, nos. 505 and 510, August 1 and September 5, 1996; and Joe Thornton, "Risk Assessment for Global Chemical Pollution? The Case for a Precautionary Policy on Chlorine Chemistry," Greenpeace Toxics Campaign, New York, February 1995.

63. Jeremy Brecher and Tim Costello, *Global Village or Global Pillage?* (Boston, MA: South End Press, 1994), p. 22; Richard Teitelbaum, "Introduction to the 500 Largest U.S. Corporations," *Fortune*, May 15, 1995; and Richard Barnet, "Lords of the Global Economy," *The Nation*, December 19, 1994, p. 756. According to Barnet, the share of federal taxes contributed by all corporations with over $250 million in assets had shrunk to 9.2 percent by 1991.

64. John H. Cushman, Jr., "Adversaries Back Pollution Rules Now on the Books," *New York Times*, February 12, 1996.

Notes to Chapter Four

1. Bill Clinton, "Remarks by the President on the 25th Anniversary of Earth Day," Earth Day Network, San Diego, California, 1995.

2. Michael Silverstein, "Clinton and Environmentalists: A Costly Parting of the Ways," *Christian Science Monitor*, September 6, 1994, p. 18.

3. Sam Hitt, "Smokescreen of Process Hides Lack of Substance," *Forest Watch*, vol. 13, no. 9, April/May 1993, p. 46.

4. Quoted in Todd Purdum, "Clinton Lashes Out at Congress, Citing Pollution and Guns," *New York Times*, August 1, 1995.

5. Timothy Egan, "Citing Space Photos, Scientists Say Forests in the Northwest Are in Danger," *New York Times*, June 11, 1992.

6. Conversation with Michael Donnelly, Friends of the Brietenbush Cascades, May 1994.

7. Michael Donnelly, "The Great Timber Famine Fallacy," *Wild Forest Review*, vol. 1, no. 2, December 1993, p. 23.

8. Bill Clinton, "Closing Remarks," *Forest Watch*, vol. 13, no. 9, April/May 1993.

9. Conversation with Jeffrey St. Clair, February 1994.

10. Timothy Egan, "Oregon, Foiling Forecasters, Thrives as it Protects Owls," *New York Times*, October 6, 1995; Donnelly, "The Great Timber Famine Fallacy"; and John H. Cushman, Jr. and Timothy Egan, "Battles on Conservation Rack Up Ratings Points," *New York Times*, July 31, 1996.

11. Jeffrey St. Clair, "The Political Science of Jack Ward Thomas," *Wild Forest Review*, vol. 1, no. 2, December 1993, pp. 15-18.

12. Western Ancient Forest Campaign, "Clinton Announces Forest Plan" and "Report from Washington," Washington, D.C., July 1993.
13. Jeffrey St. Clair, "Endgame for Northwest Forests?" *Wild Forest Review*, vol. 1, no. 6, May 1994, pp. 26-29; Gwen Fill, "Clinton Backs a $1 Billion Plan to Spare Trees and Aid Loggers," *New York Times*, July 1, 1993.
14. Tim Hilchey, "Study Raises Concern over Plan to Protect Northern Spotted Owl," *New York Times*, December 14, 1993; Western Ancient Forest Campaign "Interior Bows to Industry on Owl Protection," briefing paper, December 1993; Timothy Egan, "Upheaval in the Forests," *New York Times*, July 2, 1993; Keith Schneider, "In Peace Plan for Northwest Timber Dispute, Options May Anger Both Sides," *New York Times*, June 19, 1993; and Global Action and Information Network, "Environmentalists Alarmed by White House Forest Plans," June 1993.
15. Jim Owens, "White House Staff Steer Clinton Towards Forest Disaster," Western Ancient Forest Campaign, June 1993; Andy Kerr, "In Defense of the Deal," *Wild Forest Review*, vol. 1, no. 1, November 1993, pp. 19-20.
16. Larry Tuttle, "Five Degrees of Intimidation," and Michael Donnelly, "Toward a Politics of Inclusion, *Wild Forest Review*, vol. 1, no. 7, June 1994, pp. 28, 29.
17. Susan Meeker-Lowry, interview with Andy Stahl, December 1993.
18. Kerr, "In Defense of the Deal."
19. Jeffrey St. Clair, "Meditations on a Done Deal," *Wild Forest Review*, vol. 1, no. 1, November 1993, p. 14.
20. Conversation with Jeffrey St. Clair , February 1994.
21. Jim Owens, "Option 9 Response Overwhelms Forest Service," Western Ancient Forest Campaign, Washington, D.C., November 1993.
22. Tim McKay, "Delays and Legal Moves Dog Option Nine," *EcoNews*, April 1994; Jim Owens, "Release of Option 9," Western Ancient Forest Campaign briefing paper, February 1994.
23. Owens, "Option 9 Response Overwhelms Forest Service."
24. William Dwyer, "Order Dissolving Injunction and Setting Schedule for Summary Judgment Motions," U.S. District Court, Seattle, Washington, June 6, 1994; conversation with Tim Hermach, Native Forest Council, May 1994.
25. Jeffrey St. Clair, "Down by Law: Losing it at the Courthouse," *Wild Forest Review*, vol. 2, no. 2, December 1994, p. 4.
26. Western Ancient Forest Campaign, "Option 9 Decision Time," briefing paper, February 1994.
27. Weyerhaeuser, a major landowner in the state of Arkansas, may have played a key role in compelling then-Governor Clinton to moderate his position on clearcutting in the early 1980s. See, for example, Ken Silverstein and Alexander Cockburn, "Paper Trail: The Origins of Whitewater," *CounterPunch,* vol. 3, nos. 2-3, February 1, 1996.
28. "Congress Passes Timber Salvage Rider," *Save America's Forests*, vol. 6, no. 2, winter 1995-96; Jeffrey St. Clair, "Salvage Dreams: Reading the Future of North America's Forests in the History of the Salvage Rider," *Wild Forest Review*, vol. 3, no. 1, January/February 1996, pp. 8-21; Phil Knight, "Lawless Logging Threatens Central Montana Roadless Areas," Native Forest Network, Bozeman, Mon-

tanta, January 1996; Timothy Egan, "As Clear Cutting Returns, Motives are Questioned," *New York Times*, December 5, 1995; and Ned Daly, "Logging Without Laws: Salvage Logging on Federal Lands," Taxpayer Assets Project (Public Citizen), Washington, D.C., December 1995.

29. "Forest Service Memo Exposes Fraudulent Salvage Program," *Save America's Forests*, vol. 6, no. 2, Winter 1995-96, p. 25; "Abuse of Public Law 104-19 in the Northern Rockies: Salvage Timber Sales Violating Law and Public Process," Alliance for the Wild Rockies, Missoula, Montana, November 1995.

30. Kathie Durbin, "Boise Salvage Sale is a Real Loser," *Cascadia Times*, August 1995 (via Econet Western Lands Gopher Service).

31. Jeffrey St. Clair and Scott Greacen, "Dark Heart of the Salvage Rider," *Wild Forest Review*, vol. 3, no. 1, January/February 1996, pp. 22-25; Taxpayer Assets Project, *TAP-Resources* (Public Citizen), November 1995.

32. Arthur Partridge, "Partridge Exposes 'Salvage' Hoax," *Save America's Forests*, vol. 6, no. 2, winter 1995-96, p. 22; Mathew Jacobson, "Letter to President Clinton," Green Mountain Forest Watch, Brattleboro, Vermont, March 1996.

33. Quoted in a Western Ancient Forest Campaign alert, January 1996.

34. Julie Norman, "Citizen Resistance to the Logging Without Laws Rider," *Headwaters Journal*, vol. 5, no. 4, winter 1995-96; Karen Wood, "Environmental Movement Dignitaries Join in Sugarloaf Protest," Siskiyou Regional Education Project, Cave Junction, Oregon, November 1995. Sugarloaf arrestees included National Audubon Society vice-president Brock Evans and former Indiana Congressperson Jim Jontz, along with a wide spectrum of regional activists.

35. "Over 100 Arrested in Olympic Forest Protest," Econet Western Lands Gopher Service, February 1996; Timothy Egan, "Clinton Under Attack by Both Sides in a Renewed Logging Fight," *New York Times*, March 1, 1996; Matt Rossel, "Digging In at Warner Creek," *Earth First!*, vol. 16, no. 1, October 1995; "Salvage Rider Rewards Arsonists at Warner Creek," *Save America's Forests*, vol. 6, no. 2, winter 1995-96, p. 61; and Patrick Mazza, "Grassroots Forest Movement Sprouting—'Salvage' Rider Backfiring on Timber Industry," *Cascadia Planet*, April 22, 1996.

36. Phil Knight, "Citizens Rally in Montana to Stop Lawless Logging," Native Forest Network, Bozeman, Montana, November 1995.

37. Andy Kerr and Sally Cross, "Let's Get Political," *Wild Earth*, vol. 6, no. 1, spring 1996, pp. 72-74; Mike Roselle, "The End of Humor," *Earth First!*, May 1995, p. 23.

38. Mathew Jacobson, "The Forest Health Hoax and the Liquidation of Our Forest Ecosystems," Green Mountain Forest Watch, Brattleboro, Vermont, April 1996.

39. U.S. Department of Agriculture, *et al.*, "Memorandum of Agreement on Timber Salvage Related Activities Under Public Law 104-19," August 9, 1995; Dan Glickman, "Revised Direction for Emergency Timber Salvage Sales Conducted Under Section 2001(b) of P.L. 104-19," U.S. Department of Agriculture, July 2, 1996. Phil Knight, "Hyalite Timber Sale Shut Down," Native Forest Network, Bozeman, Montana, September 1996; Western Ancient Forest Campaign, *Logging Without Laws Bulletin*, no. 83, Washington, D.C., May 23, 1996; and Kieran Suckling, personal correspondence, August 6, 1996.

40. Scott Sonner, "Clinton Orders Halt to Logging," Associated Press, December 13, 1996; Jim Jontz and Steve Holmer, "Gore Says: Salvage Logging is 'Biggest Mistake,'" Washington, D.C.: Western Ancient Forest Campaign, September 27, 1996.

41. Steve Holmer, "Jim Baca Forced to Resign at BLM," Western Ancient Forest Campaign, February 1994; Jeff DeBonis, "The Interior Secretary is a Trojan Horse Crushing Reform," *Wild Forest Review*, vol. 1, no. 8, August 1994. DeBonis, a former Forest Service employee who now heads an organization dedicated to supporting government whistle-blowers, accused Babbitt of a rather overt and cynical betrayal of his own staff: "Babbitt's reform rhetoric flushed out some of the last of the remaining ethical activists within many of these agencies who have managed to survive numerous purges over the years."

42. Carl Hulse, "Building Near Endangered Species," *New York Times*, December 28, 1993; Keith Schneider, "Accord is Reached to Aid Forest Bird," *New York Times*, April 16, 1993; and William Stevens, "Interior Secretary Is Pushing a New Way to Save Species," *New York Times*, March 1, 1993.

43. Kieran Suckling, "Lawsuit Challenges HCP Policy," *Southwest Biodiversity Alert*, no. 40, October 30, 1996.

44. Les Line, "Songbird Population Losses Tied to Fragmentation of Forest Habitat," *New York Times*, April 4, 1995.

45. John H. Cushman, Jr., "Environmentalists Gain a Victory, at Least for the Moment," *New York Times*, June 30, 1995.

46. John H. Cushman, Jr., "Conservatives Tug at Endangered Species Act," *New York Times*, May 28, 1995; "House G.O.P. Leaders Propose to Ease Endangered Species Act," *New York Times*, September 8, 1995; Ecological Society of America, "Endangered Species Act," update, Global Action and Information Network, Santa Cruz, California, October 1995; Kieran Suckling, "Analysis of the Gilchrest 'Natural Legacy Protection Act,' HR 2375," Southwest Center for Biological Diversity, Silver City, New Mexico, October 1995; Jeffrey St. Clair and Alexander Cockburn, "The Fake Fight over the Endangered Species Act," *Wild Forest Review*, vol. 2, no. 7, October/November 1995, pp. 22-23; and Richard Stone, "Incentives Offer Hope for Habitat," *Science*, vol. 269, September 1, 1995, pp. 1212-13.

47. Sierra Club Action, "Status Report—Anti-Environmental Bills in 104th Congress," San Francisco, Califonia, August 1995; Kieran Suckling, "Analysis of the Gilchrest 'Natural Legacy Protection Act,' HR 2375," Southwest Center for Biological Diversity, October 1995; and Malcolm Wallop, "The Mother of All Property Fights," Alliance for America, Washington, D.C., November 1995.

48. Charles Mann and Mark Plummer, "Is Endangered Species Act in Danger?" *Science*, vol. 267, March 3, 1995, pp. 1256-58.

49. "Excerpts from the Report of the Committee on Scientific Issues in the Endangered Species Act of the National Research Council of the National Academy of Science, May 25, 1995," *ESA Background*, Endangered Species Coalition, Washington, D.C., January 1996.

50. Elizabeth Losos, *et al.*, "Taxpayer-Subsidized Resource Extraction Harms Species," *BioScience*, vol. 45, no. 7, July/August 1995, pp. 446-55. This study brought

together scientists from the Smithsonian Tropical Research Institute, Stanford University, University of Michigan, Environmental Defense Fund, and the Wilderness Society.

51. David Hogan, "Evisceration by Regulation: How the Fish and Wildlife Service Gutted the Endangered Species Act," *Wild Forest Review*, vol. 2, no. 7, October/November 1995, pp. 19-21.

52. "Clinton Reinstates His Own Administrative ESA Moratorium," *ESA Advocate*, no. 9, Southwest Center for Biological Diversity, Silver City, New Mexico, May 1996.

53. Kieran Suckling, "Letter to Endangered Species Coalition," Southwest Center for Biological Diversity, Silver City, New Mexico, March 1996; "Talking Points for Endangered Species Act Reauthorization," Environmental Defense Fund, March 1996; Pacifica Radio News broadcasts, April 10 and April 22, 1996; and Russell Mokhiber, "Endangered Species Coalition Ousts EDF for Working with Industry on Compromise: 'They Showed No Remorse,'" *Corporate Crime Reporter*, vol. 10, no. 13, April 1996.

54. Mike Bader, "Last, Best Chance for a Wild Rockies: Northern Rockies Ecosystem Protection Act," *Wild Forest Review*, vol. 1, no. 3, February 1994, pp. 26-30; Dave Foreman, "Beyond Rocks and Ice: Toward a Biological Model for Wilderness," *Wild Forest Review*, vol. 1, no. 3, February 1994, pp. 31-33.

55. Chad Hanson, *et al.*, "Sierra Club Sells Out Northern Rockies Wilderness," April 14, 1994.

56. Sara Rimer, "In Clear-Cutting Vote, Maine Will Define Itself," *New York Times*, September 25, 1996.

57. Conrad Heeschen, "Maine Legislator: Forest Compact Damages Democracy," *Northern Forest Forum*, Fall 1996, p. 2.

58. Dieter Bradbury, "New Vote on Forest Compact May Be a Year Away," *Portland* (Maine) *Press Herald*, November 7, 1996.

59. Mitch Lansky, "The Forest Compact: A Happy Day for Cynics," *Northern Forest Forum*, Fall 1996, pp. 8-11.

60. Alison Mitchell, "President Designates a Monument Across Utah," *New York Times*, September 19, 1996; Todd S. Purdum, "Clinton Unveils Plan to Halt Gold Mine Near Yellowstone," *New York Times*, August 13, 1996; and Jeffrey St. Clair and Alexander Cockburn, "Dave Foreman's Dream and Bill Clinton's Trail of Tears," *Nature and Politics* (syndicated column), September 1996.

61. John H. Cushman, Jr., "Swaps Broaden Federal Efforts to Shield Land," *New York Times*, September 30, 1996.

62. B. J. Bergman, "Club Endorses Bill Clinton," *Sierra*, vol. 81, no. 6, November/December 1996, p. 61; Cushman, "Swaps Broaden Federal Efforts to Shield Land."

63. Karyn Strickler, "Living Up to the Legend," *Earth First!*, vol. 16, no. 1, October 1995, p. 1.

Notes to Chapter Five

1. Keith Schneider, "As Earth Day Turns 25, Life Gets Complicated," *New York Times*, April 16, 1995.
2. Mark Dowie, "American Environmentalism: A Movement Courting Irrelevance," *World Policy Journal*, vol. 9, no. 1, Winter 1991-92, pp. 67-92.
3. Carl Pope, "Politics of the Environment: K Street Meets Main Street," speech to the National Press Club, October 9, 1996.
4. Matthew O'Malley, "Air Pollution, Past and Present," *Dollars and Sense*, no. 204, March/April 1996; World Resources Institute, *World Resources: A Guide to the Global Environment* (New York: Oxford University Press, 1994); and Dennis Hevesi, "Environmental Quality Shows Gains and Declines Since 1970, a Report Finds," *New York Times*, December 5, 1995.
5. Richard Moore, talk at the University of Vermont, Burlington, April 1995.
6. *Akwesasne Notes*, ed., *Basic Call to Consciousness* (Rooseveltown, NY: Mohawk Nation, 1978), p. 71. For an historical survey of Native Americans' ecological worldview, see Donald A. Grinde and Bruce E. Johansen, *Ecocide of Native America* (Santa Fe, NM: Clear Light Publishers, 1995).
7. Quoted in John Seed, *et al.*, *Thinking Like a Mountain: Towards a Council of All Beings* (Philadelphia, PA: New Society Publishers, 1988), p. 36.
8. Ethical interpretations of the findings of ecological science continue to inspire controversy in scholarly circles. See, for example, Yvonne Baskin, "Ecologists Dare to Ask: How Much Does Diversity Matter?" *Science*, vol. 264, April 8, 1994, pp. 202-3; William K. Stevens, "Study Bolsters Value of Species Diversity," *New York Times*, February 1, 1994; and J. Baird Callicott, "Do Deconstructive Ecology and Sociobiology Undermine Leopold's Land Ethic?" *Environmental Ethics*, vol. 18, no. 4, winter 1996, pp. 353-72.
9. For a broad overview of the origins of the idea of dominating nature in the West, see my earlier *The Green Alternative: Creating an Ecological Future* (Philadelphia, PA: New Society Publishers, revised edition, 1992), especially Chapter One; and Carolyn Merchant, *The Death of Nature* (San Francisco, CA: Harper & Row, 1980).
10. See, for example, Roderick Nash, The Rights of Nature: a History of Environmental Ethics (Madison, WI: University of Wisconsin Press, 1989).
11. David F. Noble, "Present Tense Technology," *Democracy*, vol. 3, no. 2, spring 1983; E. P. Thompson, "The Moral Economy of the English Crowd in the Eighteenth Century," *Past and Present*, vol. 50, 1971, pp. 76-136. See also Kirkpatrick Sale, *Rebels Against the Future: The Luddites and Their War On the Industrial Revolution*, New York: Addison-Wesley, 1995.
12. "The Struggle for Existence in Human Society" was the title of a famous essay by T. H. Huxley, to which Kropotkin's opus, *Mutual Aid* (first published in book form in 1902, though the individual essays therein appeared between 1890 and 1896), was largely a response.
13. See, for example, his *Fields, Factories and Workshops*, as edited by Colin Ward (New York: Harper & Row, 1975).

14. Elisée Reclus, "The Feeling for Nature in Modern Society," in John P. Clark and Camille Martin, *Liberty, Equality, Geography: The Social Thought of Elisée Reclus* (Denver, CO: Aigis Publications, 1997), p. 55.

15. Elisée Reclus, "Evolution, Revolution and the Anarchist Ideal," in Clark and Martin, *Liberty, Equality, Geography*, pp. 175-76.

16. In *The Dialectics of Nature*, for example, Fredrick Engels discussed the evolutionary origins of human intelligence, concluding that the quality that most clearly distinguishes human beings from other animals is the faculty for "impressing the stamp of their will upon nature." "In short, the animal merely *uses* external nature, and brings about changes in it simply by his presence; man by his changes makes it serve his ends, *masters* it," Engels explained. "This is the final essential distinction between man and other animals, and once again it is labor that brings about this distinction." (Emphasis in original.) This view clearly has its origins in the scientific outlook of Enlightenment figures such as Francis Bacon, and indeed, in Renaissance theology. It illustrates, however, how the Marxist hypostatization of labor as the defining principle of human existence has made it very difficult to derive an ecological outlook from Marxist principles, despite numerous thoughtful attempts to do so. To his credit, Engels did acknowledge that "conquering" nature had many unforeseen consequences, from the extremes of drought and flooding that resulted from early civilizations' destruction of the Mediterranean forests, to the contemporary link between epidemic disease and inadequate diets. See *The Dialectics of Nature* (New York: International Publishers, 1940), pp. 291-93.

17. Mark Dowie, *Losing Ground: American Environmentalism at the Close of the Twentieth Century* (Cambridge, MA: MIT Press, 1995), p. 85. E. Bruce Harrison, the public relations executive who coordinated the campaign against *Silent Spring*, has established himself as a leading proponent of corporate greenwashing, helping corporations to exploit "a tremendous opportunity to define and dominate the future of environmentalism." See *PR Watch*, vol. 1, no. 3, spring 1994.

18. Paul B. Sears, "Ecology—A Subversive Subject," *BioScience*, vol. 14, no. 7, July 1964, pp. 11-13.

19. Sears, "Ecology—A Subversive Subject," p. 13.

20. Eugene P. Odum, "The New Ecology," *BioScience*, vol. 14, no. 7, July 1964, p. 16.

21. *Our Synthetic Environment*, originally written under the pseudonym Lewis Herber, was first published by Alfred A. Knopf (New York) in 1962. It is currently available in a 1974 edition, published by Harper & Row.

22. Murray Bookchin, "Ecology and Revolutionary Thought," in *Post-Scarcity Anarchism* (San Francisco, CA: Ramparts Press, 1971), p. 58. *Post-Scarcity Anarchism* was reprinted by Black Rose Books (Montreal) in 1986.

23. Murray Bookchin, *The Ecology of Freedom* (Palo Alto, CA: Cheshire Books, 1982), p. 21.

24. See, for example, Murray Bookchin, *The Philosophy of Social Ecology*, (Montreal, Quebec: Black Rose Books, 1990).

25. Philip Shabecoff, *A Fierce Green Fire: The American Environmental Movement* (New York: Hill and Wang, 1993), p. 125.

26. From the lead editorial in *Ramparts*, vol. 8, no. 11, May 1970, p. 4.

27. While the Clamshell Alliance was actually founded a year earlier, and the basic outlines of its structure predated the 1977 action, it was in the armories that the structure was first fully realized and the bonds of solidarity that made it work were forged. Organizations inspired by Clamshell—the Abalone Alliance in California, the Crabshell Alliance in the Pacific Northwest, the Catfish Alliance, the Shad Alliance, the Peachtree Alliance, and countless others—all arose shortly after the first large Seabrook action. Many were founded or assisted by people who had been at Seabrook and spent two weeks in the New Hampshire armories.

28. Sam Dolgoff, *The Anarchist Collectives* (New York: Free Life Editions, 1974); Murray Bookchin, *The Spanish Anarchists* (New York: Harper Collophon, 1977).

29. Murray Bookchin, "A Note on Affinity Groups," in *Post-Scarcity Anarchism*, p. 221. Bookchin's more recent writings describe cities and neighborhoods as the potential locus of confrontation between communities and the state. See "A New Municipal Agenda," in *The Rise of Urbanization and the Decline of Citizenship* (San Francisco: Sierra Club Books, 1987), republished and revised as *From Urbanization to Cities: Toward a New Politics of Citizenship* (London, England: Cassell, 1995).

30. Joel Kovel, "The Affinity Group as the Unit of Antinuclear Politics," in Kovel, *Against the State of Nuclear Terror* (Boston, MA: South End Press, 1983), pp. 171-72.

31. The consensus process on the Clamshell Alliance Coordinating Committee eventually broke down, under pressure from self-proclaimed leadership factions that came to wield undue influence behind the scenes. Even after a decision to cancel a planned site occupation in June of 1978 irrevocably divided the organization, however, affinity groups and local chapters continued to organize locally and bring large numbers of people to Seabrook and other nuclear sites on many subsequent occasions. Although one of the two planned Seabrook reactors was eventually completed and brought on-line, at nearly ten times the originally proposed cost, the political and economic fallout from Seabrook clearly spelled the end of nuclear power development in New England.

32. Barbara Epstein, *Political Protest and Cultural Revolution* (Berkeley: University of California Press, 1991), p. 116.

Notes to Chapter Six

1. Jenny Labalme, *A Road to Walk: A Struggle for Environmental Justice* (Durham, N.C.: Regulator Bookshop, 1987).

2. The community of Afton, where the landfill was sited, was itself 84 percent black. See Robert D. Bullard, *Dumping in Dixie: Race, Class and Environmental Quality* (Boulder, CO: Westview Press, 1990), pp. 35-38.

3. Lois Gibbs, "The Liberation of Love Canal?" *Everyone's Backyard*, March-April 1990, pp. 3-5; Peter Montague, "Chemical Dumps Make Good Homes for Poor Families, EPA Decision Indicates," *RACHEL's Hazardous Waste News* (now *RACHEL's Environment and Health Weekly*) no. 182, May 23, 1990; and Jamie Sayen, "Love Canal, Dioxin, Environmental Justice and Rebuilding Democracy: A

Conversation with Lois Marie Gibbs," *Northern Forest Forum*, vol. 4, no. 4, April 1996, pp. 20-24.

4. Dorceta Taylor, "Environmentalism and the Politics of Inclusion," in Robert D. Bullard, *Confronting Environmental Racism: Voices from the Grassroots* (Boston: South End Press, 1993), p. 54. See also Cynthia Hamilton, "Women, Home and Community: The Struggle in an Urban Environment," in Irene Diamond and Gloria F. Orenstein, *Reweaving the World: The Emergence of Ecofeminism* (San Francisco: Sierra Club Books, 1990), pp. 215-22.
5. Conversation with Lois Gibbs, March 1996.
6. Sanford Lewis, "Communities and Workers Forge New Rules for Corporate Accountability, *Just Cause*, vol. 2, no. 4, September 1995.
7. See, for example, Ted Smith, "The Challenges Ahead," *Silicon Valley Toxics News*, vol. 13, no. 4, winter 1995, p. 2; Lenny Siegel, "High-Tech Pollution," *Sierra*, November/December 1984, pp. 58-64; Robert Howard, "Second Class in Silicon Valley," *Working Papers*, September/October 1981, pp. 21-31; John E. Young, *Global Network: Computers in a Sustainable Society*, WorldWatch Paper, no. 115, WorldWatch Institute, September 1993, pp. 35-42; and Dennis Hayes, *Behind the Silicon Curtain* (Boston: South End Press, 1989).
8. Robert Gottlieb, *Forcing the Spring: The Transformation of the American Environmental Movement* (Washington, D.C.: Island Press, 1995), pp. 296-98.
9. Eyal Press, "Union Do's: Smart Solidarity," *The Nation*, April 8, 1996, pp. 29-32.
10. Communities Concerned about Corporations, "A grassroots environmental, worker, victim and shareholder alliance organized to hold petrochemical corporations accountable to communities," Hyattsville, Maryland, 1996.
11. Les Leopold, "The Just Transition Movement," *Taking Action to Stop Dioxin Exposure*, (Citizens Clearinghouse for Hazardous Wastes, 1996), pp. 113-16.
12. Peter Montague, "Big Picture Organizing," *RACHEL's Environment and Health Weekly*, no. 417, November 24, 1994. Between 1985 and 1994, at least 280 incinerators were proposed, but only seventy were built. By burning wood and paper products at high temperatures along with plastics, municipal incinerators are a persistent source of dioxins.
13. Quoted in Hamilton, "Women, Home and Community," p. 221.
14. The NTC (originally the National Campaign Against Toxics Hazards and, for its last two years, the National Toxics Campaign Fund) folded in 1993 in the face of a divisive internal debate over race and gender issues. Many of the organization's most active constituents accused its founders of paternalism, elitism, and disrespect toward local organizers. See Cathy Hinds, *et al.*, "The National Toxics Campaign: Some Reflections, Thoughts for the Movement," 1994; also Gottlieb, *Forcing the Spring*, pp. 267-68.
15. Community Environmental Health Program, "Environment and Development in the USA," Highlander Research and Education Center, New Market, Tennessee, 1992. This weighty volume is perhaps the most thorough compilation of the experiences of grassroots environmental justice activists.
16. Susan Meeker-Lowry, "Maquiladoras: A Preview of Free Trade," *Z Magazine*, October 1992, pp. 25-30; "Texas City Says Rio Grande Pollution Can Cause Fatal Illness," *New York Times*, August 14, 1994.

17. Southwest Network for Environmental and Economic Justice, "Building a Net That Works," Albuquerque, NM, 1995.

18. Gottlieb, *Forcing the Spring*, pp. 241-244.

19. Ellen O'Loughlin, "Questioning Sour Grapes: Ecofeminism and the United Farm Workers Grape Boycott," in Greta Gaard, ed., *Ecofeminism: Women, Animals, Nature* (Philadelphia, PA: Temple University Press, 1993), p. 151.

20. See, for example, A. F. Cohen and B. L. Cohen, "Tests of the Linearity Assumption in the Dose-Effect Relationship for Radiation-Induced Cancer," *Health Physics* vol. 38, January 1980, pp. 53-69. For a broader overview of the effects of radiation exposure on nuclear industry workers and others, see Karl Z. Morgan, "Cancer and Low Level Ionizing Radiation," *Bulletin of the Atomic Scientists*, September 1978, pp. 30-41.

21. Al Geddicks, *The New Resource Wars: Native and Environmental Struggles Against Multinational Corporations* (Boston, MA: South End Press, 1993), pp. 43-44; also Gottlieb, *Forcing the Spring*, p. 251.

22. On the emergence of activism against inner city lead poisoning, see Gottlieb, *Forcing the Spring*, pp. 244-50.

23. Robert D. Bullard, "Anatomy of Environmental Racism," in Richard Hofrichter, ed., *Toxic Struggles: The Theory and Practice of Environmental Justice* (Philadelphia, PA: New Society Publishers, 1993), pp. 25-35; Bullard, *Dumping in Dixie*, pp. 40-42.

24. Bullard, *Dumping in Dixie*, especially Chapters Three and Four.

25. Benjamin Goldman and Laura Fitton, *Toxic Wastes and Race Revisited* (Washington, D.C.: Center for Policy Alternatives, 1994), especially pp. 3-9. The revised study was cosponsored by both the Commission on Racial Justice and the NAACP.

26. Eric Mann, "L.A.'s Smogbusters," The Nation, September 17, 1990, p. 268 ff.

27. "Beyond Bumper Sticker Slogans: ECO Interviews Fred Krupp of EDF," *ECO*, January 1994, pp. 26-30.

28. Gottlieb, *Forcing the Spring*, pp. 260-62; Philip Shabecoff, "Environmental Groups Told They Are Racists in Hiring," *New York Times*, February 1, 1990. In an April 1995 conversation, Moore cited the timely publication in *Z Magazine* of data on the environmental groups' corporate benefactors in as one significant impetus for this letter. See Brian Tokar, "Marketing the Environment," *Z Magazine*, February 1990, pp. 15-20. Also Joni Seager, *Earth Follies: Coming to Feminist Terms with the Global Environmental Crisis* (New York: Routledge, 1993), p. 182.

29. John H. Cushman, Jr., "U.S. to Weigh Blacks' Complaints About Pollution," *New York Times*, November 19, 1993; Goldman and Fitton, *Toxic Wastes and Race Revisited*, pp. 13-16; Charles Lee, "Beyond Toxic Wastes and Race," in Bullard, *Confronting Environmental Racism*, pp. 41-52; and "For the Poor, A Legal Assist In the Cleanup of Pollution," *New York Times*, December 16, 1994.

30. "Exposing Racism in Green: Clinton Issues Environmental Justice EO," *The OMB Watcher*, April 1994, p. 9.

31. Robert D. Bullard, "Anatomy of Environmental Racism and the Environmental Justice Movement," in Bullard, *Confronting Environmental Racism*, p. 23.

32. George Johnson, "Apache Tribe Rejects Move to Store Nuclear Waste on Reservation, *New York Times*, February 2, 1995; George Johnson, "Nuclear Waste Dump Gets Tribe's Approval in Re-vote," *New York Times*, March 11, 1995; and Randel Hanson, "Indian Burial Grounds for Nuclear Waste," *Multinational Monitor*, vol. 16, no. 9, September 1995.

33. Rick Whaley and Walter Bressette, *Walleye Warriors* (Philadelphia, PA: New Society Publishers, 1994); also Geddicks, *The New Resource Wars*.

34. Al Geddicks, "Ladysmith Mine Battle Heats Up," *GreenNet*, July 1992; also Geddicks, *The New Resource Wars*.

35. Keith Schneider, "Concerned About Pollution From Proposed Mine, Wisconsin Tribe Takes On a Giant," *New York Times*, December 26, 1994.

36. Tom Goldtooth, at the Third Citizens Conference on Dioxin and Other Synthetic Hormone Disruptors, Baton Rouge, Louisiana, March 16, 1996. See also Winona LaDuke, "Like Tributaries to a River," *Sierra*, vol. 81, no. 6, November/December 1996, pp. 38-45.

37. Paul Stark, "Why Detroit Summer?" *Green Letter* (now *GroundWork*), Fall 1991, pp. 2-3.

38. Lois Marie Gibbs, ed., *Dying from Dioxin* (Boston, MA: South End Press, 1995).

39. Keith Schneider, "Fetal Harm, Not Cancer, Is Called The Primary Threat From Dioxin," *New York Times*, May 11, 1994; Peter Montague, "Potent Immune System Poison: Dioxin," "Dioxin Inquisition," and "Dioxin and Health," *RACHEL's Environment and Health Weekly*, nos. 414 (November 3, 1994), 457 (August 31, 1995), and 463 (October 12, 1995), respectively.

40. Conversation with Gary Cohen, March 1996.

41. See Brian Tokar, "Campaigning Against Dioxin," *Z Magazine*, May 1996, pp. 50-53; also *Taking Action to Stop Dioxin Exposure*, Citizens Clearinghouse for Hazardous Wastes, 1996.

42. Sayen, "Love Canal, Dioxin, Environmental Justice and Rebuilding Democracy," p. 24.

43. Cynthia Hamilton, "Coping with Industrial Exploitation," in Bullard, *Confronting Environmental Racism*, p. 66.

44. See, for example, Liane Clorfene-Casten, *Breast Cancer: Poisons, Profits and Prevention* (Monroe, ME: Common Courage Press, 1996); Susan Liroff, "Challenging the Establishment," in Judith Brady, ed., *1 in 3: Women with Cancer Confront an Epidemic* (Pittsburgh: Cleis Press, 1991), pp. 260-65; and Steven Epstein, "Democratic Science? AIDS Activism and the Contested Construction of Knowledge," *Socialist Review*, vol. 21, no. 2, April-June 1991, pp. 35-64.

45. "Interview with Dr. Sandra Steingraber," *Safe Food News* (now *Food & Water Journal*), winter 1995, p. 13.

Notes to Chapter Seven

1. One classic text in the field is Michael Soule, ed., *Conservation Biology: The Science of Scarcity and Diversity* (Sunderland, MA: Sinauer Associates, 1986). A popular source for ongoing discussions in conservation biology is the journal *Wild Earth*, published in Richmond, Vermont.

2. Rik Scarce, *Eco-Warriors: Understanding the Radical Environmental Movement* (Chicago, IL: Noble Press, 1990), pp. 23-26. Scarce's book is probably the most balanced, though somewhat idealized, account of the origins of Earth First! More popular—and more thoroughly sensationalized—accounts include Christopher Manes, *Green Rage* (Boston, MA: Little, Brown, 1990) and Susan Zakin, *Coyotes and Town Dogs: Earth First! and the Environmental Movement* (New York: Viking, 1993).

3. Steve Chase, ed. *Defending the Earth: A Dialogue Between Murray Bookchin and Dave Foreman* (Boston, MA: South End Press, 1991), pp. 38-39.

4. For an examination of the roots of the various ideological conflicts in the movement, see Brian Tokar, "Exploring the New Ecologies: Social Ecology, Deep Ecology and the Future of Green Political Thought," *Alternatives*, vol. 15, no. 4, 1988, pp. 31-43. An earlier version of the same article appeared in *The Ecologist*, vol. 18, no. 4/5 (1988), pp. 132-41.

5. Quoted in Judi Bari, "Review of Dave Foreman's *Confessions of an Eco-Warrior*", *Anderson Valley Advertiser*, April 3, 1991, reprinted in Judi Bari, *Timber Wars* (Monroe, ME: Common Courage Press, 1994), p. 107.

6. Judi Bari, "1990: A Year in the Life of Earth First!" in *Timber Wars*, pp. 67-81.

7. Dave Foreman and Nancy Morton, "Co-Founder Dave Foreman Resigns from Earth First!," resignation letter, reprinted in *The Glacial Erratic*, Fall 1990, p. 3.

8. Judi Bari, "The Earth First! Divorce,"*Anderson Valley Advertiser*, September 1990, reprinted as "Breaking Up is Hard to Do," *Timber Wars*, pp. 55-57.

9. Quoted in "Environmentalists Say Deal on Redwoods is Inadequate," *New York Times*, October 5, 1996. See also Carey Goldberg, "Glint of Hope for a Grove of Redwoods," *New York Times*, April 21, 1996; Elliot Diringer and Carolyn Lochhead, "Deal Struck to Preserve Headwaters," *San Francisco Chronicle*, September 28, 1996; Mark Bult, "Headwaters Agreement Announced: Only a Fraction to be Protected," *Rally Cry*, September 30, 1996; John H. Cushman, Jr., "Agreement May Avert Cutting of Ancient Redwoods in California," *New York Times*, September 29, 1996; Ned Daly, "Ravaging the Redwood," *Multinational Monitor*, September 1994; Mark Bult, "Pacific Lumber Logs Ancient Grove," *Rally Cry*, October 9, 1996; Mark Bult "Forest Activists Scale Golden Gate Bridge to Protest Public Property Trade to Texas Tycoon," *Rally Cry*, November 23, 1996; and "40 Headwaters Activists Remain in Jail," North Coast (CA) Earth First!, November 19, 1996.

10. "Takin' It to the (City) Streets: Earth First's! Campaign to End Corporate Dominance," *Bay Area Earth First! Update*, vol. 16, no. 1, Fall 1996.

11. These campaigns are described in Heartwood's occasional journal, *Bloodroot*, nos. 1, 2, Fall 1995 and Winter 1995-96.

12. Quoted in "The Central Appalachians: The Mother Forest," *Heartwood Annual*, 1995.

13. David Solnit, "Fighting the Clearcutting of Canada's Last Rainforest: An Interview with Tzeporah Berman," *GroundWork*, no.4, March 1994, pp. 38-39; Heather Rosemarin, "Science Panel: End Clayoquot Clearcutting," Rainforest Action Network, July 1995; Greenpeace press releases, June-August 1996; and

Friends of Clayoquot Sound newsletters, (Tofino, British Columbia), Summer 1993, Winter 1993-94, and Fall/Winter 1996-97.

14. Rainforest Action Network, "*New York Times* Drops MacMillan Bloedel," update, December 1995; conversation with John Freide, April 1996.

15. Quoted in The Northeastern U.S., "Native Forest Network Fact Sheet," Burlington, Vermont, 1994.

16. Jerry A. Bley, *et al.*, *Finding Common Ground: Conserving the Northern Forest* (Concord, NH: Northern Forest Lands Council, September 1994).

17. *Native Forest News*, special edition, Winter 1993-94.

18. Conversation with Orin Langelle and Anne Petermann, November 1993.

19. "Chips Hit the Fan in Mobile," *Earth First!*, vol. 16, no. 3, February 1996; "Hotspot Updates," *Native Forest News International*, no. 9, first quarter 1996, p. 10. Mobile now leads the nation in raw forest exports (whole logs, chips, etc.), according to NFN.

20. Leslie Hemstreet and Jake Kreilick, "Defending the Last Big Wild," *Z Magazine*, May 1993, pp. 14-17.

21. Sierra Club, "Sears Island Export Facility: Chipping and Shipping the Maine Woods," Portland, Maine, October 1995; Melissa Burch, "Fish or Chips? The Struggle for Maine's Sears Island," *Native Forest Network Bulletin*, Fall 1995; Daniel Sosland, "Wood Chips and White Elephants," *Conservation Matters*, Summer 1995.

22. Melissa Burch, *et al.*, "Beyond Reform: A Revolutionary Ecological Perspective on Forest Protection," Native Forest Network, Burlington, Vermont, 1996.

23. See, for example, Reed Noss, "The Wildlands Project Land Conservation Strategy," *Wild Earth*, special issue, 1992, pp. 10-21; David Johns and Michael Soulé, "Getting from Here to There," *Wild Earth*, vol. 5, no. 4, Winter 1995-96, pp. 32-36. In a recent radio interview, one Wildlands Project representative described their goal as reconciling wilderness preservation with the "benefits" of the present economic system, making room for "both malls and grizzly bears" (WGDR, Plainfield, Vermont, December 8, 1995). The Wildlands Project has been critiqued in scientific as well as political terms by activists and scholars in the Northeast and Northwest: Tim Bechtold, *et al.*, "Letter to the Wildlands Board," November 10, 1994.

24. "A Vision for an Autonomous Traditional Ecological Zone," Native Forest Network, 1995.

25. Panel discussion at the Native Forest Network's First North American Temperate Forest Conference, Burlington, Vermont, November 1993.

26. Chad Hanson, *et al.*, "Sierra Club Sells Out Northern Rockies Wilderness," April 14, 1994.

27. See, for example, Hannah Creighton, "Not Thinking Globally: The Sierra Club Immigration Policy Wars," *Race, Poverty and the Environment*, Summer 1993, pp. 24-29.

28. Brian Lipsett, "'Dirty Money' for Green Groups?" *The Workbook*, vol. 18, no. 1, Spring 1983, pp. 5, 11, with follow-up letters to the editor in the summer and fall issues.

29. Quoted in Alex Barnum, "Sierra Club Votes on Logging Stand," *San Francisco Chronicle*, April 20, 1996. See also, "The Great Zero Cut Debate," *Earth First!*, vol. 15, no. 8, September 1995, pp. 24-27.

30. Native Forest Council press release, April 21, 1996; Patrick Mazza, "Driving the timber industry off national forests: Back to the future for the Sierra Club," *Cascadia Planet*, May 21, 1996 (http://www.tnews.com).

31. Michael Donnelly, "How to Reinvigorate the Forest Movement," *Cascadia Planet*, March 1, 1996.

Notes to Chapter Eight

1. While some commentators dismiss the term Third World as a Cold War archaism, in favor of more neutral terms like "the South," many activists in Asia, Africa, and Latin America embrace a "Third World" identity. Eschewing the images of poverty and "underdevelopment" that the term evokes for many in the industrialized world, for these activists "Third World" recalls the best traditions of the Non-Aligned Movement of the 1950s and 1960s, and the national independence and "third path" economic currents of the 1960s and 1970s.

2. For a comprehensive analysis of this process and its effects on traditional, land-based peoples, see "Whose Common Future," *The Ecologist*, vol. 22, no. 4, July/August 1992, pp. 121-210 (available in book form from New Society Publishers).

3. Shiva, *Staying Alive: Women, Ecology and Development* (London, England: Zed Books, 1988), pp. 1-2.

4. "The Green Belt Movement in Kenya," interview with Wangari Maathai, in Steve Lerner, ed., *Beyond the Earth Summit* (Bolinas, CA: Common Knowledge Press, 1992), pp. 47-64.

5. Vandana Shiva, *Staying Alive*, pp. 55-89; interview with Vandana Shiva in Lerner, *Beyond the Earth Summit*, pp. 77-87.

6. Larry Lohmann, "Visitors to the Commons: Approaching Thailand's 'Environmental' Struggles from a Western Starting Point," in Bron Raymond Taylor, ed., *Ecological Resistance Movements: The Global Emergence of Radical and Popular Environmentalism* (Albany, NY: State University of New York Press, 1995), p. 117.

7. Ben Wisner, "*Luta*, Livelihood and Lifeworld in Contemporary Africa," in Taylor, *Ecological Resistance Movements*, p. 184.

8. Yash Tandon, "Grassroots Resistance to Dominant Land-Use Patterns in Southern Africa," in Taylor, *Ecological Resistance Movements*, p. 173.

9. On toxic dumping in the Third World, see Mitchel Cohen, "Toxic Imperialism: Exporting Pentagonorrhea," *Z Magazine*, October 1990, pp. 78-79; Mitchel Cohen, *Haiti and Somalia: The International Trade in Toxic Waste*, Brooklyn, NY: Red Balloon, 1995; Chin Oy Sim, "Basel Convention to Ban Waste Exports?" *Third World Resurgence*, no. 44, April 1994, pp. 10-12.

10. "Biopiracy Update: A Global Pandemic," *RAFI Communiqué*, September/October 1995; "The Struggle Against Biopiracy" (feature section), *Third World Resurgence*, no. 63, November 1995, pp. 9-30.

11. Pat Mooney, "Indigenous Person from Papua New Guinea Claimed in U.S. Government Patent," Rural Advancement Foundation International, October 1995, also reprinted in *Third World Resurgence*, no. 63, p. 30. See also Andrew Kimbrell, *The Human Body Shop* (San Francisco, CA: HarperCollins, 1993), especially Chapters Fourteen and Fifteen.

12. Martin Khor, "A worldwide fight against biopiracy and patents on life," Third World Resurgence, no. 63, p. 11.

13. Shiva, *Staying Alive*, Chapter Five; see also Vandana Shiva, *The Violence of the Green Revolution: Third World Agriculture, Ecology and Politics* (London, England: Zed Books, 1993).

14. Vandana Shiva, "Quit India! Indian farmers burn Cargill plant and send message to multinationals," *Third World Resurgence*, no. 36, August 1993, pp. 40-41.

15. Martin Khor, "500,000 Indian farmers rally against GATT and patenting of seeds," *Third World Resurgence*, no. 39, November 1993, pp. 20-22.

16. S. M. Mohamed Idris, "Doublespeak and the new biological colonialism," *Third World Resurgence*, no. 39, November 1993, pp. 30-31.

17. S.M. Mohamed Idris, letter protesting the arrest of Professor M. D. Nanjundaswamy and others, February, 1996; Ong Ju Lynn, "Activists force India's first KFC outlet to be closed down," *Third World Resurgence*, no. 63, p. 42; Vandana Shiva, "More than a matter of two flies: Why KFC is an ecological issue," *Third World Resurgence*, no. 67, March 1996, pp. 2-4.

18. Conservation International World Wide Web page, http://www.conservation.org/aboutci/strategy/dfnswap.htm.

19. Georgeann Potter, "Debt Swaps," reprinted in *Dialogue on Debt: Alternative Analysis and Solutions* (Washington, D.C.: Center of Concern, 1988); James Painter, "Unpaid Debt to Nature," *South*, August 1989, pp. 108-9; Kenneth Margolis, "Light in the Forest," *Orion Nature Quarterly*, Winter 1989; and Peter Truell, "What Some Monkeys in Bolivia Have to Do with the Debt Crisis," *Wall Street Journal*, January 20, 1988.

20. Brad Erickson, "Are Debt-for-Nature Swaps the Answer," *EPOCA Update*, summer 1990, pp. 2-3; "Debt Swap Questioned," *Bolivia Bulletin*, September 1988.

21. William F. Allman, "The Preservation Paradox," *U.S. News and World Report*, April 25, 1988, pp. 53-54.

22. Quoted in Carmelo Ruiz, "Liberal and Corporate Environmentalism," M.A. thesis: Institute for Social Ecology/Goddard College, Plainfield, Vermont, January 1995, p. 131.

23. Manuel Baquedano, in *The Ecologist*, May-June 1992, quoted in Ruiz, "Liberal and Corporate Environmentalism," p. 132.

24. Joe Kane, "With Spears from All Sides," *New Yorker*, vol. 69, no. 31, September 27, 1993, pp. 54-79; Joe Kane, *Savages* (New York: Alfred A. Knopf, 1995); also Al Geddicks, *The New Resource Wars: Native and Environmental Struggles Against Multinational Corporations* (Boston, MA: South End Press, 1993), pp. 33-38.

25. Moringe Parkipuny, "To Save the Elephants, Help Their Protectors," *Toward Freedom*, January 1990, p. 13.

26. See, for example, Amartya Sen, "Population: Delusion and Reality," *New York Review of Books*, September 22, 1994, pp. 62-71; Jonathan Lieberson, "Too Many

People?," *New York Review of Books*, June 26, 1986, pp. 36-41; Murray Bookchin, "The Population Myth," in *Which Way for the Ecology Movement?* (San Francisco: AK Press, 1994); and Frances Moore Lappé and Joseph Collins, *Food First: Beyond the Myth of Scarcity* (Boston: Houghton Mifflin, 1977).

27. Canadian planners Mathis Wackernagel and William Rees have estimated that the basic food, fuel, forest, and other needs of the Netherlands consume an equivalent land area fifteen times the country's size. Mathis Wackernagel and William Rees, *Our Ecological Footprint: Reducing Human Impact on the Earth* (Gabriola Island, British Columbia: New Society Publishers, 1996), pp. 93-95.

28. Robert D. Kaplan, "The Coming Anarchy," *Atlantic Monthly*, February 1994, especially pp. 46-54.

29. Quoted in Pratap Chatterjee and Matthias Finger, *The Earth Brokers: Power, Politics and World Development* (London, England: Routledge, 1994), p. 70.

30. Tom Athanasiou, *Divided Planet: The Ecology of Rich and Poor* (Boston: Little, Brown, 1996), p 45.

31. The World Bank, *World Development Report, 1989*, quoted in Jim MacNeill, *et al.*, *Beyond Interdependence* (New York: Oxford University Press, 1991). The 1992 UN Development Program's *Human Development Report* revealed that the 20 percent of the world's population that live in the richest countries receive 82.7 percent of the world's income (David Korten, "The Limits of the Earth," *The Nation*, July 15, 1996, p. 16).

32. MacNeill, *et al, Beyond Interdependence*, p. 3.

33. Martin Khor, "Earth Summit Ends with Disappointment and Hope," Third World Network, June 1992.

34. Ichiyo Muto, "For an Alliance of Hope," in Jeremy Brecher, *et al.*, eds., *Global Visions: Beyond the New World Order* (Boston, MA: South End Press, 1993), pp. 148.

35. On the legacy of Bhopal, see David Denbo, *et al.*, *Abuse of Power* (New York: New Horizons Press, 1990); Peter Montague, "Things to Come," *RACHEL's Environment and Health Weekly*, no. 523, December 5, 1996.

36. Oliver Tickell and Nicholas Hildyard, "Green Dollars, Green Menace," *The Ecologist*, vol. 22, no. 3, May/June 1992, p. 82.

37. Quoted in Tom Barry, "Seeing Green: The A.I.D.ing of the Environment," *Covert Action Quarterly*, no. 58, Fall 1996, p. 47.

38. Barry, "Seeing Green," p. 49.

39. Vandana Shiva, "The Politics of Diversity," *The Permaculture Activist*, vol. 7, no. 1, Spring 1991, p. 6.

40. World Commission on Environment and Development, *Our Common Future* (New York: Oxford University Press, 1988). For an analysis of the outcome of the Rio summit and Third World activists' response, see Brian Tokar, "After the 'Earth Summit,'" *Z Magazine*, September 1992, pp. 8-14. On the co-optation of international environmentalists at Rio, see Chatterjee and Finger, *The Earth Brokers*.

41. MacNeill, *et. al., Beyond Interdependence*, p. 5.

42. Maria Mies, "The Need for a New Vision: The Subsistence Perspective," in Maria Mies and Vandana Shiva, *Ecofeminism* (London, England: Zed Books, 1993), pp. 297-324.

43. *The Ecologist*, "Whose Common Future?," pp. 197-200.

44. Jo Bedingfield, "Golf Course Tees Off Mexican Village," *San Francisco Chronicle*, November 12, 1995; Alberto Ruz Buenfil, "The Revolution in Tepotztlán," *Revista ArcoRedes*, April 1996. For background on the Zapatista movement, see John Ross, *Rebellion from the Roots* (Monroe, ME: Common Courage Press, 1995).
45. *The Ecologist*, "Whose Common Future?," p. 204.
46. Martin Khor, "Sustainable Development and Sustainability: Ten points to clarify the concepts," *Earth Summit Briefings*, no. 4, Third World Network, 1992.
47. Vandana Shiva, "The Greening of the Global Reach," in Brecher, *Global Visions*, pp. 53-54.
48. Shiva, "The Greening of the Global Reach," p. 58. See also Vandana Shiva, *Monocultures of the Mind* (Penang, Malaysia: Third World Network, 1993).
49. Athanasiou, *Divided Planet*, p. 304.

Notes to Chapter Nine

1. On the origins of the Greens in the United States, see Brian Tokar, *The Green Alternative: Creating an Ecological Future* (Philadelphia, PA: New Society Publishers, 1992, revised edition); on the debate over electoralism in the U.S. Greens, see Brian Tokar, "The Greens: To Party or Not?," *Z Magazine*, October 1991, pp. 42-46, and "The Nader for President Fiasco," *Z Magazine*, November 1996, pp. 26-30.
2. *The Greens/Green Party U.S.A. Program*, Kansas City, Missouri, 1992, p. 8 (reprinted as a Summer 1996 supplement to *Green Politics*). For a detailed account of the Green program and how it was developed, see Brian Tokar, "Into the Future with the Greens," *Z Magazine*, November 1990, pp. 61-66.
3. On the origins of the Green Action Plan and of the debates around Green Party organization, see Tokar, "The Greens: To Party or Not?"; also Howard Hawkins, "Can the Greens Unite for 1996?" *Z Magazine*, May 1995, pp. 10-14. Greta Gaard's forthcoming book, *Ecological Politics: Ecofeminists and the Greens* (Philadelphia: Temple University Press), offers the most complete history to date of the development of the U.S. Greens, both as a social movement and a political party. For a view in support of the Greens' turn toward more traditional party politics, see John Rensenbrink, *The Greens and the Politics of Transformation* (San Pedro, CA: R. & E. Miles, 1992).
4. The quarterly tabloid *Green Politics* offers the most up-to-date information on Green activities around the country (c/o Greens Clearinghouse, P. O. Box 100, Blodgett Mills, NY 13738). On the development and consequences of the 1996 Ralph Nader campaign, see Tokar, "The Nader for President Fiasco."
5. On the mapping of bioregions and watersheds, see Doug Aberley, *Boundaries of Home: Mapping for Local Empowerment* (Gabriola Island, British Columbia: New Society Publishers, 1993).
6. The most comprehensive collection of bioregional movement writings is Van Andruss, *et al.*, *Home: A Bioregional Reader* (Philadelphia, PA: New Society Publishers, 1990).

7. David Haenke, *Ecological Politics and Bioregionalism* (Drury, MO: New Life Farm, 1984), p. 25; see also Peter Berg, "Amble Towards Continent Congress," (San Francisco: Planet Drum Foundation, 1976).

8. See Chapter Eight, note 44.

9. *Proceedings of the Third North American Bioregional Congress* (San Francisco: Planet Drum Foundation, 1989), p. 70.

10. *Proceedings of the Fourth North American Bioregional Congress,* 1991, p. 64.

11. For a political critique of bioregionalism as a sensibility, see Donald Alexander, "Bioregionalism: Science or Sensibility," *Environmental Ethics,* vol. 12, no. 2, Summer 1990, pp. 161-73.

12. Quoted in Adrienne Harris and Ynestra King, *Rocking the Ship of State: Toward a Feminist Peace Politics* (Boulder, CO: Westview Press, 1989), pp. 287-88.

13. Ynestra King, "Healing the Wounds: Feminism, Ecology and the Nature/Culture Dualism," in Irene Diamond and Gloria Fenman Orenstein, eds., *Reweaving the World: The Emergence of Ecofeminism* (San Francisco, CA: Sierra Club Books, 1990), pp. 117-18.

14. Starhawk, foreword to Irene Diamond, *Fertile Ground: Women, Earth and the Limits of Control* (Boston, MA: Beacon Press, 1994), p. ix.

15. One of the foremost critiques of ecofeminist eclecticism is Janet Biehl, *Rethinking Ecofeminist Politics* (Boston, MA: South End Press, 1991). A complementary critical view is expressed by Kate Sandilands, who argues that an ecological feminism needs to be more fully distinguished from the essentialist views of cultural feminists, and acknowledge the social construction of the idea of nature. See her "Ecofeminism and its Discontents: Notes Toward a Politics of Diversity," *The Trumpeter,* vol. 8, no. 2, Spring 1991, pp. 90-96.

16. See, for example, Lori Gruen, "Dismantling Oppression: An Analysis of the Connection Between Women and Animals," in Greta Gaard, ed., *Ecofeminism: Women, Animals, Nature* (Philadelphia, PA: Temple University Press, 1993), pp. 60-90.

17. See, for example, Michelle Summer Fike and Sarah Kerr, "Making the Links: Why Bioregionalism Needs Ecofeminism," *Alternatives,* vol. 21, no. 2, 1995, pp. 22-27. On the role of ecofeminists in the Greens, see Greta Gaard, *Ecological Politics,* especially Chapter Four.

18. Val Plumwood, *Feminism and the Mastery of Nature* (London, England: Routledge, 1993), pp. 5, 22.

19. See, for example, Chaia Heller, "For the Love of Nature: Ecology and the Cult of the Romantic," in Gaard, *Ecofeminism,* pp. 219-42; and *The Desire for Nature/The Nature of Desire* (Denver, CO: Aigis Press forthcoming); also Diamond, *Fertile Ground.*

20. Maria Mies and Vandana Shiva, *Ecofeminism* (London, England: Zed Books, 1993), p. 6.

21. One of the more comprehensive overviews of deep ecology is Alan Drengson and Yuichi Inoue, *The Deep Ecology Movement* (Berkeley, CA: North Atlantic Books, 1995). The foundational work in social ecology is Murray Bookchin, *The Ecology of Freedom* (Palo Alto, CA: Cheshire Books, 1982, Revised ed., Montreal: Black Rose Books, 1991). A comparative work addressing these various philoso-

phies is Michael Zimmerman, *et al.*, *Environmental Philosophy: From Animal Rights to Radical Ecology* (Englewood Cliffs, NJ: Prentice-Hall, 1993, Revised edition 1997).

22. Murray Bookchin, "Social Ecology vs. Deep Ecology," *Green Perspectives*, no. 4-5, July 1987, reprinted in *Socialist Review*, vol. 18, no. 3, July 1988, pp. 9-29.

23. David Orton, "Deep Ecology Lessons," *Green Web Bulletin*, no. 52, October 1996.

24. Thomas Berry, *The Dream of the Earth* (San Francisco: Sierra Club Books, 1988), p. 42. The misanthropic pole of deep ecology is best represented by Christopher Manes, *Green Rage* (Boston, MA: Little, Brown, 1990), a book unfortunately plagued by frequent misrepresentations of others' points of view.

25. See Murray Bookchin, *The Ecology of Freedom* (Palo Alto, CA: Cheshire Books, 1982), Epilogue; "Freedom and Necessity in Nature: A Problem in Ecological Ethics," *Alternatives*, vol. 13, no. 4, November 1986, pp. 29-38; an updated version appears in *The Philosophy of Social Ecology: Essays on Dialectical Naturalism* (Montreal, Quebec: Black Rose Books, 1990, revised 1995) . See also Hans Jonas, *The Phenomenon of Life* (Chicago, IL: University of Chicago Press, 1966).

26. Murray Bookchin, *Re-enchanting Humanity* (London, England: Cassell, 1995), p. 32.

27. Many critics have correctly pointed out that the very concept of a worldview, or indeed a "self," is a singular product of human cultural evolution. For social critic Tim Luke, this belies the claim of deep ecologists that their biocentrism transcends the assumptions of post-Enlightenment thought. See Tim Luke, "The Dreams of Deep Ecology," *Telos*, Summer 1988, pp. 65-92.

28. Murray Bookchin, "A New Municipal Agenda," in *The Rise of Urbanization and the Decline of Citizenship* (San Francisco: Sierra Club Books, 1987) republished and revised as *From Urbanization to Cities: Toward a New Politics of Citizenship* (London, England: Cassell, 1995); also Howard Hawkins, "A Left Municipal Program," *Z Magazine*, December 1996, pp. 14-19.

29. Bookchin's theory of social ecology is most fully developed in *The Philosophy of Social Ecology*, along with *The Ecology of Freedom*. For a more comprehensive overview, see his *Remaking Society: Pathways to a Green Future* (Boston, MA: South End Press, 1990).

30. Other works informed by social ecology include John Clark, *The Anarchist Moment: Reflections on Culture, Nature and Power* (Montreal, Quebec: Black Rose Books, 1984); Biehl, *Rethinking Ecofeminist Politics*; Pratap Chatterjee and Matthias Finger, *The Earth Brokers: Power, Politics and World Development* (London, England: Routledge, 1994); Chaia Heller, *The Desire for Nature/The Nature of Desire* (Denver: Aigis Publications), forthcoming; Mike Small, *Zoon Politikon: Democracy, Ecology and Selfhood*, forthcoming. See also, John Clark's anthology, *Renewing the Earth: The Promise of Social Ecology* (London, England: Green Print, 1990), and various essays in the journal *Democracy and Nature* (formerly *Society and Nature*). Social ecology has also been influential among Green writers and activists in Germany, Italy, Norway, Greece, and other European countries.

31. Dave Foreman's notorious comments about the 1980s famine in Ethiopia first appeared in Bill Devall, "A Spanner in the Woods: An Interview with Dave Foreman," *Simply Living*, vol. 2, no. 12, 1987, pp. 40-43.

32. An historical and bioregional analysis of the deep ecology/social ecology debate appears in Tokar, "Exploring the New Ecologies" (see Chapter Seven, note 4).

33. Theodore Roszak, "Environmentalism and the Mystique of Whiteness: An Interview with Carl Anthony," in Theodore Roszak, *et al.*, eds., *Ecopsychology: Restoring the Earth, Healing the Mind* (San Francisco, CA: Sierra Club Books, 1995), p. 265.

34. Peggy Sue McRae, "Deep and Wide: Deep Ecology and the Male Ego," *Earth First!*, vol. 15, no. 8, September 1995.

35. Bill Devall, "The Ecological Self," in Drengson and Inoue, *The Deep Ecology Movement*, p. 119.

36. Judi Bari, "Revolutionary Ecology," *The Alarm*, 1995, p. 6 ff. It is noteworthy that the qualities of deep ecology that Bari invokes in its defense include aspects that many deep ecologists call into question and that are more widely embraced by social ecologists.

37. David Orton, "Deep Ecology Lessons," also "Struggling Against Sustainable Development," *Z Papers*, vol. 3, no. 1, winter 1994, pp. 13-19. The deep ecology platform originally appeared in Bill Devall and George Sessions, *Deep Ecology: Living as if Nature Mattered* (Salt Lake City, UT: Gibbs M. Smith, 1985), p. 70. Another thoughtful attempt at a left/deep ecology synthesis is Andrew McLaughlin, *Regarding Nature: Industrialism and Deep Ecology* (Albany, NY: State University of New York Press, 1993).

38. See, for example, Bookchin, "Freedom and Necessity in Nature."

39. See, for example, Robyn Eckersley, "Divining Evolution: The Ecological Ethics of Murray Bookchin," *Environmental Ethics*, vol. 11, no. 2, spring 1989, pp. 99-116, and Bookchin's response, "Recovering Evolution: A Reply to Eckersley and Fox," *Environmental Ethics*, vol. 12, no. 3, Fall 1990, pp. 253-74.

40. One recent critique that raises important philosophical issues, but is clearly limited by its oversights, is Joel Kovel, "Negating Bookchin," in Andrew Light, ed., *Anarchism, Nature and Society: Critical Perspectives on Murray Bookchin's Social Ecology* (New York, NY: Guilford Publications, forthcoming).

41. See, for example, Herman Daly and John Cobb, *For the Common Good* (Boston, MA: Beacon Press, 1989), especially Chapter Three.

42. Peter Passell, "The Wealth of Nations: A 'Greener' Approach Turns List Upside Down," *New York Times*, September 19, 1995.

43. Japanese companies also borrow 80 percent of their capital from banks and, thus, may be structurally less dependent on more speculative stock and bond markets. See Richard Barnet and John Cavanagh, *Global Dreams* (New York: Simon and Schuster, 1994), p. 410.

44. Rainforest Action Network, "About the Mitsubishi Campaign," San Francisco, California, 1996.

45. Zhores Medvedev, "The Environmental Destruction of the Soviet Union," *The Ecologist*, vol. 20, no. 1, January/February 1990. See also Marlise Simons, "East Europe Sniffs Freedom's Air, and Gasps," *New York Times*, November 3, 1994.

46. Patrick Tyler, "A Tide of Pollution Threatens China's Prosperity," *New York Times*, September 25, 1994; Todd Lappin, "Environmentalism in China: Can Green Mix with Red?," *The Nation*, February 14, 1994, pp. 191-96.

47. Elmar Altvater, *The Future of the Market* (London and New York: Verso, 1993), p. 183 ff. A California-based school of "socialist ecologists" has also demonstrated the anti-ecological nature of capitalist economics and capitalist society. Under the theoretical leadership of political economist James O'Connor, they have shown that environmental pollution and resource depletion are necessary consequences of capitalist accumulation. Their Marxist political orientation, however, has restrained their full acceptance of an ecological orientation that acknowledges the natural world as more than an "external factor of production," or human society as capable of being organized around anything but its economic activity. See, for example, James O'Connor, "Capitalism, Nature, Socialism: A Theoretical Introduction," *Capitalism, Nature, Socialism*, no. 1, Fall 1988, pp. 11-38.

48. Many critics have adopted a focus on industrialism as the basis for an analysis encompassing the technological, cultural, as well as economic, roots of contemporary society. While critiques of industrialism often shed much light on these various interrelated factors, they tend to obscure the unique role of capitalism in shaping contemporary technology and culture, with its relentless commodification of all areas of life. Hence the compelling need for an historical analysis of capitalism, industrialism, and the nation-state as simultaneously co-evolving social principles.

49. Karl Polanyi, *The Great Transformation* (Boston, MA: Beacon Press, 1957, original edition, 1944), p. 33.

50. Randall Smith, "The Big Casino: How Currency Traders Play for High Stakes Against Central Banks," *Wall Street Journal*, September 18, 1992.

51. For a comprehensive and up-to-date overview of such experiments, see Susan Meeker-Lowry, *Invested in the Common Good* (Philadelphia, PA: New Society Publishers, 1995). On the socially transformative potential of urban gardens, see H. Patricia Hynes, *A Patch of Eden: America's Inner City Gardeners* (White River Junction, VT: Chelsea Green, 1996).

52. Roy Morrison, *We Build the Road as We Travel* (Philadelphia, PA: New Society Publishers, 1991); and *Ecological Democracy* (Boston, MA: South End Press, 1995), especially Chapter Seven; Richard Evanoff, "Learning from Japanese Cooperatives," *Aoyama Journal of International Politics and Economics*, no. 27, June 1993, pp. 113-35; various authors, "Can We Build On and Towards Seikatsu?," *GEO*, no. 13, June/July 1994.

53. The most comprehensive and detailed proposal for community-based democratic planning of economic decisions has been developed by Michael Albert and Robin Hahnel in their book, *Looking Forward: Participatory Economics for the Twenty-First Century* (Boston, MA: South End Press, 1991). Albert and Hahnel offer a cooperative model of production, consumption, and allocation based on the principles of participatory democracy, community-based planning, and democratic coordination of decentralized economic activities. Their model, however, achieves equity through a national system of distribution that aspires to function as a fully integrated cybernetic system, with little consideration for the social and ecological benefits of a more localist, bioregionally centered approach.

54. Polanyi, *The Great Transformation*, pp. 46-47. On the concept of reciprocity in Native-American cultures and its lessons for the ecology movement, see Winona LaDuke, "Environmentalism, Racism and the New Age Movement," *Left Green Notes*, no. 4, September/October 1990, pp. 15-18 (reprinted from *Left Field*, no. 4, summer 1990); "Building Bridges," *Proceedings of the First North American Temperate Forest Conference*, Native Forest Network, Burlington, VT, pp. 15-22.

55. Polanyi, *The Great Transformation*, p. 71.

56. Murray Bookchin, "Market Economy or Moral Economy," in *The Modern Crisis* (Philadelphia: New Society Publishers, 1986), pp. 77-95; E. P. Thompson, "The Moral Economy of the English Crowd in the Eighteenth Century," *Past and Present*, vol. 50, 1971, pp. 76-136.

57. Tokar, *The Green Alternative*, pp. 114-17, 145-47. For an historical outlook on the development of cooperative movements, see Chapter Seven of Martin Buber, *Paths in Utopia* (Boston, MA: Beacon Press, 1958).

58. Buber, *Paths in Utopia*, p. 14.

Notes to Chapter Ten

1. Mike Roselle, "Barricades for the Bears," *Earth First!*, vol. 16, no. 7, August 1996, p. 23.

2. Michael Colby, "Activist Malpractice," *Safe Food News*, Fall 1994, p. 4 (reprinted in *RACHEL's Environment and Health Weekly*, no. 413, October 27, 1994).

3. Michael Colby, "Activist Malpractice."

4. Statement by Mark Van Putten, CEO-elect of the National Wildlife Federation, May 1996.

5. "Sierra Club Passes Torch to Youngest President," *Sierra Club Action*, no. 210, May 22, 1996.

6. "Take one minute to save our environment!," NRDC fundraising letter, 1996.

7. John Entine, "Let Them Eat Brazil Nuts," *Dollars and Sense*, March/April 1996, pp. 30-33; "Shattered Image: Is the Body Shop Too Good to be True?" *Business Ethics*, September/October 1994, pp. 23-38; and Stephen Corry, "The Rainforest Harvest: Who Reaps the Benefit?" *The Ecologist*, vol. 23, no. 4, July/August 1993, pp. 148-53.

8. Gordon Durnill, *The Making of a Conservative Environmentalist* (Bloomington, IN: University of Indiana Press, 1995), pp. 121, 176, 178.

9. Michael Crozier, et al., *The Crisis of Democracy: Report on the Governability of Democracies to the Trilateral Commission* (New York: New York University Press, 1975), p. 8.

10. Samuel Huntington, "The United States," in *The Crisis of Democracy*, p. 114.

11. Richard Flacks, *Making History* (New York: Columbia University Press, 1988), p. 36.

12. Daniel Singer, "Mittérand Le Pétit," *The Nation*, October 10, 1994, p. 381.

13. "Text of President Clinton's acceptance speech at the Democratic National Convention in Chicago on Thursday, August 29, 1996," Associated Press. Just as Clinton was delivering this speech on the floor of the Democratic Convention, political activists meeting in a warehouse that had been a headquarters for pub-

lic demonstrations during the convention were being arrested, pepper-sprayed, and roughed up by Chicago police, according to various reports by the Chicago-based CounterMedia collective.

14. The daily barrage of television brings the mentality and sensibility of suburbia into urban and rural communities as well.

15. Susan Sontag, "A Lament for Bosnia," *The Nation*, December 25, 1995, p. 820.

16. Sara Diamond, "Dominion Theology: The Truth About the Christian Right's Bid for Power," *Z Magazine*, February 1995, pp. 37-41.

17. Stanley Tarrow, *Power in Movement: Social Movements, Collective Action and Politics* (New York, NY: Cambridge University Press, 1994), especially Chapter Nine; Bill Moyer, "The Movement Action Plan: A Strategic Framework Describing the Eight Stages of Successful Social Movements," Social Movement Empowerment Project, San Francisco, California, 1987.

18. John H. Cushman, Jr., "Many States Give Polluting Firms New Protections," *New York Times*, April 5, 1996.

19. Tarrow, *Power in Movement*, pp. 144-45.

20. Stanley Aronowitz, "Towards Radicalism: The Death and Rebirth of the American Left," in David Trend, ed., *Radical Democracy: Identity, Citizenship and the State* (New York, NY: Routledge, 1996), p. 95. Emphasis in original.

21. Richard Flacks, "Reviving Democratic Activism: Thoughts About Strategy in a Dark Time," in Trend, *Radical Democracy*, p. 111.

22. Flacks, "Reviving Democratic Activism," p. 110.

23. Ivan Illich, "Useful Unemployment and its Professional Enemies," in *Toward a History of Needs* (Berkeley, CA: Heyday Books, 1977), p. 17.

24. Of the dozen anti-environmental members of Congress cited by the League, six lost their re-election bids, most significantly Larry Pressler of South Dakota, who was the only incumbent U.S. Senator to be defeated in 1996. A seventh, Rep. Steve Stockman of Texas, was forced into a runoff. The League's advertising, direct mail, and voter turnout campaigns may have provided the margin of victory for opponents of the "Dirty Dozen" in several instances. See League of Conservation Voters, "'Dirty Dozen' Campaigns at a Glance," http://www.lcv.org/dirty12/dirty12results.

25. National Public Radio, "All Things Considered," October 19, 1996; John H. Cushman, Jr., "Environmentalists Ante Up to Sway a Number of Races," *New York Times*, October 23, 1996; and "For Environmentalists, Mixed Results in Election Efforts," *New York Times*, November 8, 1996.

26. Author and activist Helena Norberg-Hodge has termed this strategy "counter-development": exposing the myths of development by raising awareness in Third World countries of the real consequences of commercialism and consumerism in the industrialized world. See, for example, Chapter Seventeen of her *Ancient Futures: Learning from Ladakh* (San Francisco, CA: Sierra Club Books, 1991).

27. Jamin B. Raskin, "Challenging the 'Wealth Primary,'" *The Nation*, November 21, 1994, pp. 609-11.

28. One recent poll revealed that more than three-quarters of the respondents were seriously concerned about stagnant wages and reduced benefits, as well as

widespread layoffs of workers, in a period of rising corporate profits and climbing CEO salaries. Nearly half of those surveyed (46 percent) viewed corporate greed as the main source of economic troubles, and almost a quarter (22 percent) said that corporations and government were equally responsible. EDK Associates, "Corporate Irresponsibility: There Ought to Be Some Laws," Preamble Center for Public Policy, New York, 1996, quoted in *RACHEL's Environment and Health Weekly*, no. 507, August 15, 1996.

29. See, for example, Brian Tokar, "Biotechnology: The Debate Heats Up," *Z Magazine*, June 1995, pp. 49-55, reprinted in *Third World Resurgence*, no. 63, November 1995.

Index

A

AIDS 140, 189
ARCO 19-20, 22, 35, 129
Abalone Alliance 122
Abbey, Edward 189
acid rain 35, 37-38, 40-1, 195
Adler, Jonathan 226-27
affinity groups 120-21
African American 27, 130, 132
Agency for International Development (AID) 170
Alabama 96, 110, 152, 247
Alaska *xiii*, 14, 19, 77, 86
Albert, Michael 255
Albuquerque 130
Allen, Robert 11
Alliance for America 35, 226
Alliance for the Wild Rockies *xxi*, 96, 146
Altvater, Elmar 195
Amazon 87, 160, 167, 222
American Bar Association 11
American Cyanamid 12
American Enterprise Institute 34, 44, 72
American Indian Movement *ix*
American Institute of Biological Sciences 115

American Mining Congress 72
American Petroleum Institute 10, 72
AmeriCorps 95
Ames, Amyas 11
Amherst 183
Anthony, Carl 190
Apache 135
Appalachia 110
Archer Daniels Midland 26, 226
Arctic National Wildlife Refuge 19
Arizona 75, 80, 104, 143, 151
Arkansas 236
Arnold, Ron 72
Aronowitz, Stanley 212
Associated Press 155
Athanasiou, Tom *xiv*, 168, 174
Atlanta 130
Audubon Magazine 18
Audubon Society *xx*, 9, 12, 23, 24, 25, 35, 68, 70, 92-93, 99, 102, 154, 155, 237
Audubon, John James 9
Australia 111, 151, 152, 185, 193

B

BASF 128, 194
BFI (Browning Ferris Industries) 75

About South End Press

South End Press is a nonprofit, collectively run book publisher with over 200 titles in print. Since our founding in 1977, we have tried to meet the needs of readers who are exploring, or are already committed to, the politics of radical social change.

Our goal is to publish books that encourage critical thinking and constructive action on the key political, cultural, social, economic, and ecological issues shaping life in the United States and in the world. In this way, we hope to give expression to a wide diversity of democratic social movements and to provide an alternative to the products of corporate publishing.

Through the Institute for Social and Cultural Change, South End Press works with other political media projects—*Z Magazine*; Speak Out!, a speakers bureau; Alternative Radio; and the Publishers Support Project—to expand access to information and critical analysis. If you would like a free catalog of South End Press books, please write to us at: South End Press, 116 Saint Botolph Street, Boston, MA 02115.

Visit South End Press, *Z Magazine*, Z Media Institute, Left On-Line University, and the Chomsky Archive on Z Net at http://www.lbbs.org

Related Titles

Dying from Dioxin
A Citizen's Guide to Reclaiming our Health and Building Democracy
by Lois Gibbs and the Citizens Clearinghouse for Hazardous Waste

Global Village or Global Pillage:
Economic Reconstruction from the Bottom Up
by Jeremy Brecher and Tim Costello

Biopiracy
The Plunder of Nature and Knowledge
Vandana Shiva